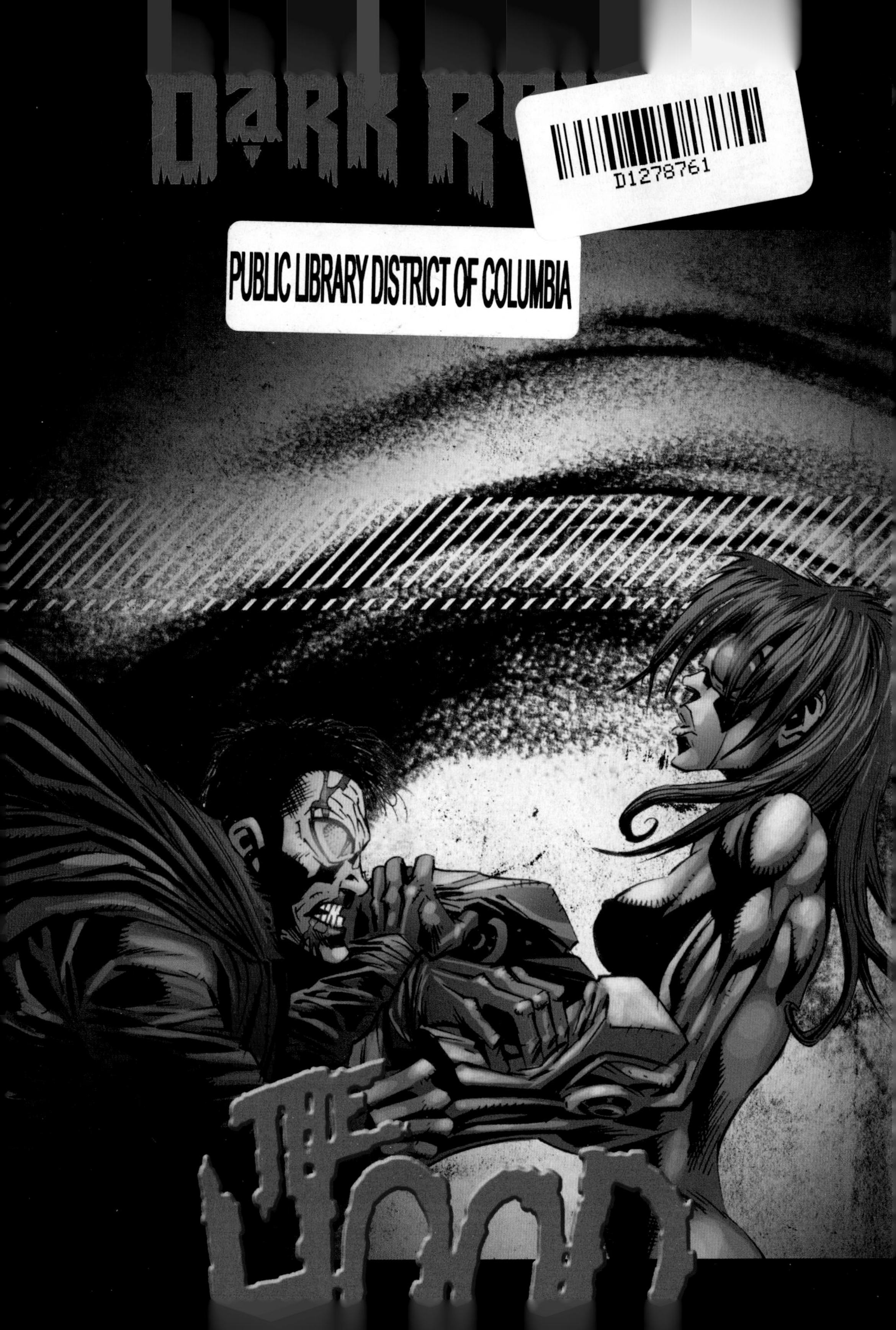
THE

Writer: **JEFF PARKER**
Artist: **KYLE HOTZ**
Inker, Issue #5: **SCOTT HANNA**
Colorist: **FRANK MARTIN**
Letterer: **DAVE SHARPE**
Cover Artist: **MARKO DJURDJEVIC**

"FAMILY TRUST"
Writer: **RICK REMENDER**
Artist: **MAX FIUMARA**
Colorist: **NESTOR PEREYRA**
Letterer: **JEFF ECKLEBERRY**
Cover Artist: **DANIEL ACUÑA**

Assistant Editor: **MICHAEL HORWITZ**
Editor: **BILL ROSEMANN**

Collection Editor: **CORY LEVINE**
Assistant Editors: **ALEX STARBUCK & JOHN DENNING**
Editors, Special Projects: **JENNIFER GRÜNWALD & MARK D. BEAZLEY**
Senior Editor, Special Projects: **JEFF YOUNGQUIST**
Senior Vice President of Sales: **DAVID GABRIEL**
Book Design: **RODOLFO MURAGUCHI**

Editor in Chief: **JOE QUESADA**
Publisher: **DAN BUCKLEY**
Executive Producer: **ALAN FINE**

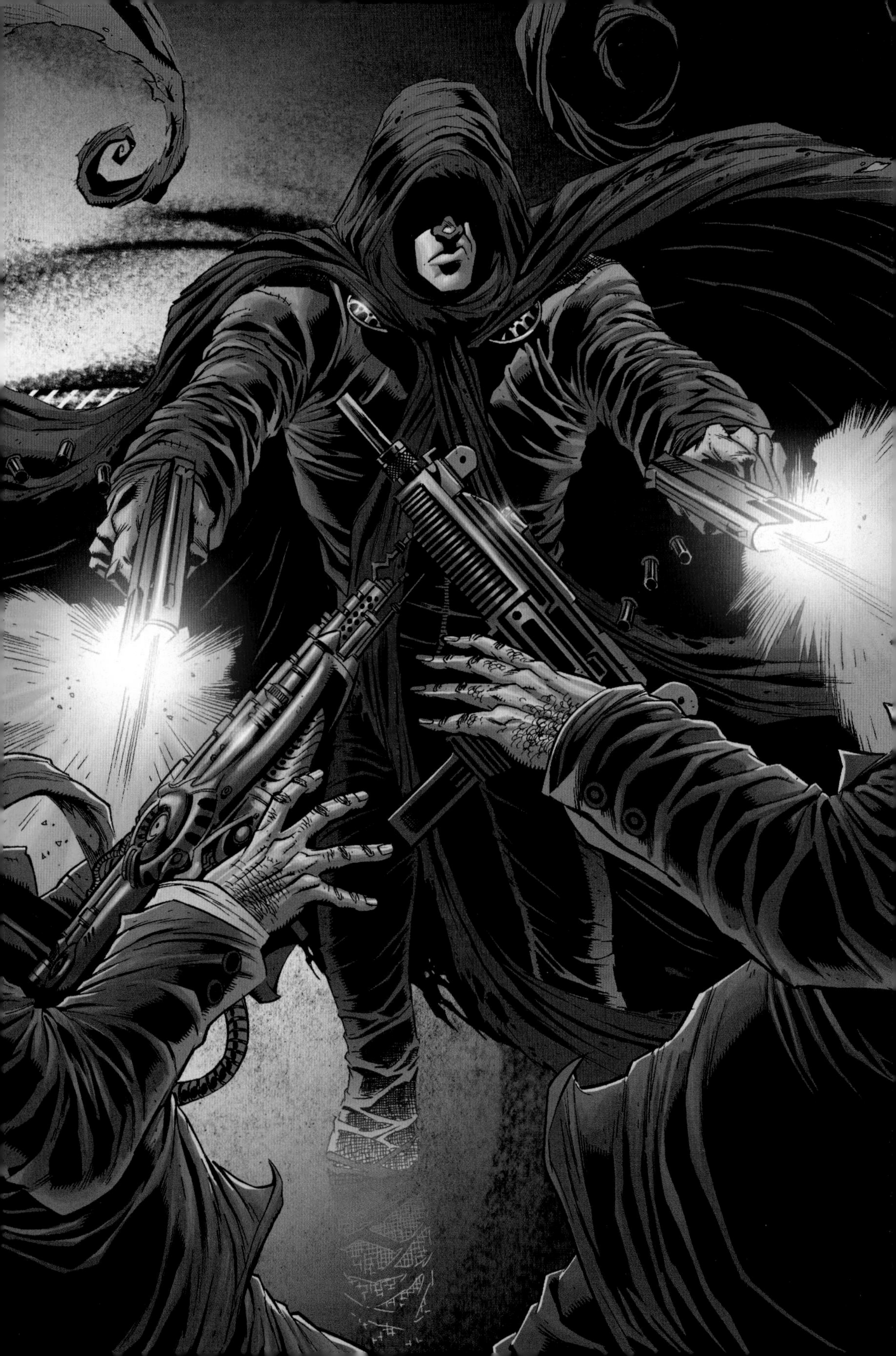

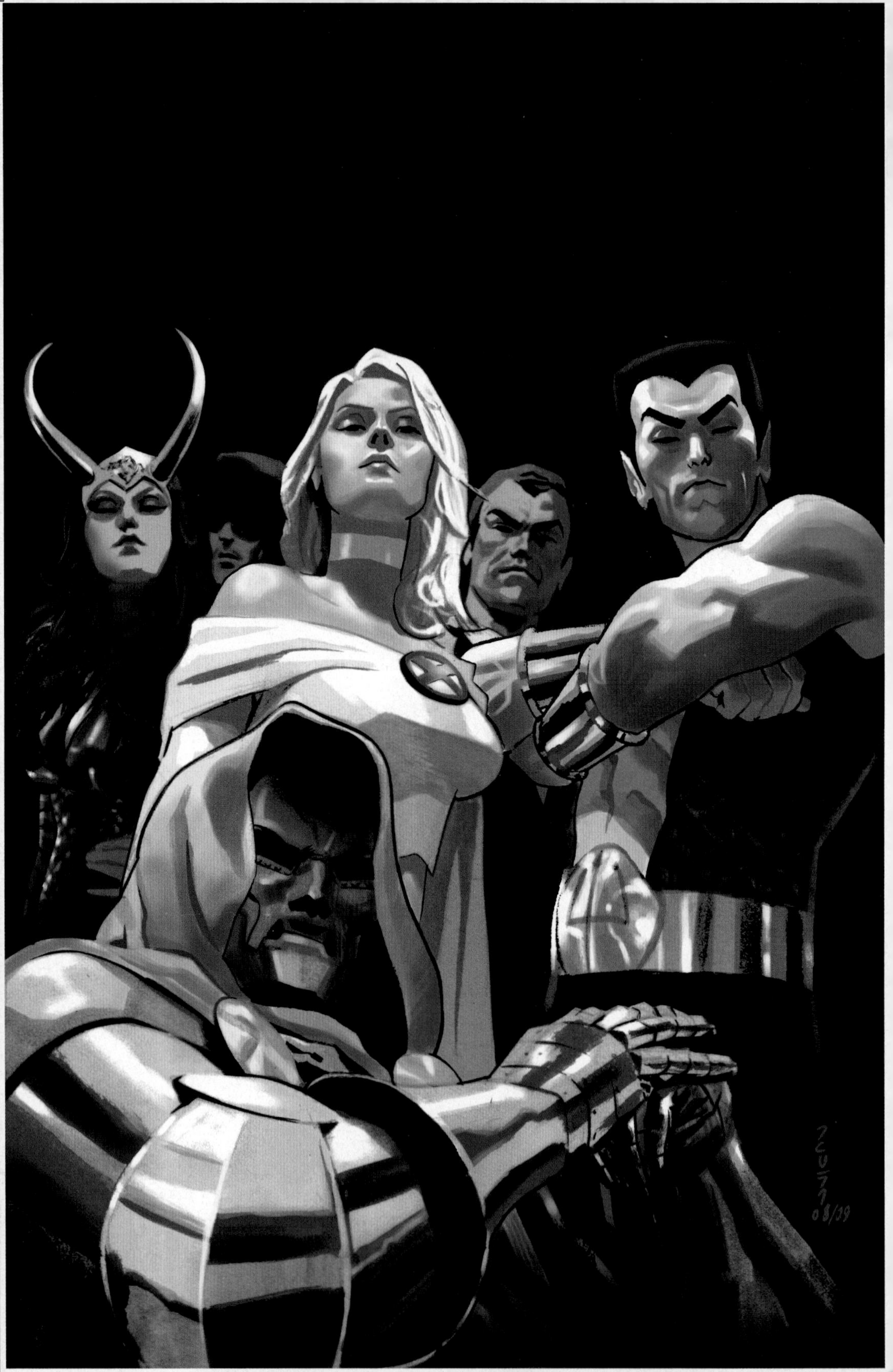

DARK REIGN: THE CABAL

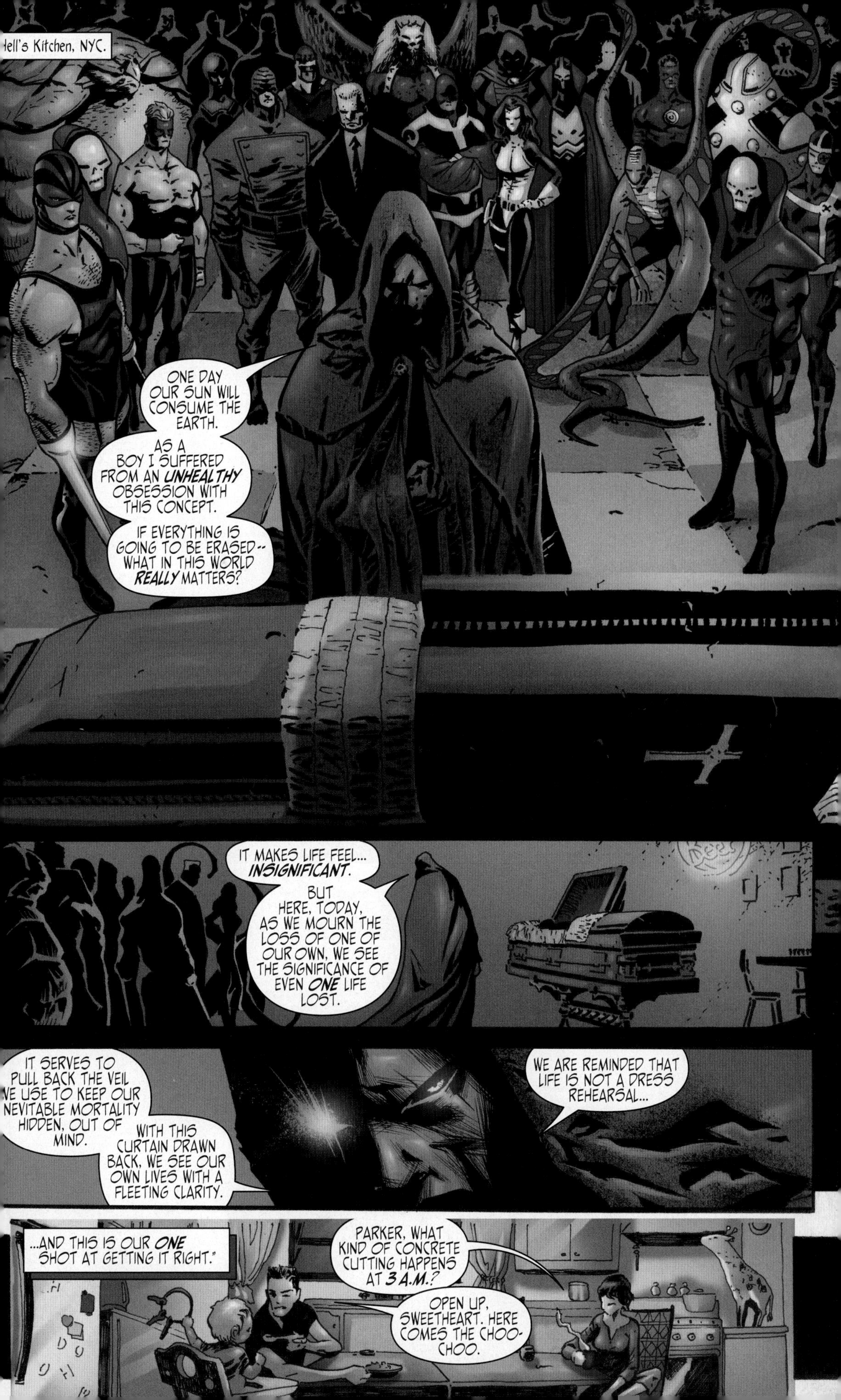

Hell's Kitchen, NYC.
ONE DAY OUR SUN WILL CONSUME THE EARTH.
AS A BOY I SUFFERED FROM AN UNHEALTHY OBSESSION WITH THIS CONCEPT.
IF EVERYTHING IS GOING TO BE ERASED--WHAT IN THIS WORLD REALLY MATTERS?
IT MAKES LIFE FEEL... INSIGNIFICANT.
BUT HERE, TODAY, AS WE MOURN THE LOSS OF ONE OF OUR OWN, WE SEE THE SIGNIFICANCE OF EVEN ONE LIFE LOST.
IT SERVES TO PULL BACK THE VEIL WE USE TO KEEP OUR INEVITABLE MORTALITY HIDDEN, OUT OF MIND.
WITH THIS CURTAIN DRAWN BACK, WE SEE OUR OWN LIVES WITH A FLEETING CLARITY.
WE ARE REMINDED THAT LIFE IS NOT A DRESS REHEARSAL...
...AND THIS IS OUR ONE SHOT AT GETTING IT RIGHT."
PARKER, WHAT KIND OF CONCRETE CUTTING HAPPENS AT 3 A.M.?
OPEN UP, SWEETHEART. HERE COMES THE CHOO-CHOO.

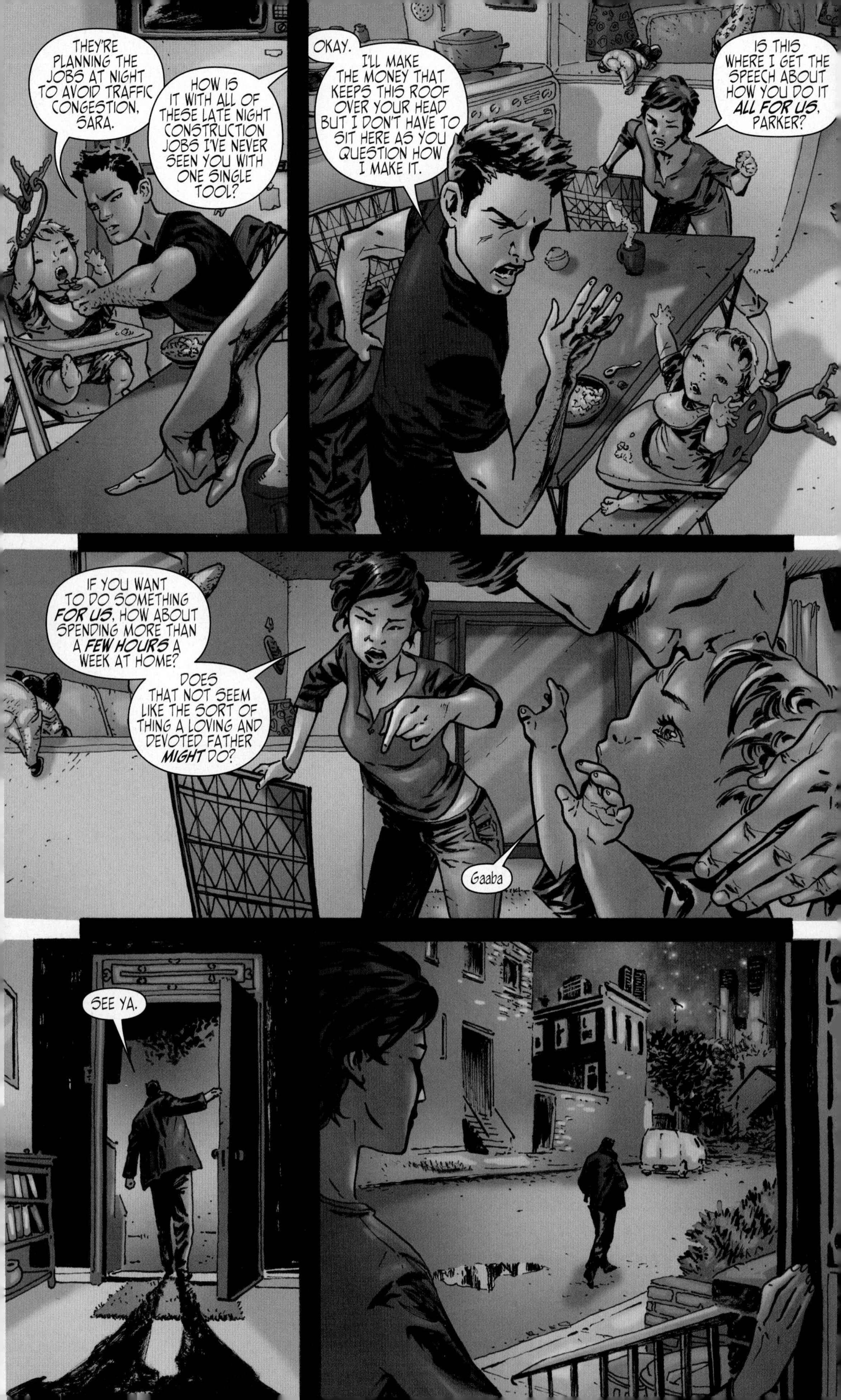

THEY'RE PLANNING THE JOBS AT NIGHT TO AVOID TRAFFIC CONGESTION, SARA.
HOW IS IT WITH ALL OF THESE LATE NIGHT CONSTRUCTION JOBS I'VE NEVER SEEN YOU WITH ONE SINGLE TOOL?
OKAY.
I'LL MAKE THE MONEY THAT KEEPS THIS ROOF OVER YOUR HEAD BUT I DON'T HAVE TO SIT HERE AS YOU QUESTION HOW I MAKE IT.
IS THIS WHERE I GET THE SPEECH ABOUT HOW YOU DO IT ***ALL FOR US***, PARKER?
IF YOU WANT TO DO SOMETHING ***FOR US***, HOW ABOUT SPENDING MORE THAN A ***FEW HOURS*** A WEEK AT HOME?
DOES THAT NOT SEEM LIKE THE SORT OF THING A LOVING AND DEVOTED FATHER ***MIGHT*** DO?
Gaaba
SEE YA.

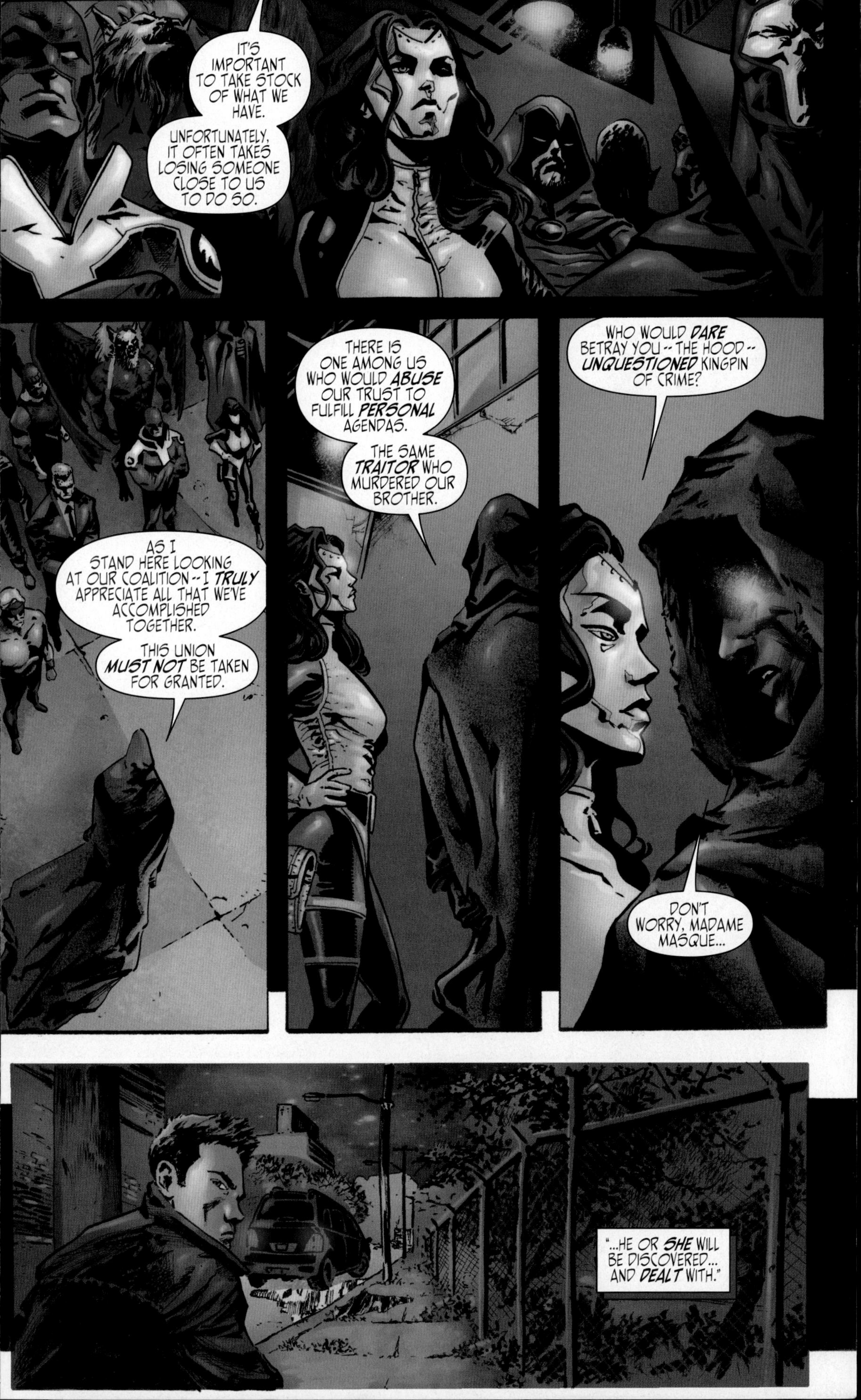
IT'S IMPORTANT TO TAKE STOCK OF WHAT WE HAVE.
UNFORTUNATELY, IT OFTEN TAKES LOSING SOMEONE CLOSE TO US TO DO SO.
AS I STAND HERE LOOKING AT OUR COALITION -- I TRULY APPRECIATE ALL THAT WE'VE ACCOMPLISHED TOGETHER.
THIS UNION MUST NOT BE TAKEN FOR GRANTED.
THERE IS ONE AMONG US WHO WOULD ABUSE OUR TRUST TO FULFILL PERSONAL AGENDAS.
THE SAME TRAITOR WHO MURDERED OUR BROTHER.
WHO WOULD DARE BETRAY YOU -- THE HOOD -- UNQUESTIONED KINGPIN OF CRIME?
DON'T WORRY, MADAME MASQUE...
"...HE OR SHE WILL BE DISCOVERED... AND DEALT WITH."

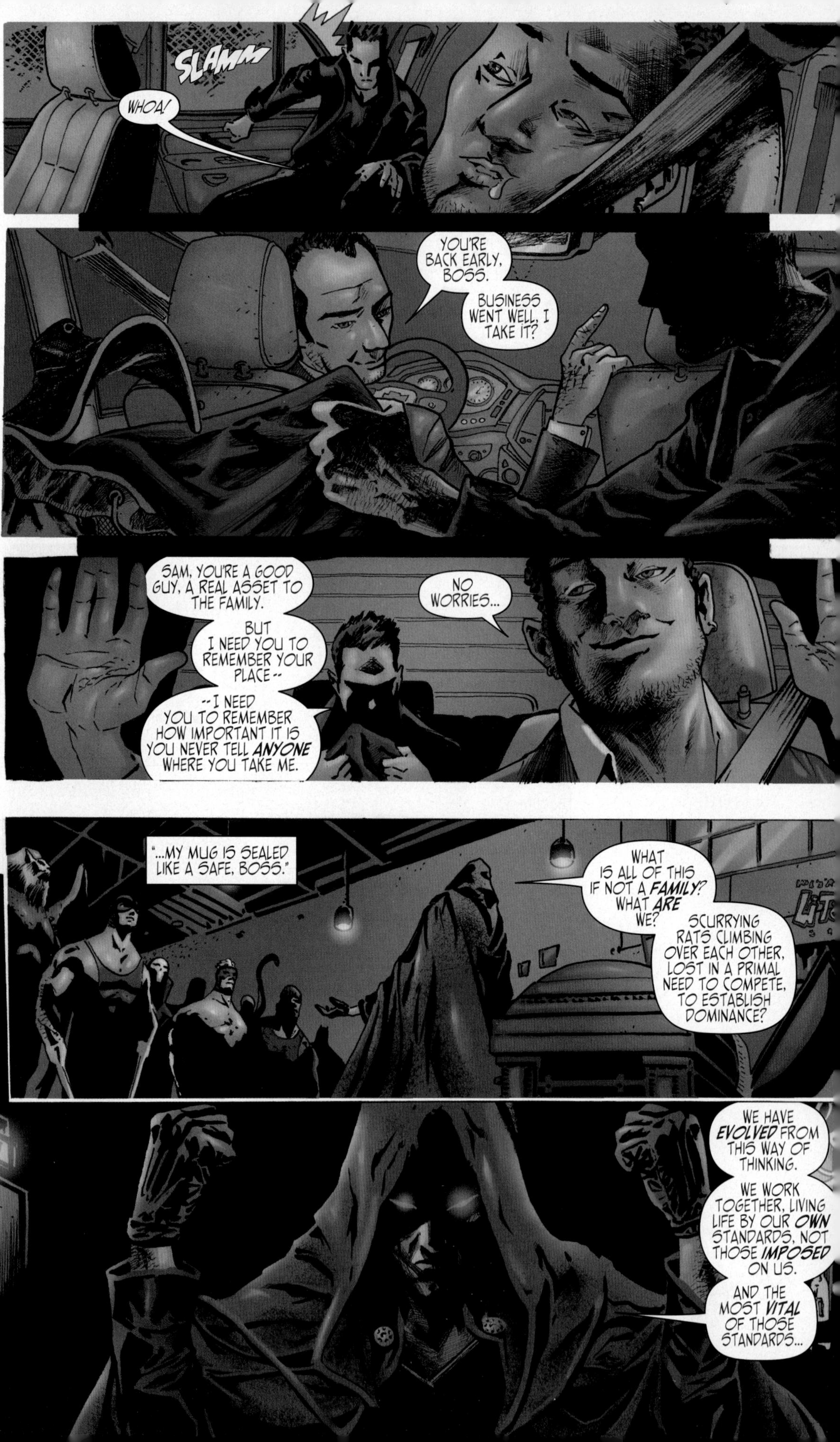
SLAMM
WHOA!
YOU'RE BACK EARLY, BOSS.
BUSINESS WENT WELL, I TAKE IT?
SAM, YOU'RE A GOOD GUY, A REAL ASSET TO THE FAMILY.
BUT I NEED YOU TO REMEMBER YOUR PLACE--
--I NEED YOU TO REMEMBER HOW IMPORTANT IT IS YOU NEVER TELL ANYONE WHERE YOU TAKE ME.
NO WORRIES...
"...MY MUG IS SEALED LIKE A SAFE, BOSS."
WHAT IS ALL OF THIS IF NOT A FAMILY? WHAT ARE WE?
SCURRYING RATS CLIMBING OVER EACH OTHER, LOST IN A PRIMAL NEED TO COMPETE, TO ESTABLISH DOMINANCE?
WE HAVE EVOLVED FROM THIS WAY OF THINKING.
WE WORK TOGETHER, LIVING LIFE BY OUR OWN STANDARDS, NOT THOSE IMPOSED ON US.
AND THE MOST VITAL OF THOSE STANDARDS...

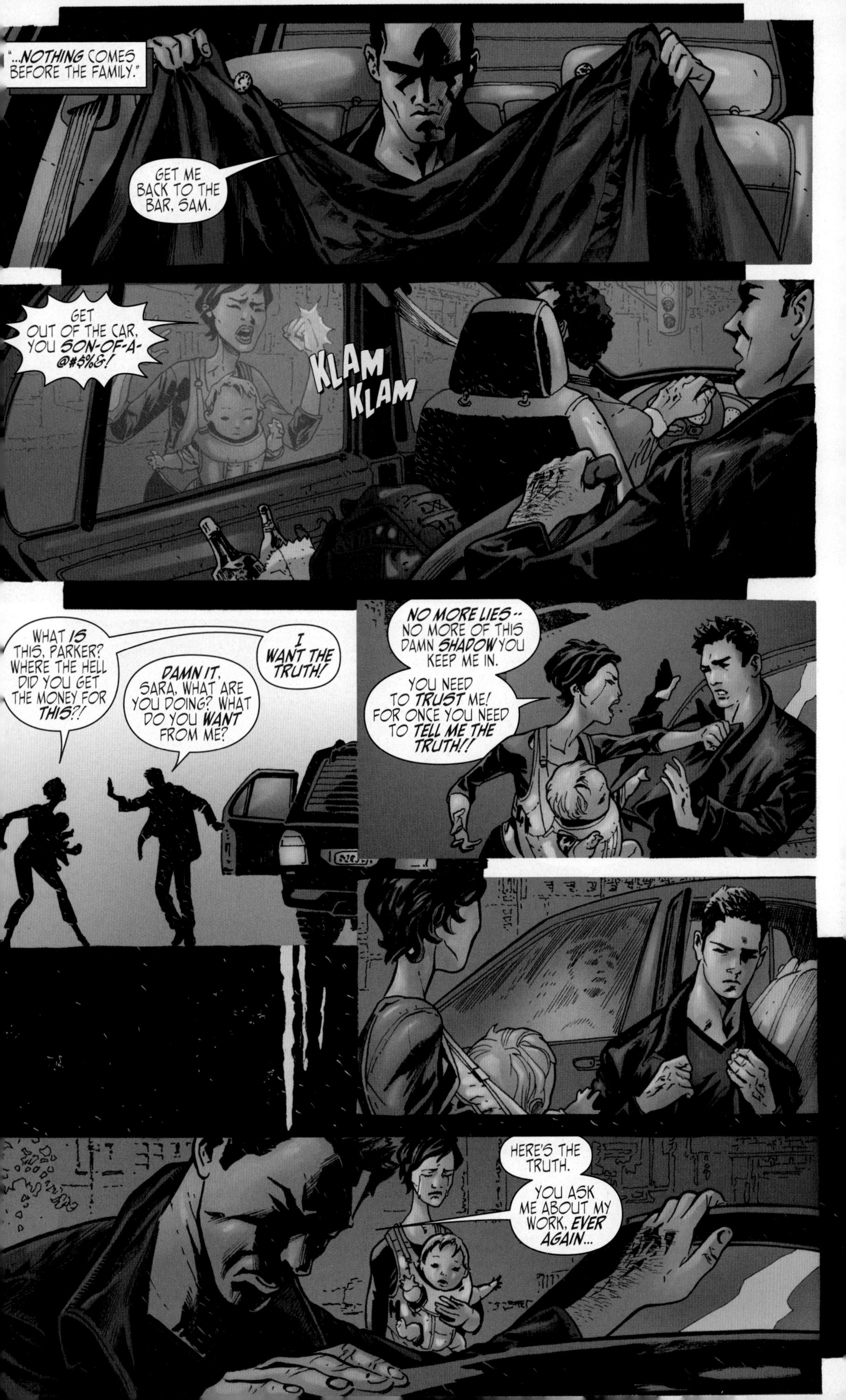

"...NOTHING COMES BEFORE THE FAMILY."
GET ME BACK TO THE BAR, SAM.
GET OUT OF THE CAR, YOU SON-OF-A-@#$%&!
KLAM KLAM
WHAT IS THIS, PARKER? WHERE THE HELL DID YOU GET THE MONEY FOR THIS?!
DAMN IT, SARA, WHAT ARE YOU DOING? WHAT DO YOU WANT FROM ME?
I WANT THE TRUTH!
NO MORE LIES-- NO MORE OF THIS DAMN SHADOW YOU KEEP ME IN.
YOU NEED TO TRUST ME! FOR ONCE YOU NEED TO TELL ME THE TRUTH!!
HERE'S THE TRUTH.
YOU ASK ME ABOUT MY WORK, EVER AGAIN...

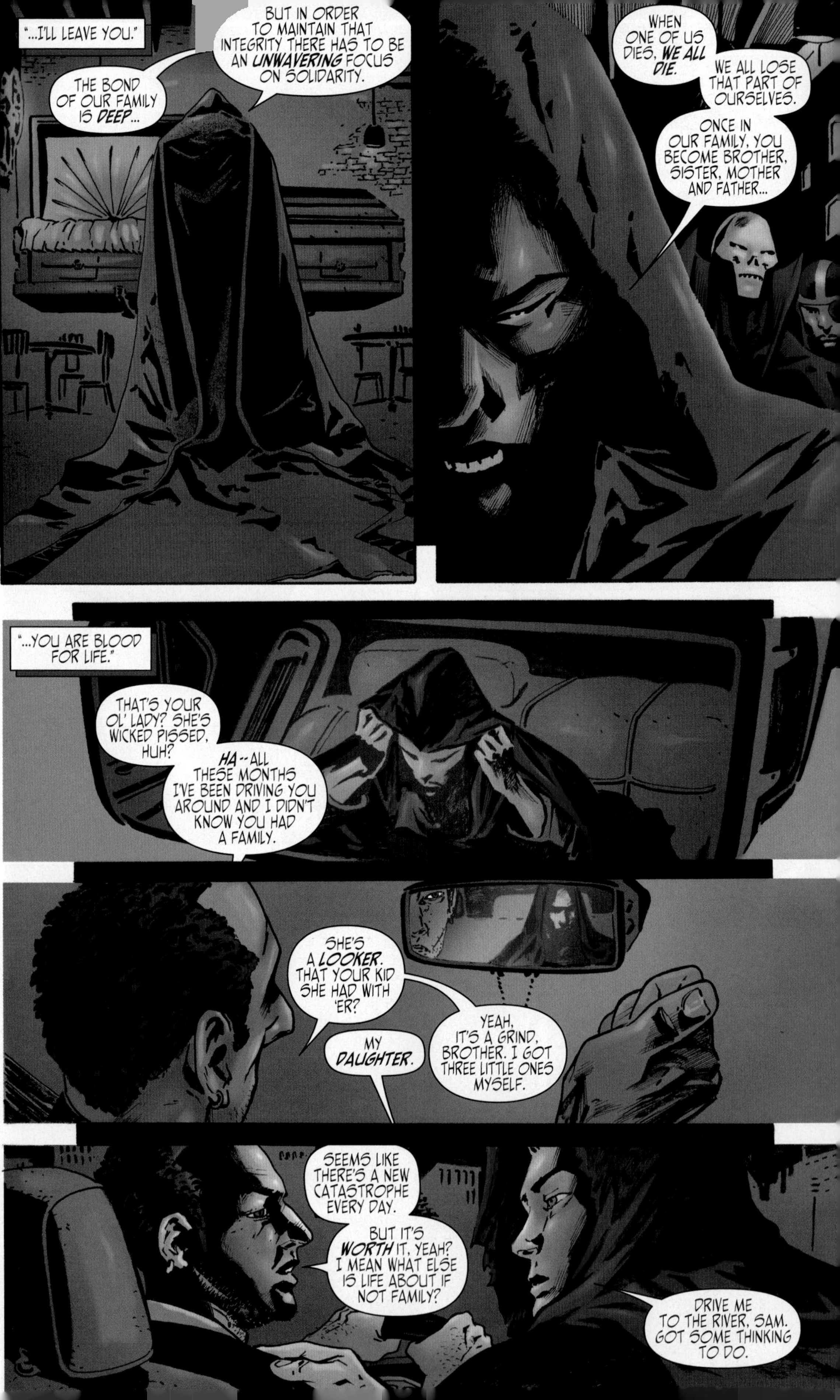
"...I'LL LEAVE YOU."
THE BOND OF OUR FAMILY IS DEEP...
BUT IN ORDER TO MAINTAIN THAT INTEGRITY THERE HAS TO BE AN UNWAVERING FOCUS ON SOLIDARITY.
WHEN ONE OF US DIES, WE ALL DIE.
WE ALL LOSE THAT PART OF OURSELVES.
ONCE IN OUR FAMILY, YOU BECOME BROTHER, SISTER, MOTHER AND FATHER...
"...YOU ARE BLOOD FOR LIFE."
THAT'S YOUR OL' LADY? SHE'S WICKED PISSED, HUH?
HA--ALL THESE MONTHS I'VE BEEN DRIVING YOU AROUND AND I DIDN'T KNOW YOU HAD A FAMILY.
SHE'S A LOOKER. THAT YOUR KID SHE HAD WITH 'ER?
MY DAUGHTER.
YEAH, IT'S A GRIND, BROTHER. I GOT THREE LITTLE ONES MYSELF.
SEEMS LIKE THERE'S A NEW CATASTROPHE EVERY DAY.
BUT IT'S WORTH IT, YEAH? I MEAN WHAT ELSE IS LIFE ABOUT IF NOT FAMILY?
DRIVE ME TO THE RIVER, SAM. GOT SOME THINKING TO DO.

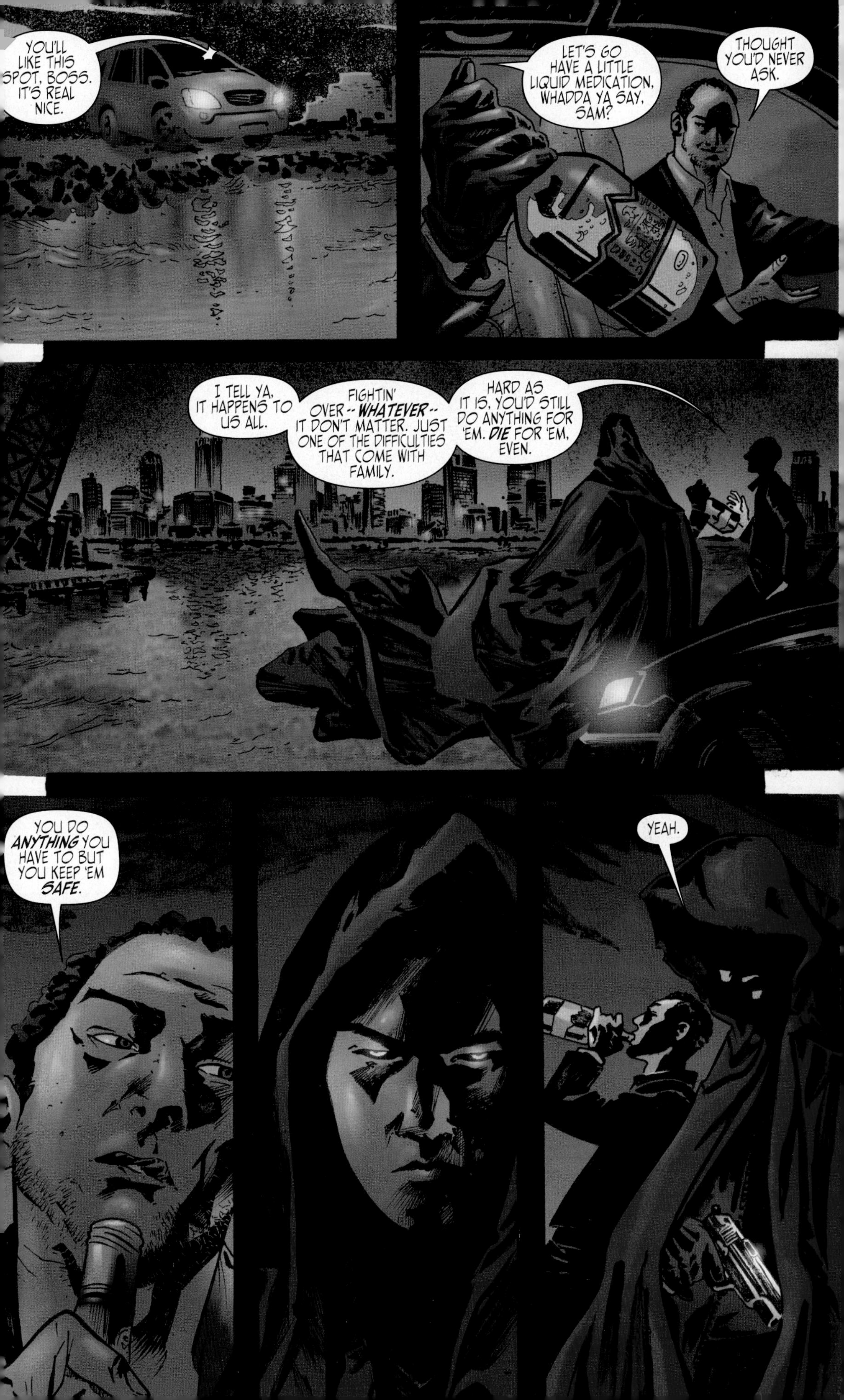

YOU'LL LIKE THIS SPOT, BOSS. IT'S REAL NICE.
LET'S GO HAVE A LITTLE LIQUID MEDICATION, WHADDA YA SAY, SAM?
THOUGHT YOU'D NEVER ASK.
I TELL YA, IT HAPPENS TO US ALL.
FIGHTIN' OVER -- WHATEVER -- IT DON'T MATTER. JUST ONE OF THE DIFFICULTIES THAT COME WITH FAMILY.
HARD AS IT IS, YOU'D STILL DO ANYTHING FOR 'EM. DIE FOR 'EM, EVEN.
YOU DO ANYTHING YOU HAVE TO BUT YOU KEEP 'EM SAFE.
YEAH.

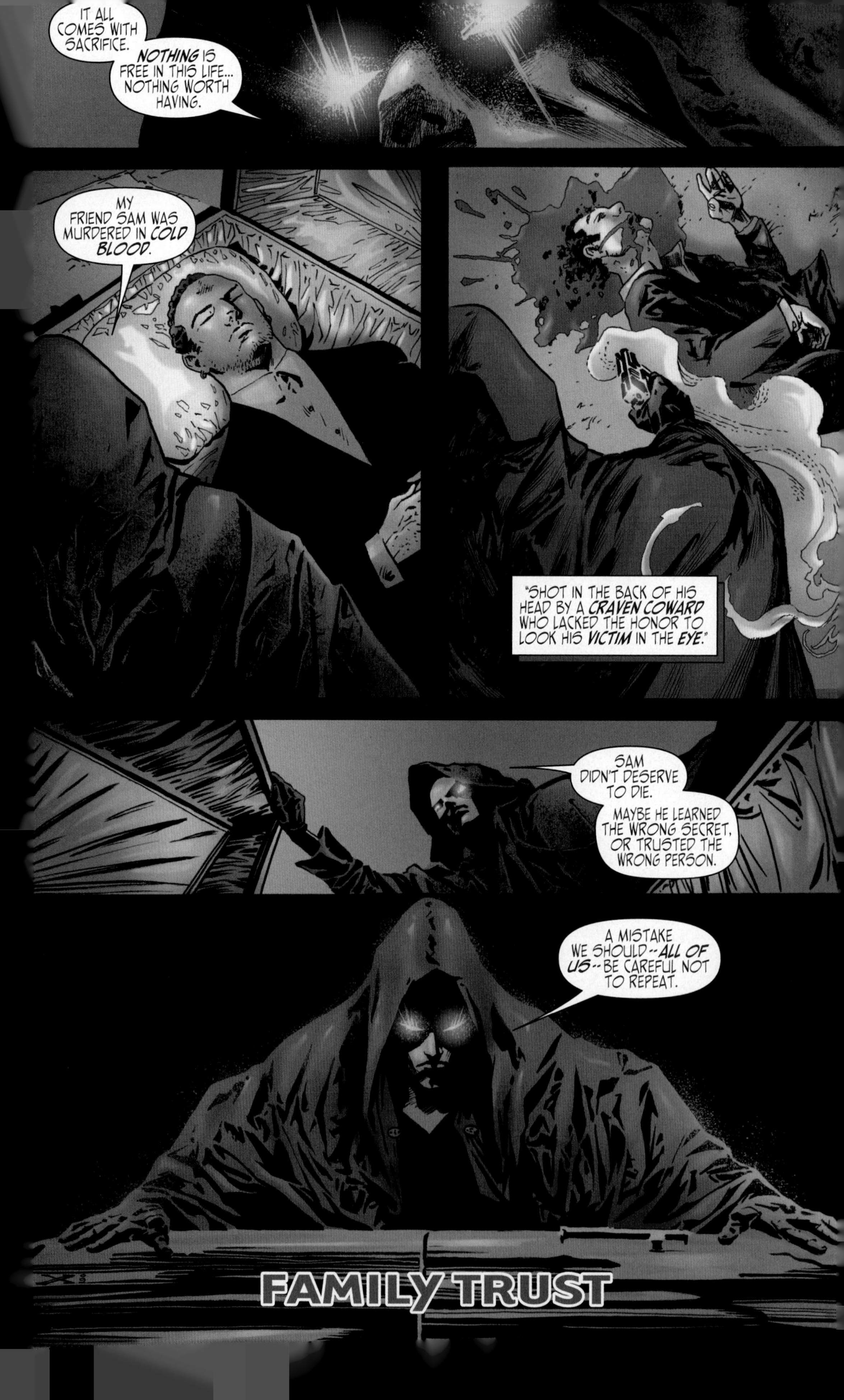

IT ALL COMES WITH SACRIFICE.
NOTHING IS FREE IN THIS LIFE... NOTHING WORTH HAVING.
MY FRIEND SAM WAS MURDERED IN COLD BLOOD.
"SHOT IN THE BACK OF HIS HEAD BY A CRAVEN COWARD WHO LACKED THE HONOR TO LOOK HIS VICTIM IN THE EYE."
SAM DIDN'T DESERVE TO DIE.
MAYBE HE LEARNED THE WRONG SECRET, OR TRUSTED THE WRONG PERSON.
A MISTAKE WE SHOULD--ALL OF US--BE CAREFUL NOT TO REPEAT.
FAMILY TRUST

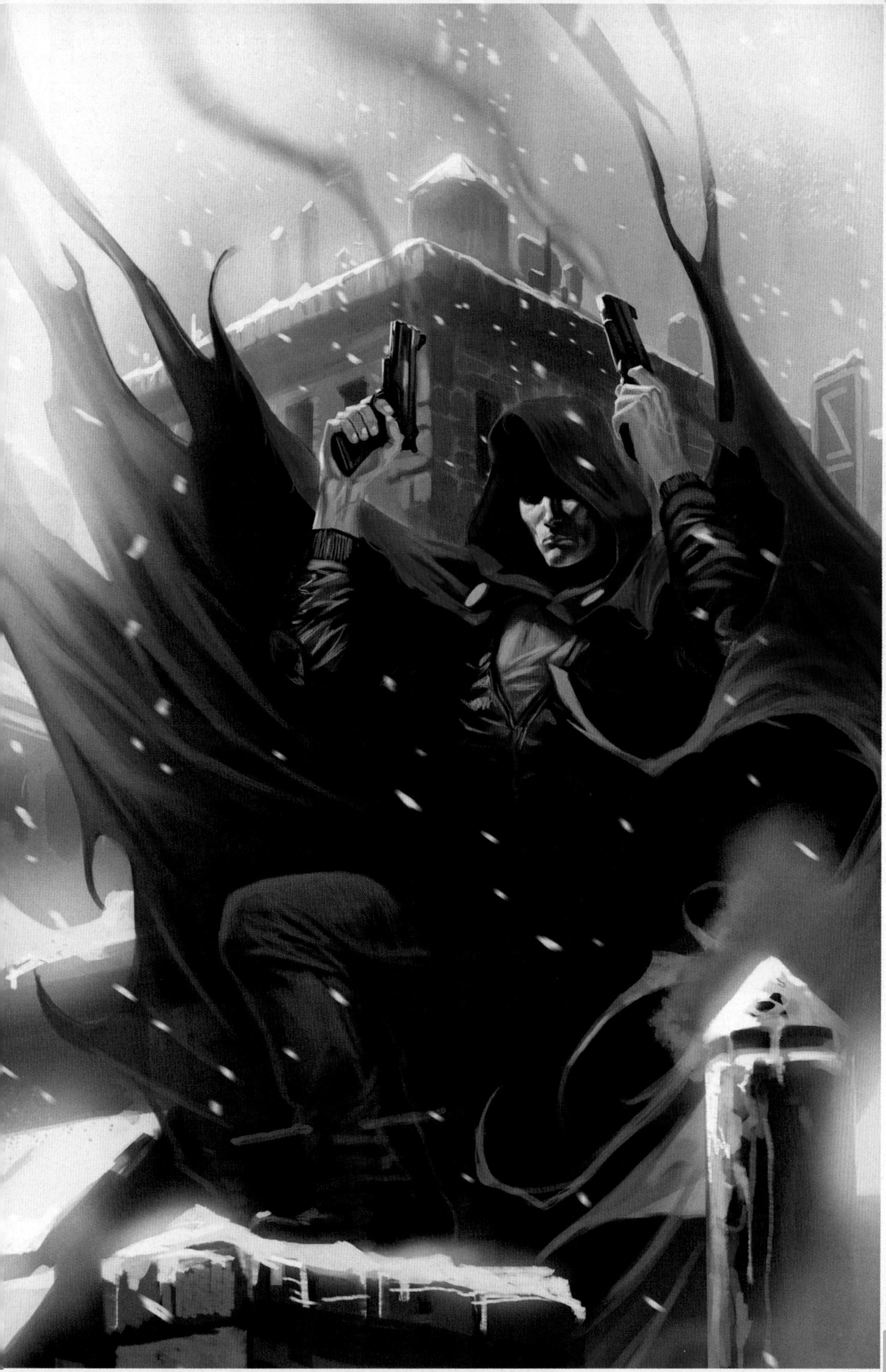

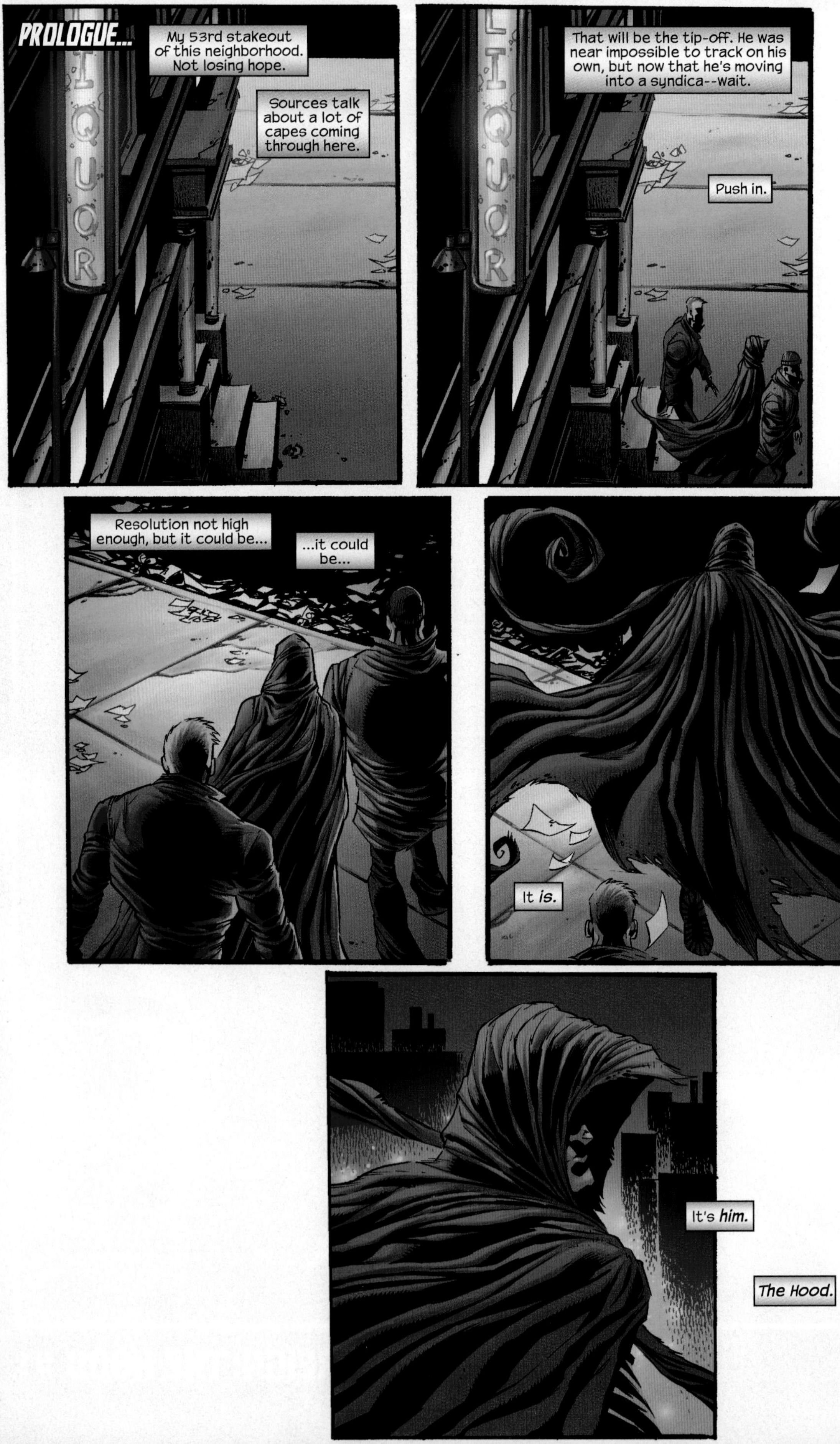
PROLOGUE...
My 53rd stakeout of this neighborhood. Not losing hope.
Sources talk about a lot of capes coming through here.
LIQUOR
That will be the tip-off. He was near impossible to track on his own, but now that he's moving into a syndica--wait.
LIQUOR
Push in.
Resolution not high enough, but it could be...
...it could be...
It *is*.
It's *him.*
The Hood.

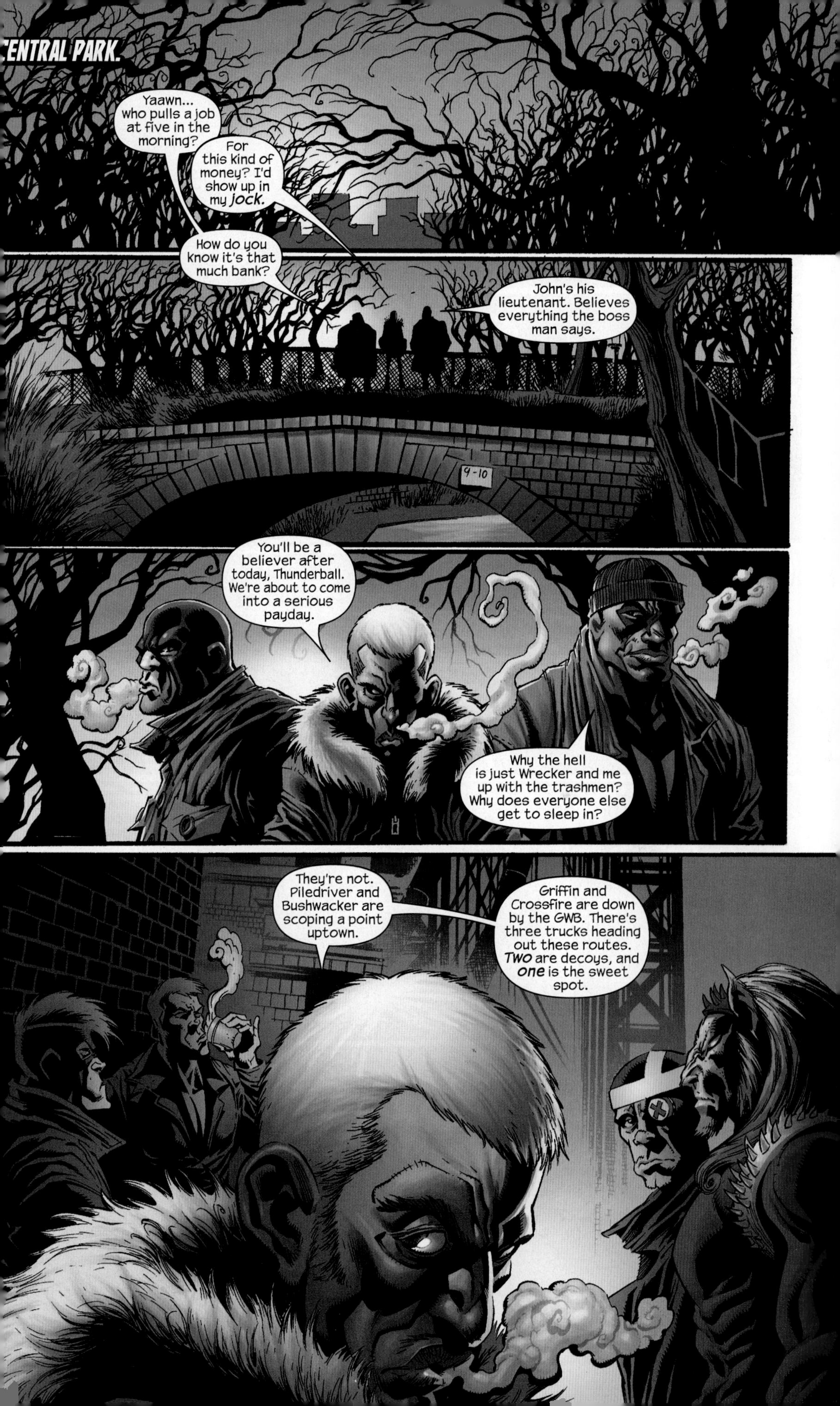

CENTRAL PARK.
Yaawn... who pulls a job at five in the morning?
For this kind of money? I'd show up in my jock.
How do you know it's that much bank?
John's his lieutenant. Believes everything the boss man says.
9-10
You'll be a believer after today, Thunderball. We're about to come into a serious payday.
Why the hell is just Wrecker and me up with the trashmen? Why does everyone else get to sleep in?
They're not. Piledriver and Bushwacker are scoping a point uptown.
Griffin and Crossfire are down by the GWB. There's three trucks heading out these routes. TWO are decoys, and ONE is the sweet spot.

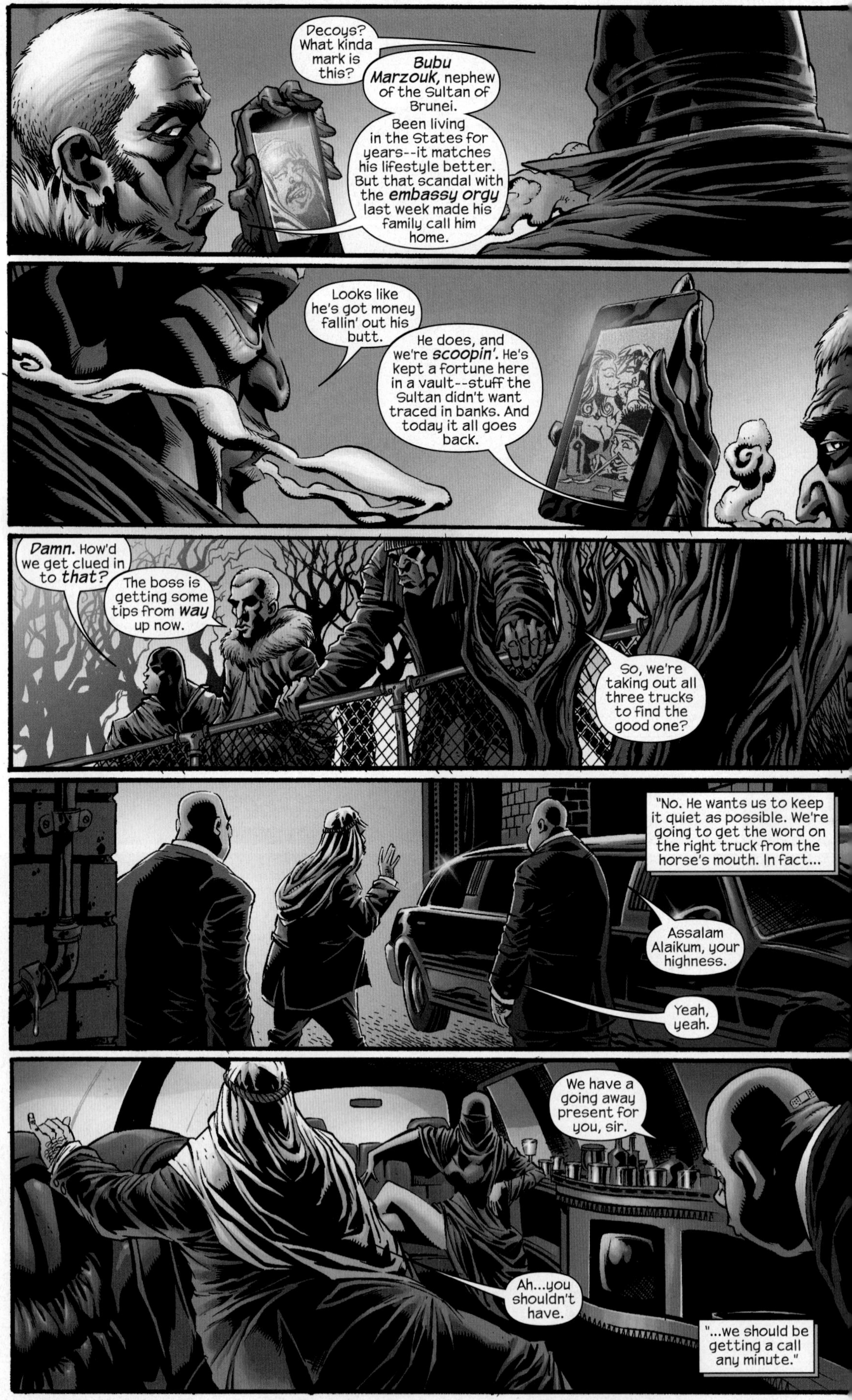

Decoys? What kinda mark is this?
Bubu Marzouk, nephew of the Sultan of Brunei.
Been living in the States for years--it matches his lifestyle better. But that scandal with the embassy orgy last week made his family call him home.
Looks like he's got money fallin' out his butt.
He does, and we're scoopin'. He's kept a fortune here in a vault--stuff the Sultan didn't want traced in banks. And today it all goes back.
Damn. How'd we get clued in to that?
The boss is getting some tips from way up now.
So, we're taking out all three trucks to find the good one?
"No. He wants us to keep it quiet as possible. We're going to get the word on the right truck from the horse's mouth. In fact...
Assalam Alaikum, your highness.
Yeah, yeah.
We have a going away present for you, sir.
Ah...you shouldn't have.
"...we should be getting a call any minute."

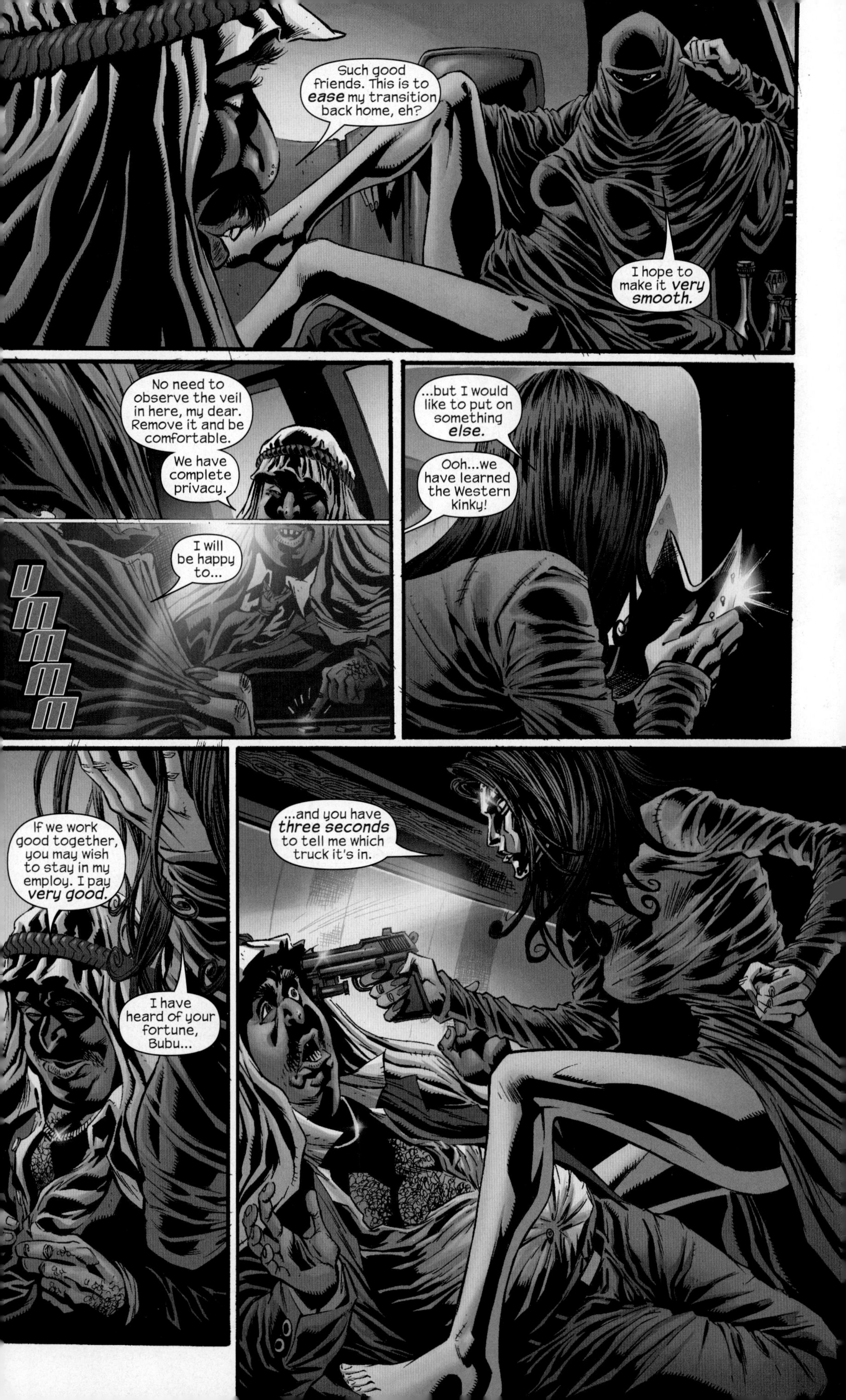
Such good friends. This is to ease my transition back home, eh?
I hope to make it very smooth.
No need to observe the veil in here, my dear. Remove it and be comfortable.
We have complete privacy.
I will be happy to...
VMMMM
...but I would like to put on something else.
Ooh...we have learned the Western kinky!
If we work good together, you may wish to stay in my employ. I pay very good.
I have heard of your fortune, Bubu...
...and you have three seconds to tell me which truck it's in.

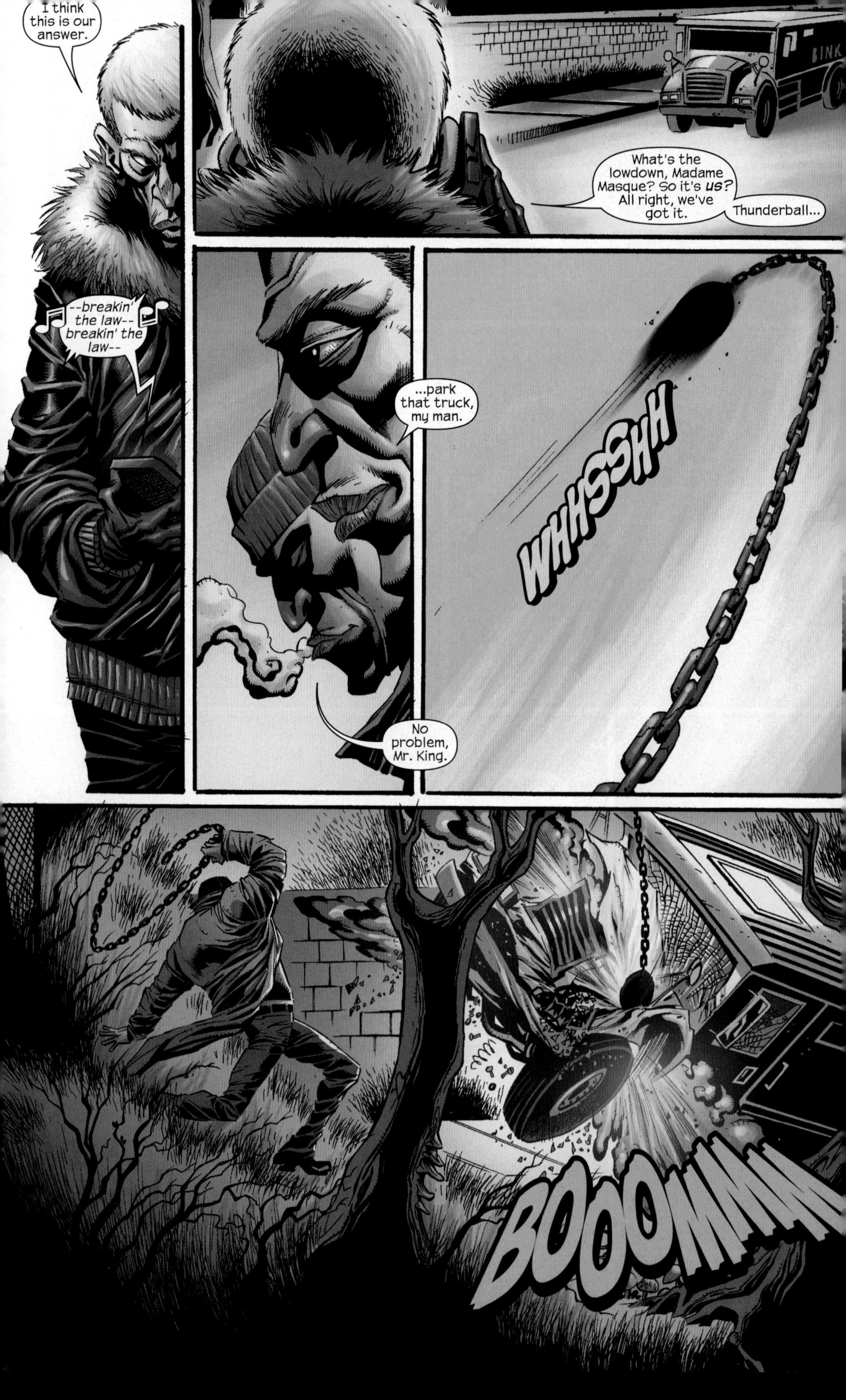
I think this is our answer.
What's the lowdown, Madame Masque? So it's *us*? All right, we've got it.
Thunderball...
--breakin' the law-- breakin' the law--
...park that truck, my man.
No problem, Mr. King.
WHHSSHH
BOOOMMM

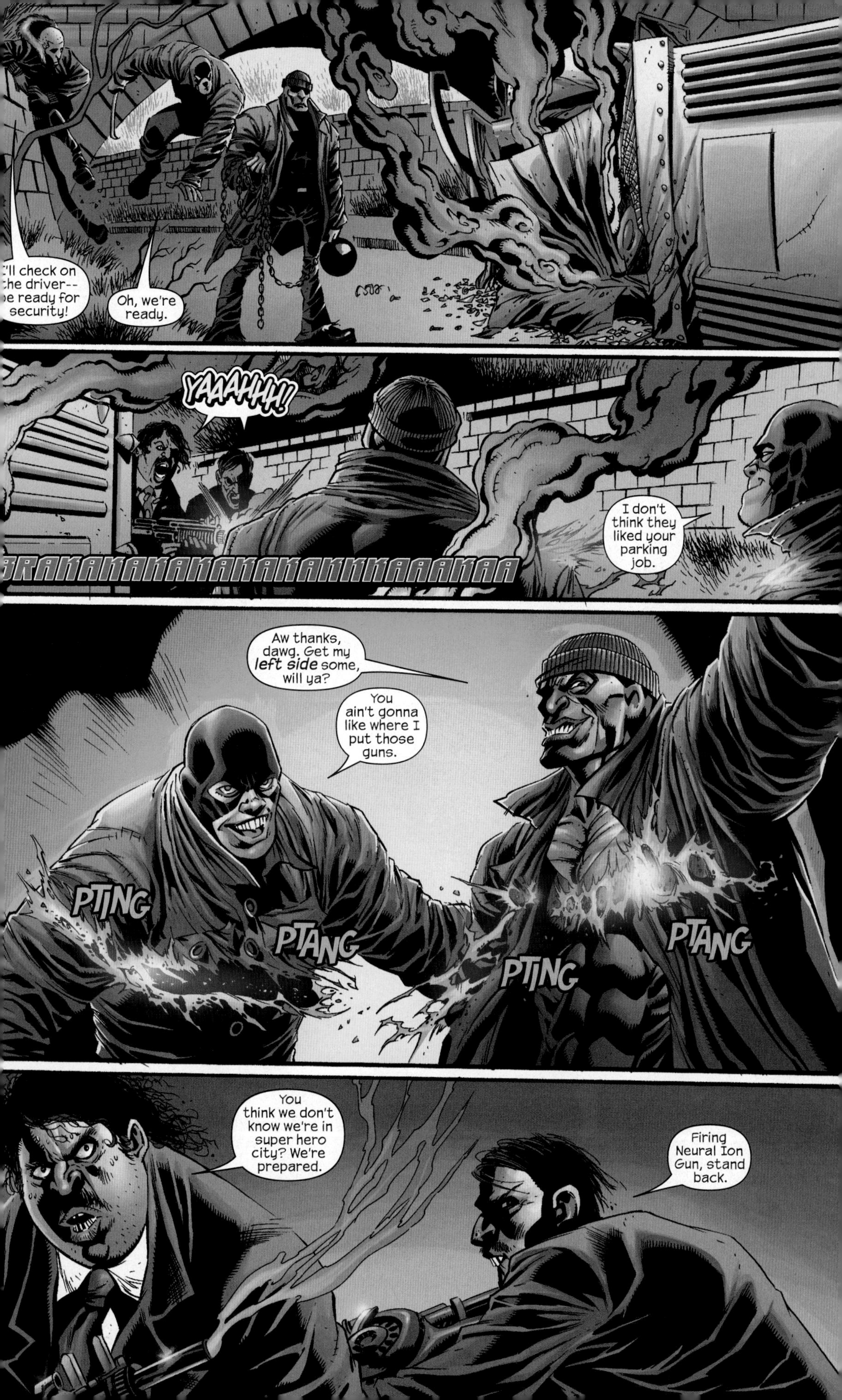
'll check on
he driver--
e ready for
security!
Oh, we're ready.
YAAAHHH!
BRAKAKAKAKAKAKAKKKAAAKAA
I don't think they liked your parking job.
Aw thanks, dawg. Get my *left side* some, will ya?
You ain't gonna like where I put those guns.
PTING
PTANG
PTING
PTANG
You think we don't know we're in super hero city? We're prepared.
Firing Neural Ion Gun, stand back.

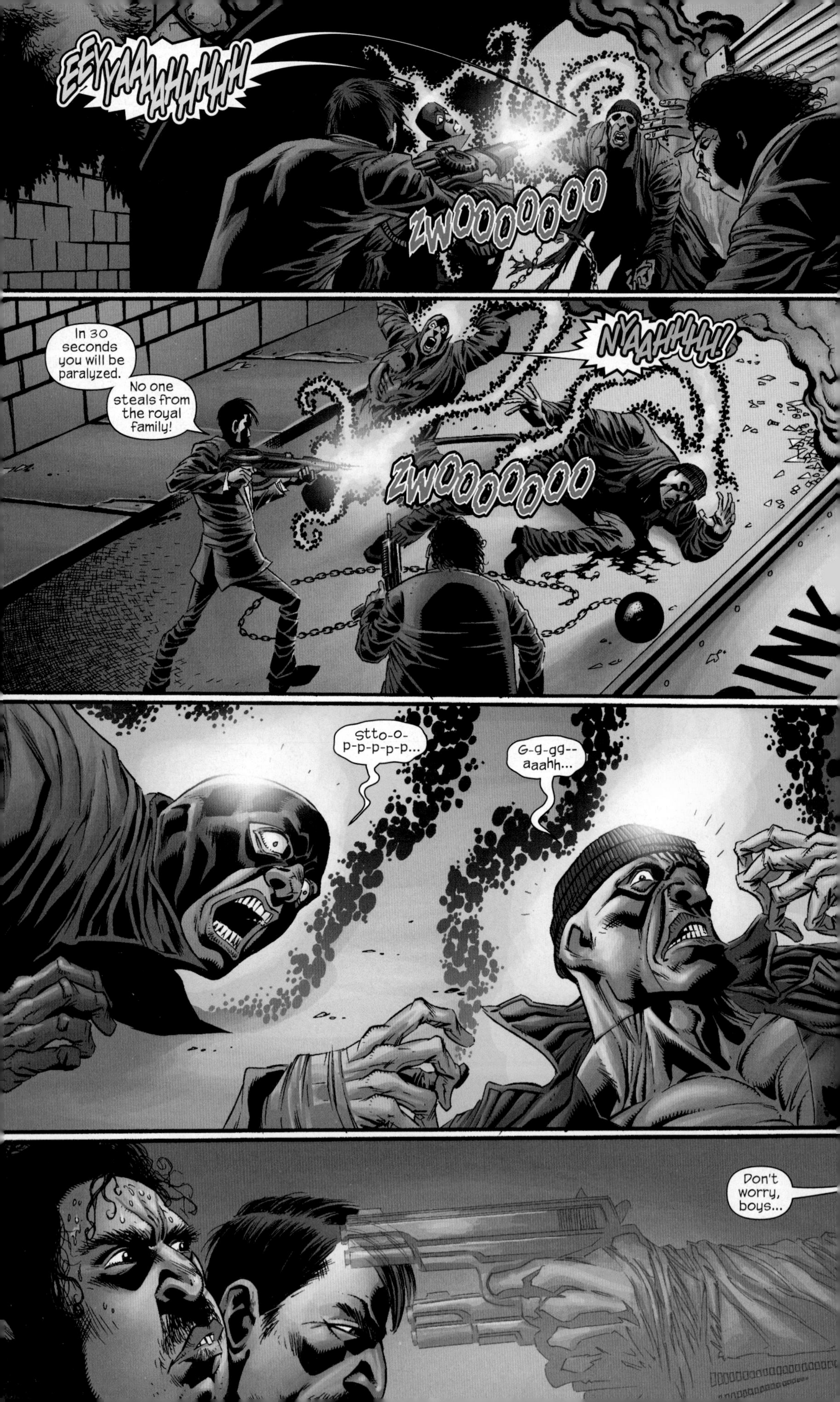
EEYYAAAAHHHHH
ZWOOOOOOO
In 30 seconds you will be paralyzed.
No one steals from the royal family!
NYAAHHHH!
ZWOOOOOOO
DINK
Stto-o-p-p-p-p-p...
G-g-gg--aaahh...
Don't worry, boys...

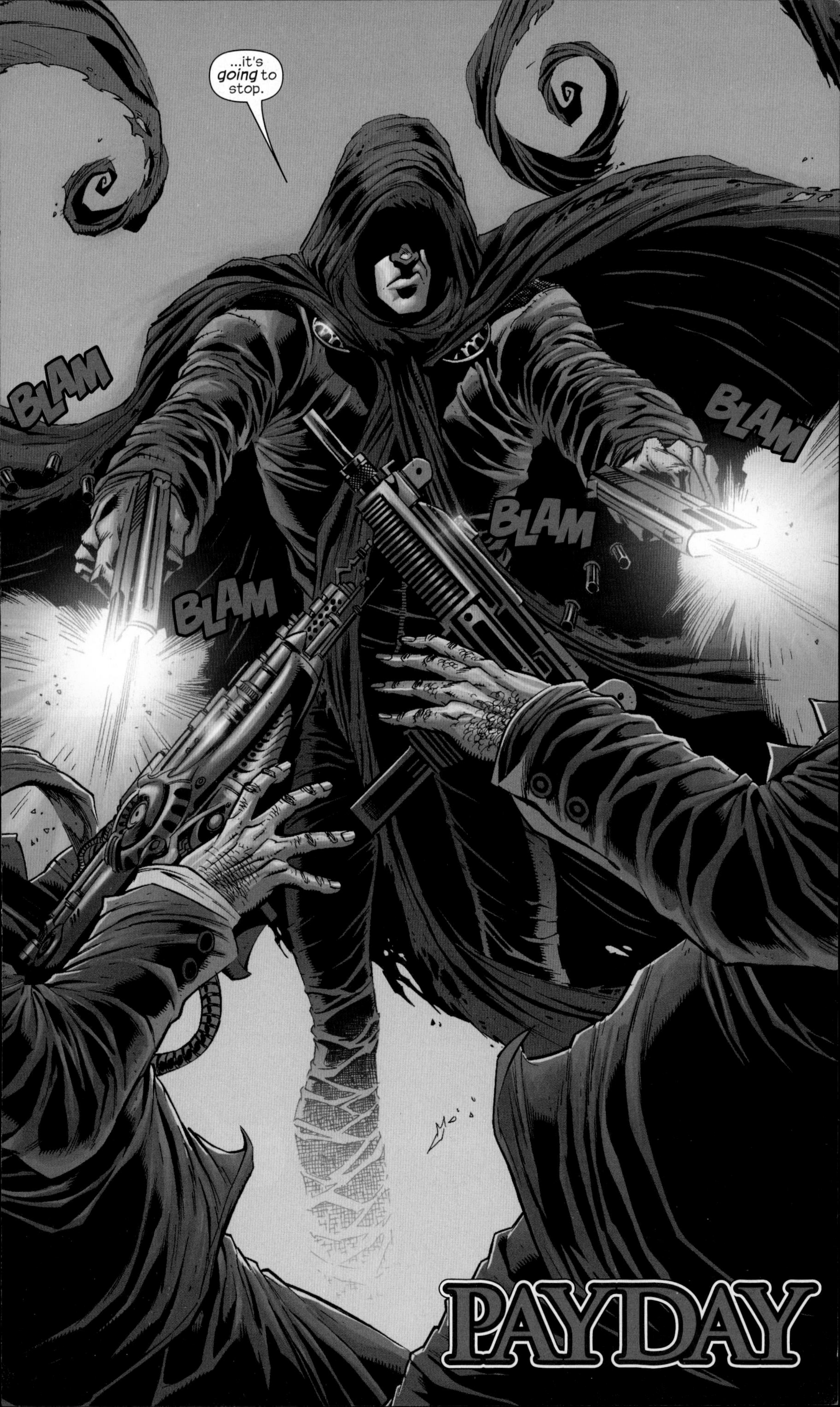
...it's *going* to stop.
BLAM
BLAM
BLAM
BLAM
PAYDAY

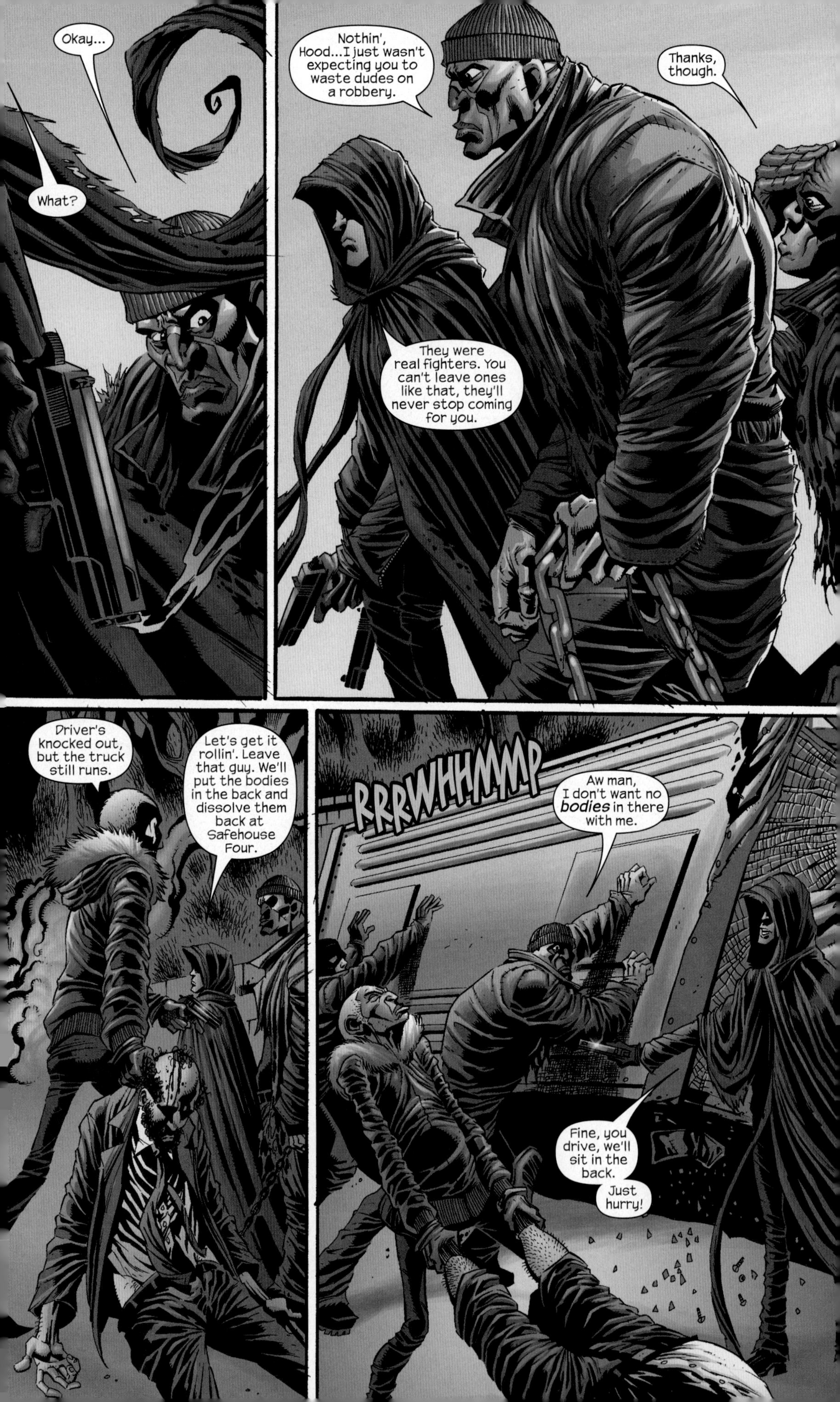

Okay...
What?
Nothin', Hood...I just wasn't expecting you to waste dudes on a robbery.
Thanks, though.
They were real fighters. You can't leave ones like that, they'll never stop coming for you.
Driver's knocked out, but the truck still runs.
Let's get it rollin'. Leave that guy. We'll put the bodies in the back and dissolve them back at Safehouse Four.
RRRWHHMMP
Aw man, I don't want no *bodies* in there with me.
Fine, you drive, we'll sit in the back.
Just hurry!

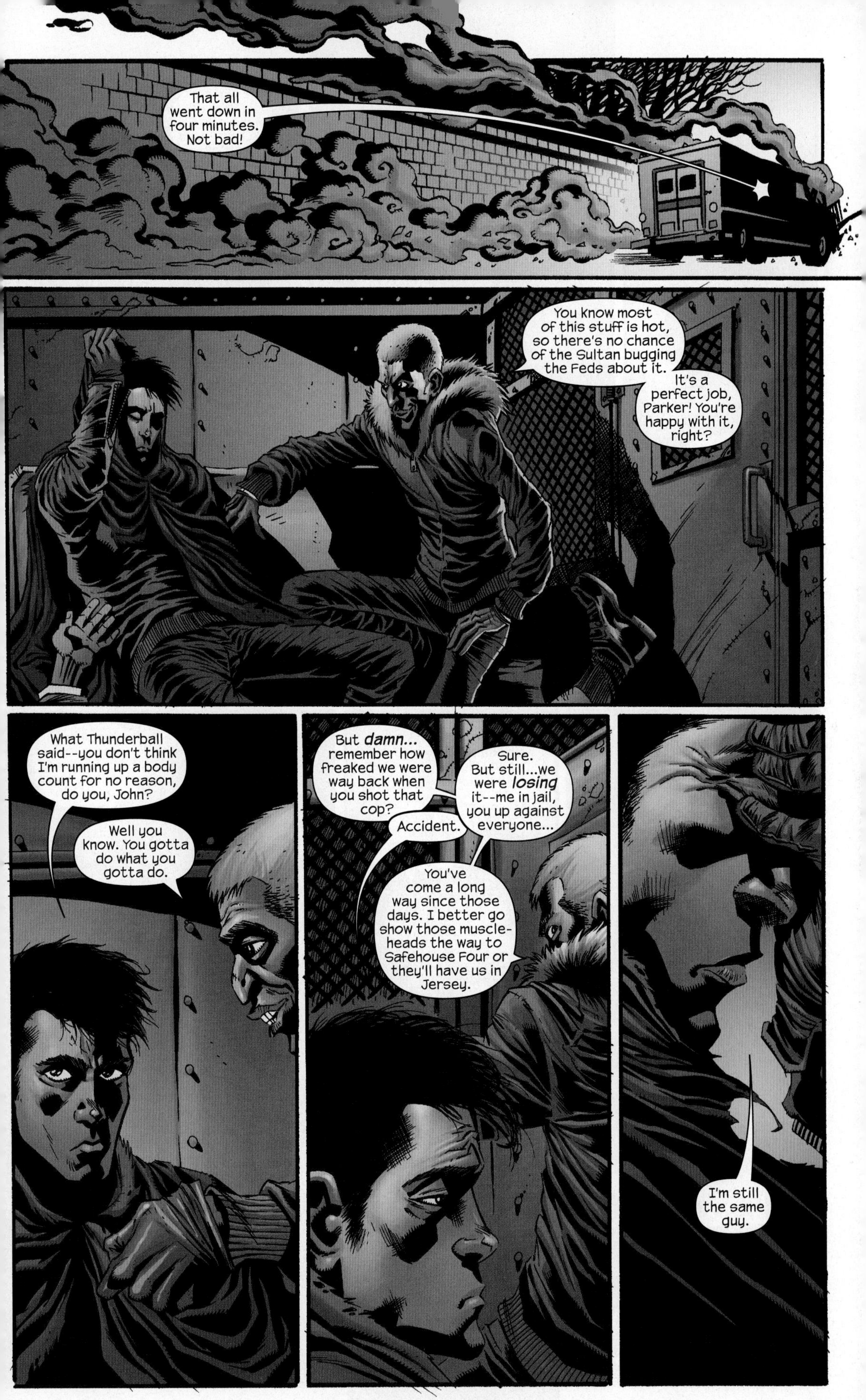

That all went down in four minutes. Not bad!
You know most of this stuff is hot, so there's no chance of the Sultan bugging the Feds about it.
It's a perfect job, Parker! You're happy with it, right?
What Thunderball said--you don't think I'm running up a body count for no reason, do you, John?
Well you know. You gotta do what you gotta do.
But *damn*... remember how freaked we were way back when you shot that cop?
Accident.
Sure. But still...we were *losing* it--me in jail, you up against everyone...
You've come a long way since those days. I better go show those muscle-heads the way to Safehouse Four or they'll have us in Jersey.
I'm still the same guy.

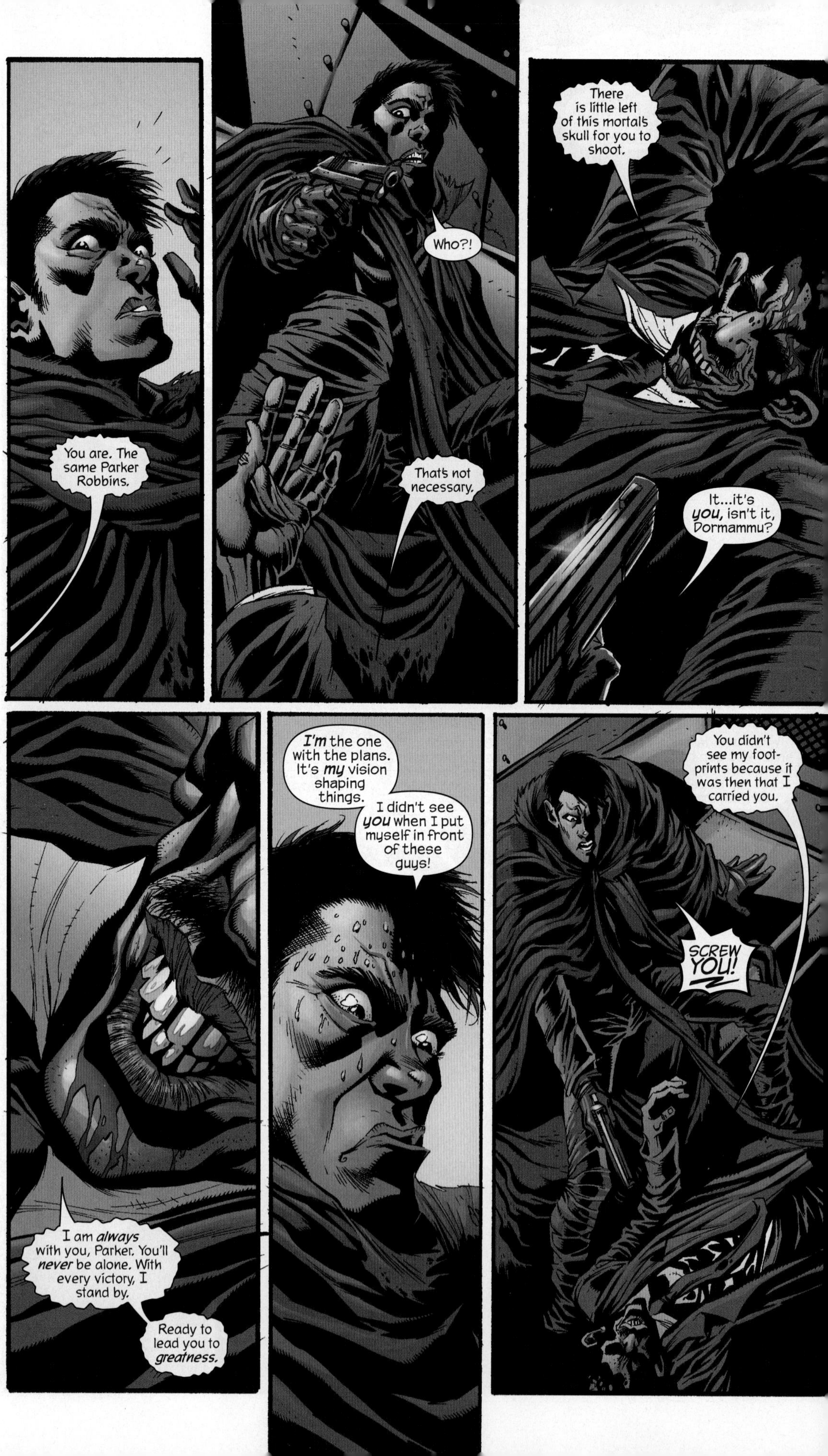
You are. The same Parker Robbins.
Who?!
That's not necessary.
There is little left of this mortal's skull for you to shoot.
It...it's *you*, isn't it, Dormammu?
I am *always* with you, Parker. You'll *never* be alone. With every victory, I stand by.
Ready to lead you to *greatness.*
I'm the one with the plans. It's *my* vision shaping things.
I didn't see *you* when I put myself in front of these guys!
You didn't see my foot-prints because it was then that I carried you.
SCREW YOU!

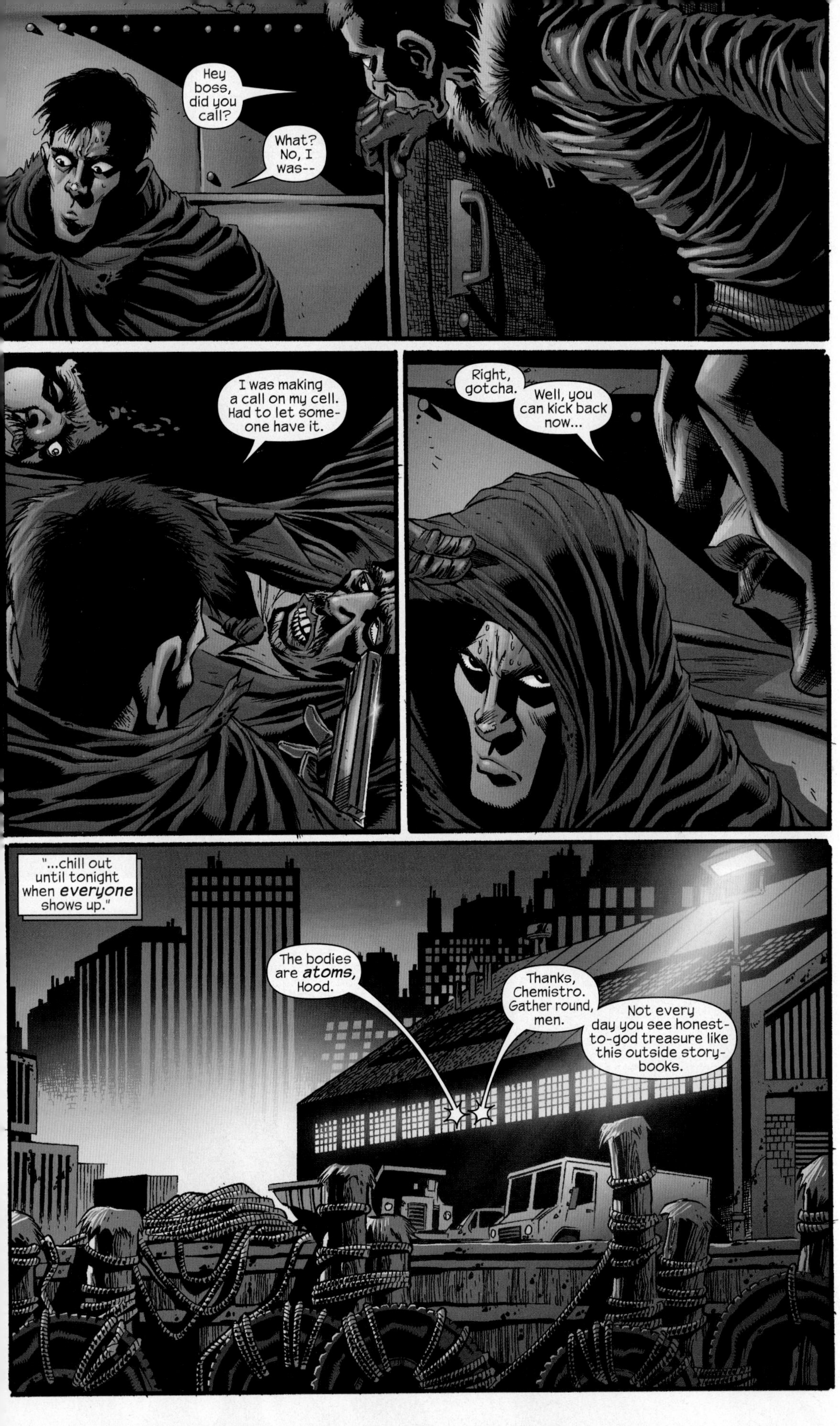

Hey boss, did you call?
What? No, I was--
I was making a call on my cell. Had to let some-one have it.
Right, gotcha.
Well, you can kick back now...
"...chill out until tonight when *everyone* shows up."
The bodies are *atoms,* Hood.
Thanks, Chemistro. Gather round, men.
Not every day you see honest-to-god treasure like this outside story-books.

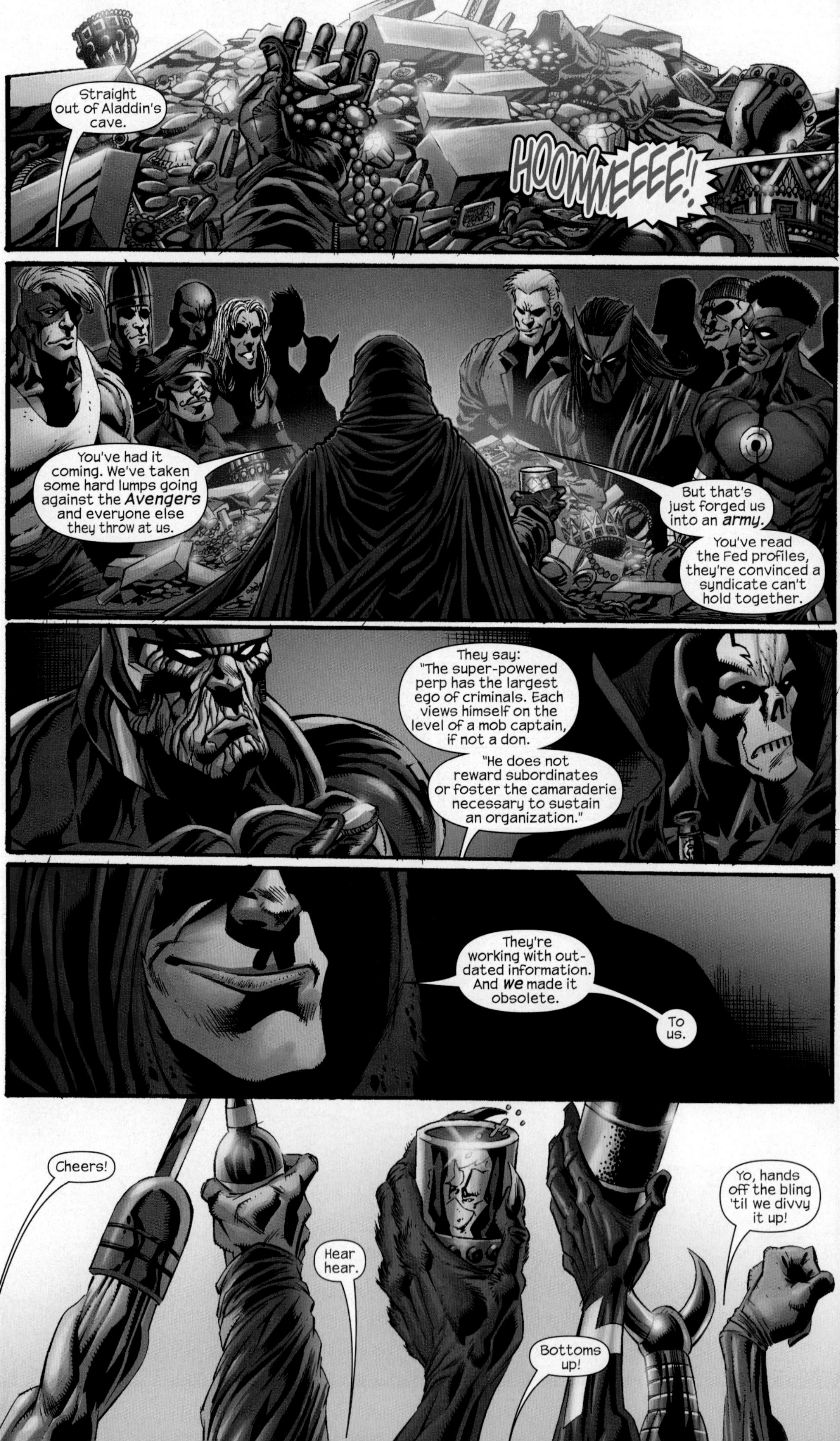
Straight out of Aladdin's cave.
HOOWWEEEE!!
You've had it coming. We've taken some hard lumps going against the Avengers and everyone else they throw at us.
But that's just forged us into an army.
You've read the Fed profiles, they're convinced a syndicate can't hold together.
They say: "The super-powered perp has the largest ego of criminals. Each views himself on the level of a mob captain, if not a don.
"He does not reward subordinates or foster the camaraderie necessary to sustain an organization."
They're working with out-dated information. And we made it obsolete.
To us.
Cheers!
Hear hear.
Bottoms up!
Yo, hands off the bling 'til we divvy it up!

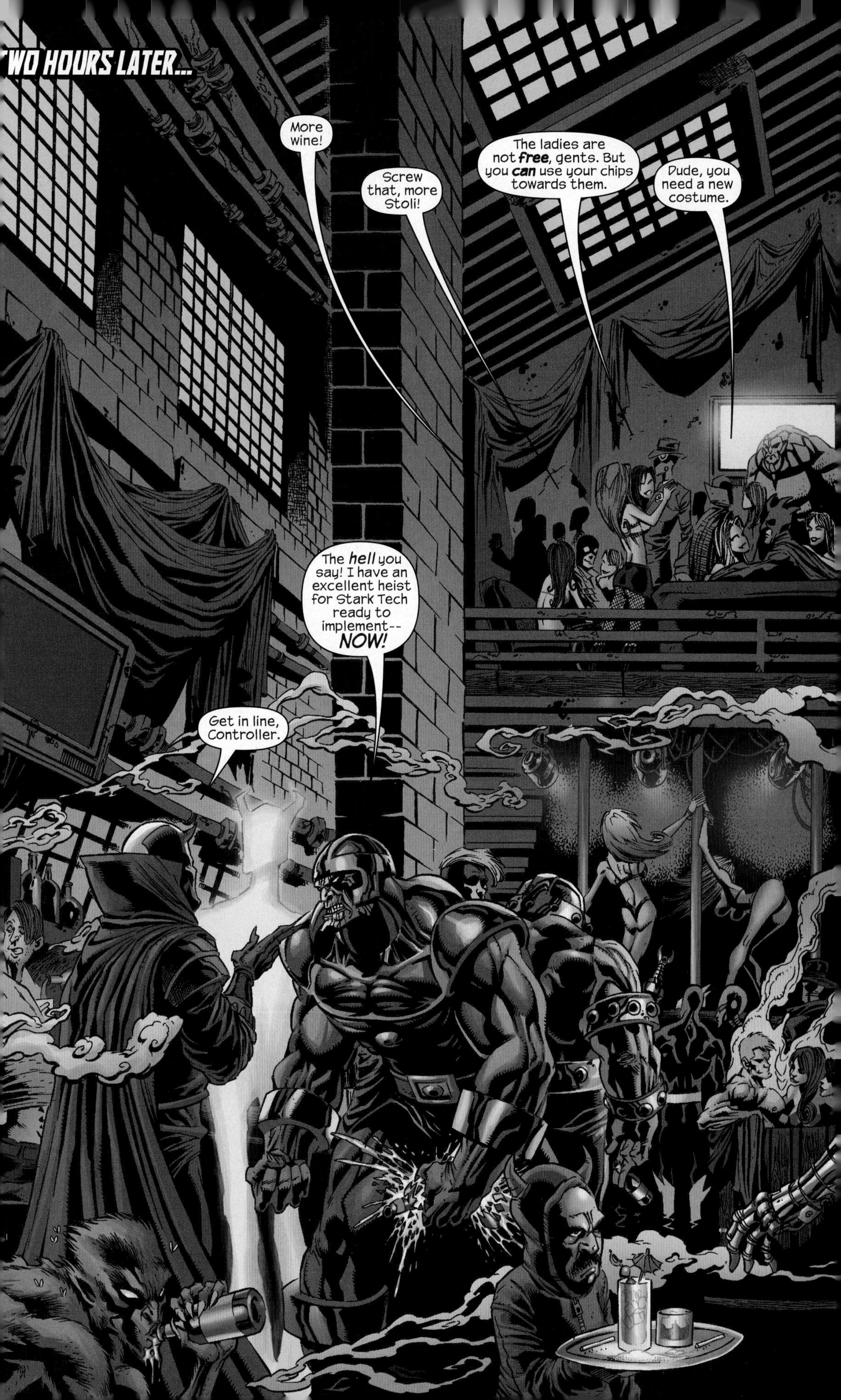

WO HOURS LATER...
More wine!
Screw that, more Stoli!
The ladies are not free, gents. But you can use your chips towards them.
Dude, you need a new costume.
The hell you say! I have an excellent heist for Stark Tech ready to implement-- NOW!
Get in line, Controller.

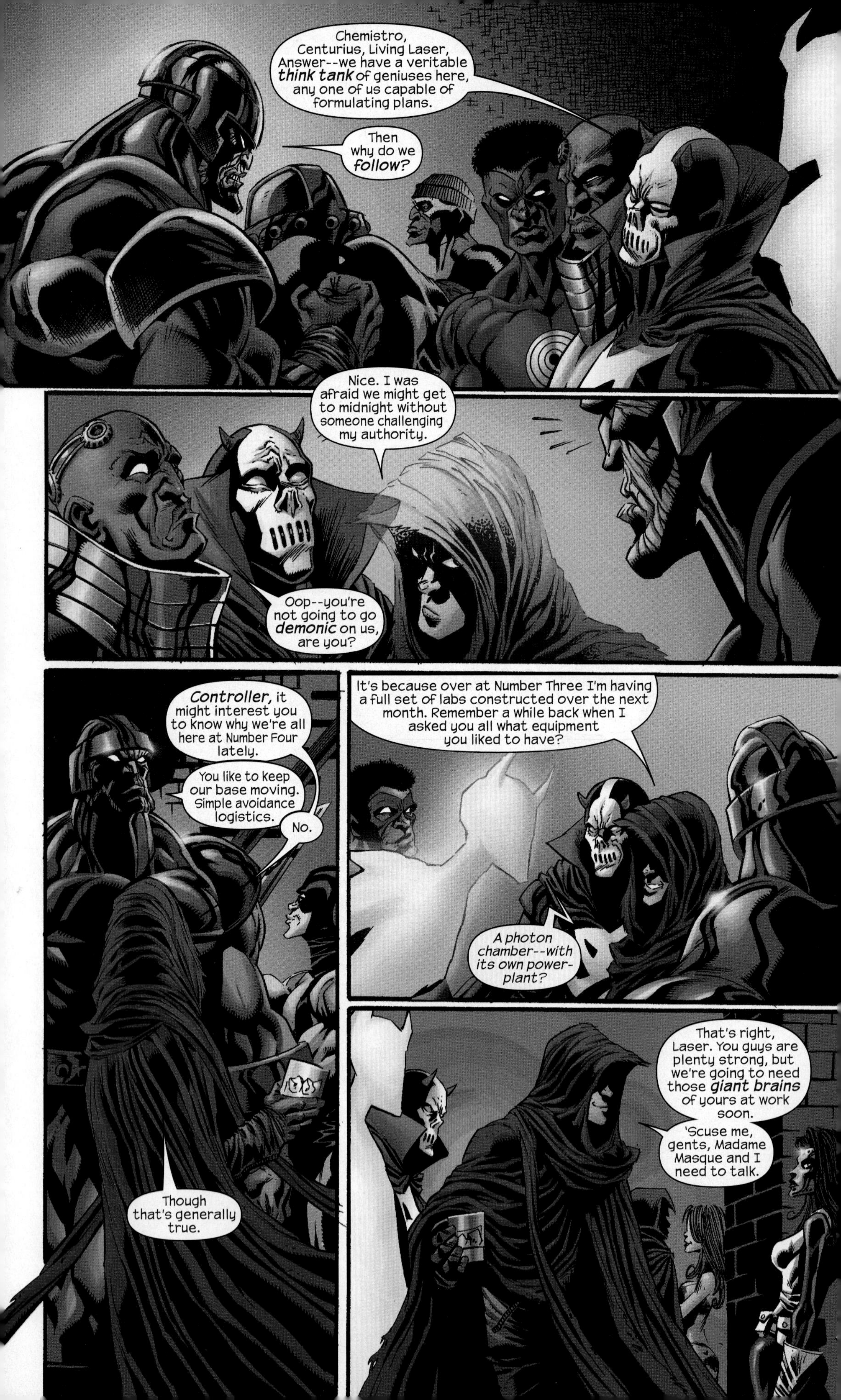

Chemistro, Centurius, Living Laser, Answer--we have a veritable think tank of geniuses here, any one of us capable of formulating plans.
Then why do we follow?
Nice. I was afraid we might get to midnight without someone challenging my authority.
Oop--you're not going to go demonic on us, are you?
Controller, it might interest you to know why we're all here at Number Four lately.
You like to keep our base moving. Simple avoidance logistics.
No.
Though that's generally true.
It's because over at Number Three I'm having a full set of labs constructed over the next month. Remember a while back when I asked you all what equipment you liked to have?
A photon chamber--with its own power-plant?
That's right, Laser. You guys are plenty strong, but we're going to need those giant brains of yours at work soon.
'Scuse me, gents, Madame Masque and I need to talk.

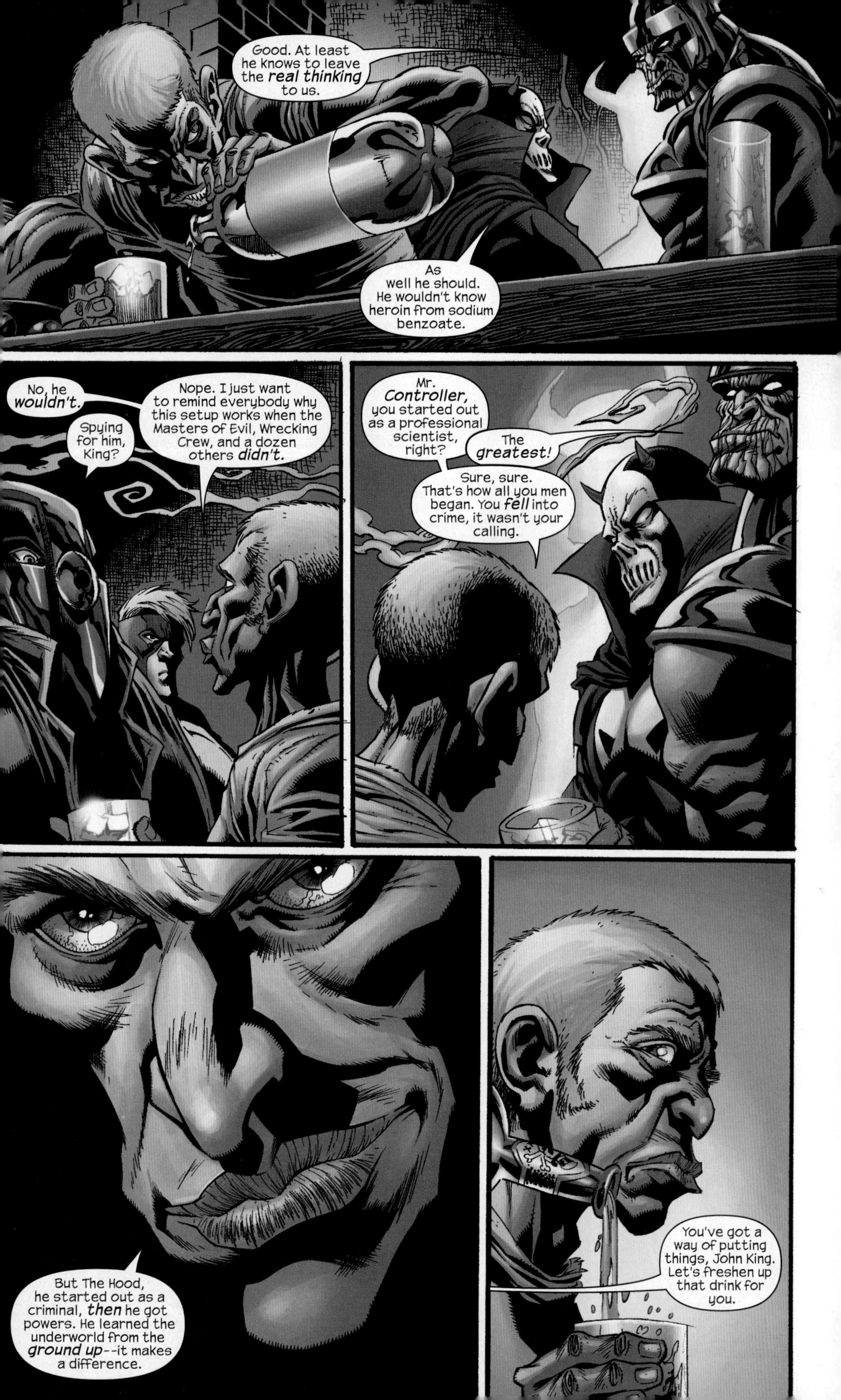

Good. At least he knows to leave the *real thinking* to us.
As well he should. He wouldn't know heroin from sodium benzoate.
No, he *wouldn't.*
Spying for him, King?
Nope. I just want to remind everybody why this setup works when the Masters of Evil, Wrecking Crew, and a dozen others *didn't.*
Mr. *Controller,* you started out as a professional scientist, right?
The *greatest!*
Sure, sure. That's how all you men began. You *fell* into crime, it wasn't your calling.
But The Hood, he started out as a criminal, *then* he got powers. He learned the underworld from the *ground up*--it makes a difference.
You've got a way of putting things, John King. Let's freshen up that drink for you.

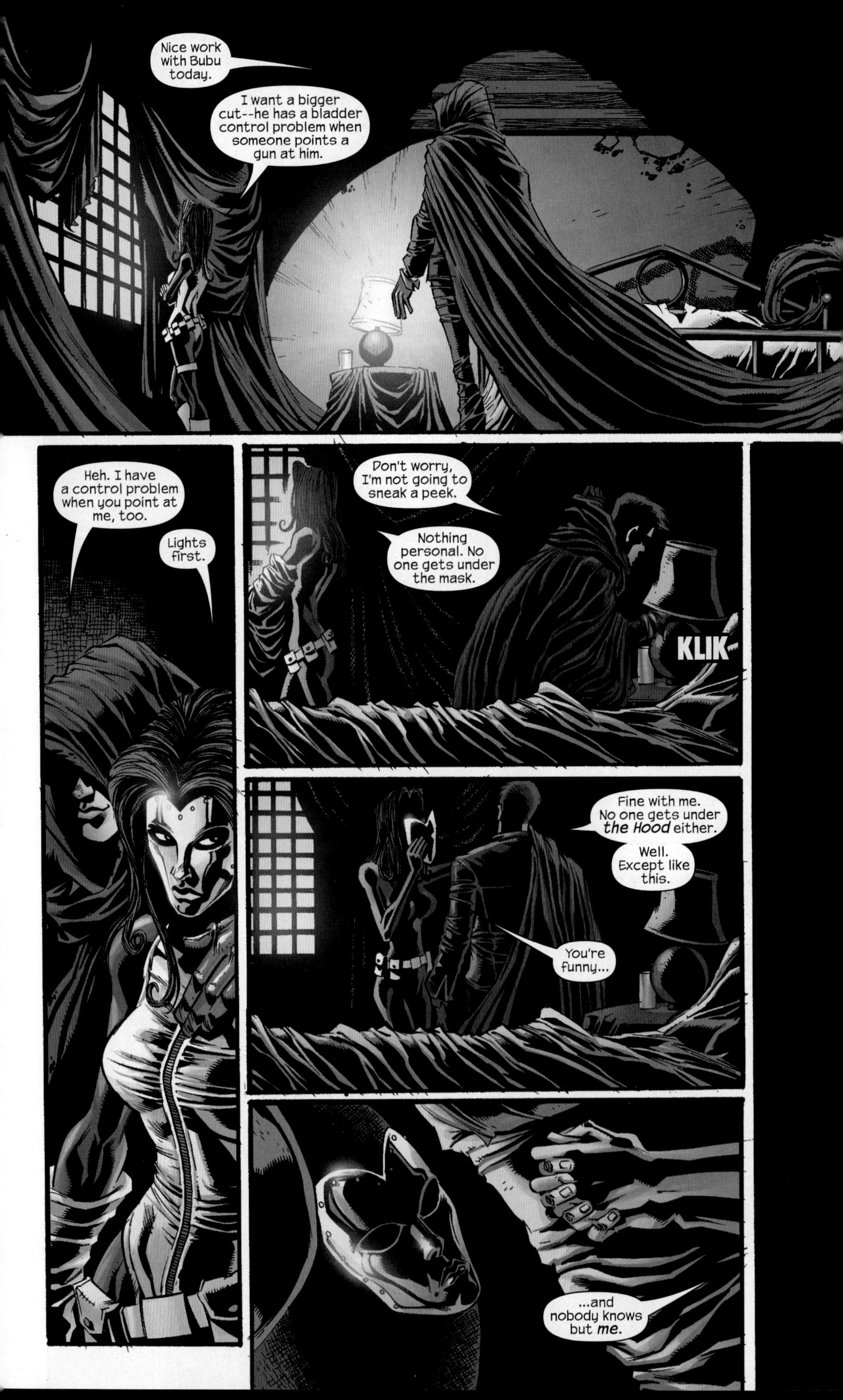
Nice work with Bubu today.
I want a bigger cut--he has a bladder control problem when someone points a gun at him.
Heh. I have a control problem when you point at me, too.
Lights first.
Don't worry, I'm not going to sneak a peek.
Nothing personal. No one gets under the mask.
KLIK
Fine with me. No one gets under *the Hood* either.
Well. Except like this.
You're funny...
...and nobody knows but *me.*

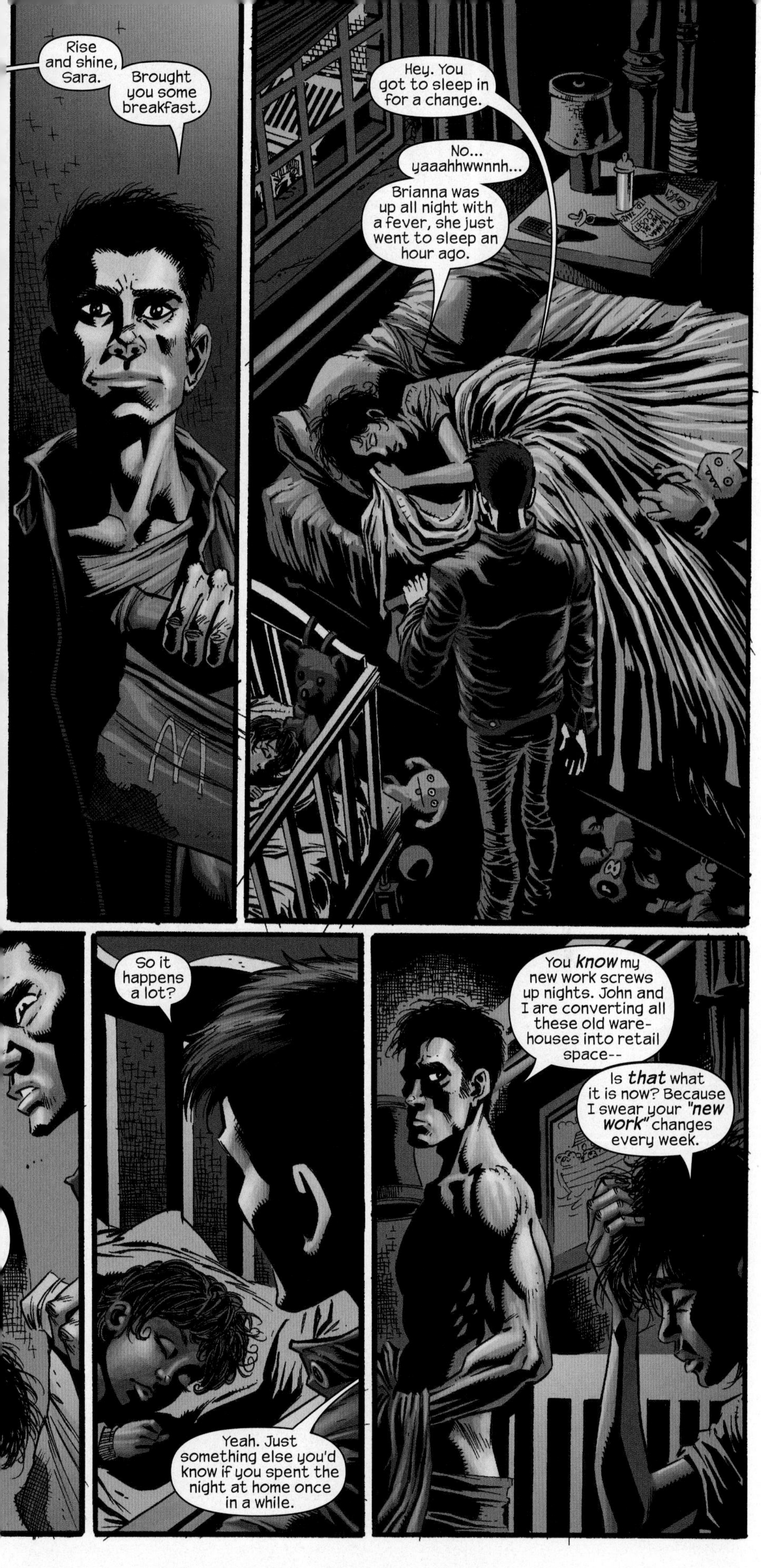

Rise and shine, Sara.
Brought you some breakfast.
Hey. You got to sleep in for a change.
No... yaaahhwwnnh...
Brianna was up all night with a fever, she just went to sleep an hour ago.
So it happens a lot?
Yeah. Just something else you'd know if you spent the night at home once in a while.
You *know* my new work screws up nights. John and I are converting all these old ware-houses into retail space--
Is *that* what it is now? Because I swear your *"new work"* changes every week.

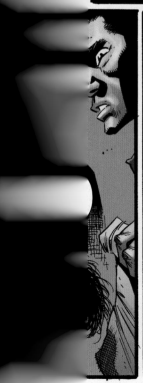

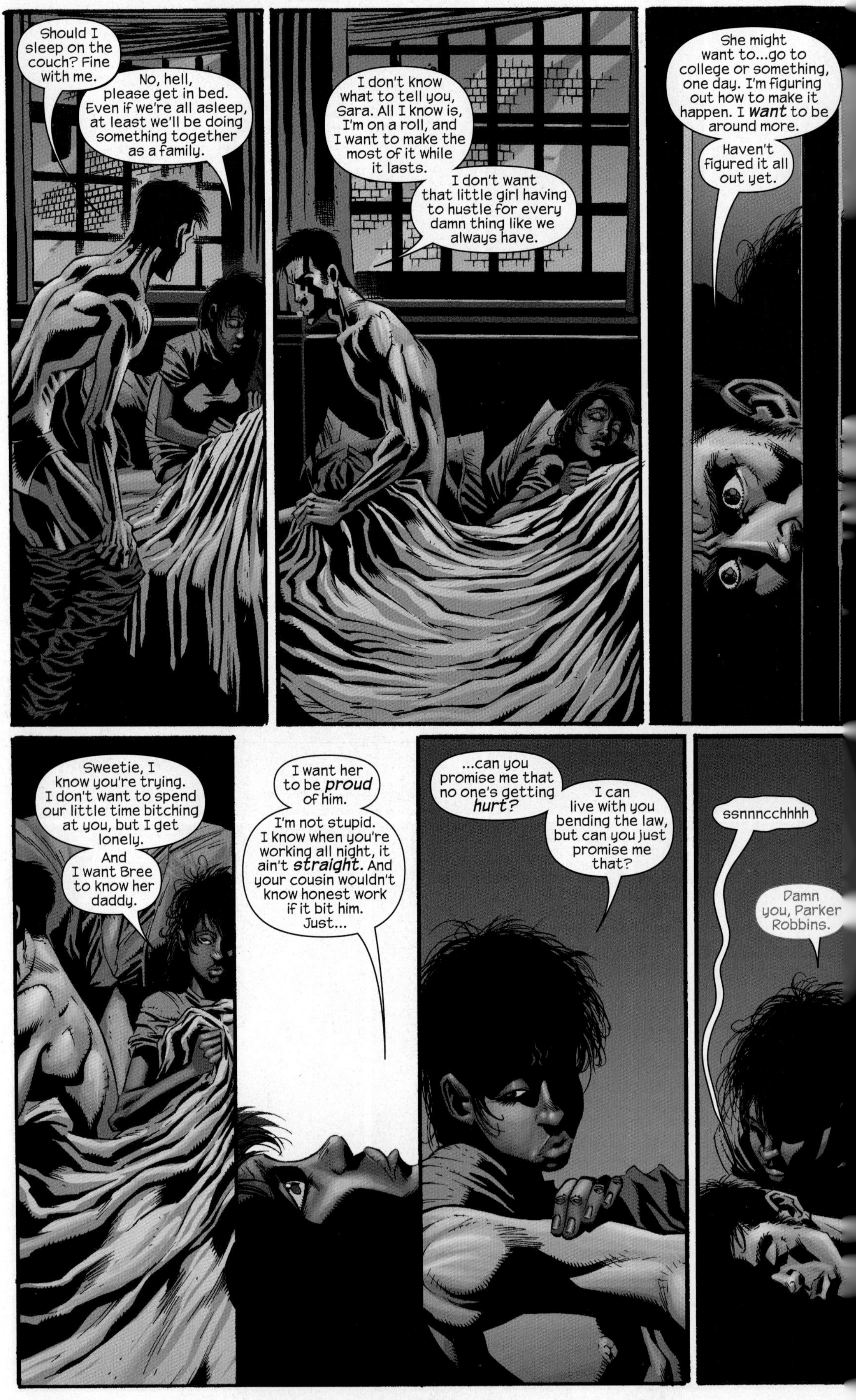
Should I sleep on the couch? Fine with me.
No, hell, please get in bed. Even if we're all asleep, at least we'll be doing something together as a family.
I don't know what to tell you, Sara. All I know is, I'm on a roll, and I want to make the most of it while it lasts.
I don't want that little girl having to hustle for every damn thing like we always have.
She might want to...go to college or something, one day. I'm figuring out how to make it happen. I *want* to be around more.
Haven't figured it all out yet.
Sweetie, I know you're trying. I don't want to spend our little time bitching at you, but I get lonely.
And I want Bree to know her daddy.
I want her to be *proud* of him.
I'm not stupid. I know when you're working all night, it ain't *straight*. And your cousin wouldn't know honest work if it bit him. Just...
...can you promise me that no one's getting *hurt?*
I can live with you bending the law, but can you just promise me that?
ssnnncchhhh
Damn you, Parker Robbins.

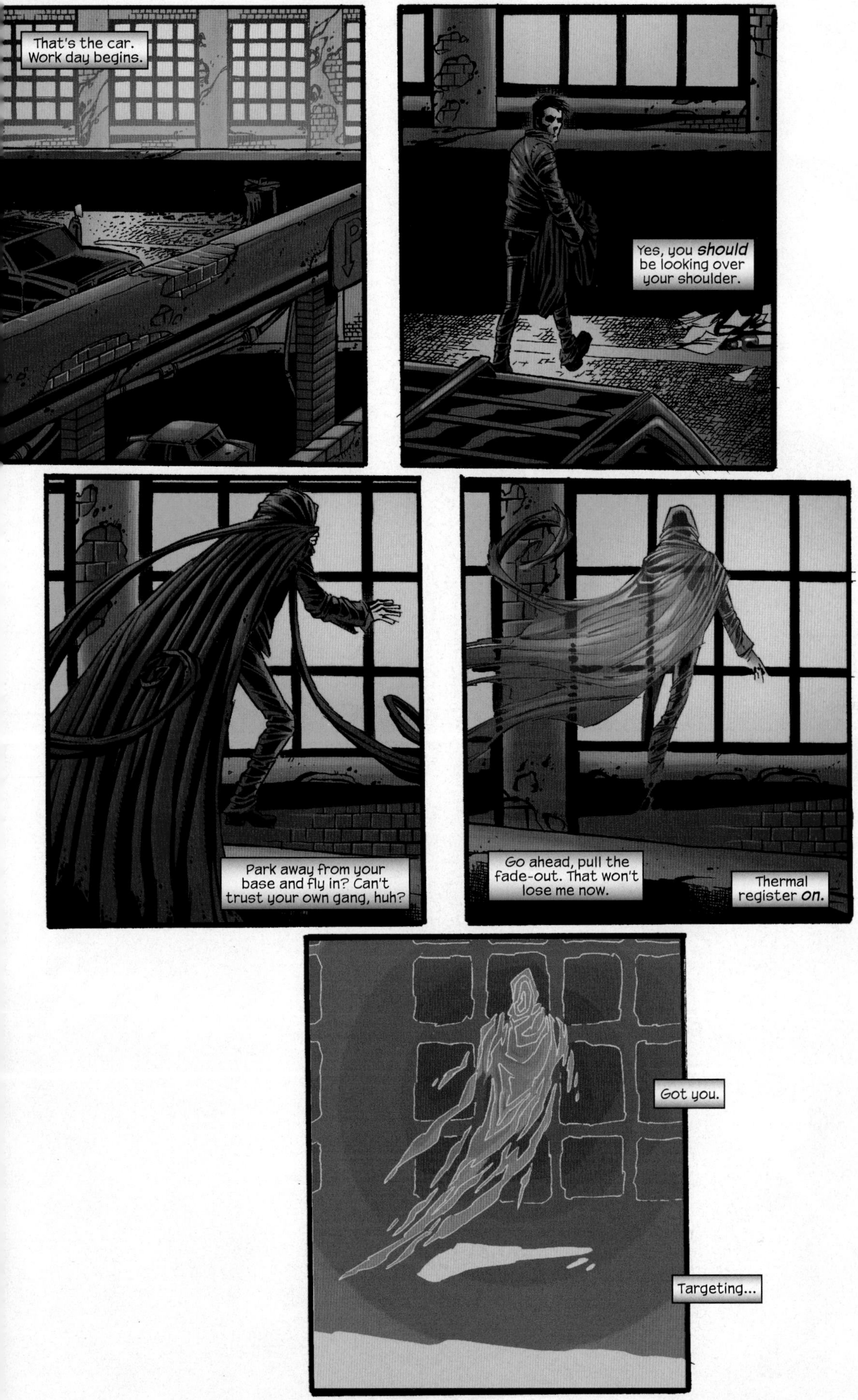

That's the car. Work day begins.
Yes, you *should* be looking over your shoulder.
Park away from your base and fly in? Can't trust your own gang, huh?
Go ahead, pull the fade-out. That won't lose me now.
Thermal register *on.*
Got you.
Targeting...

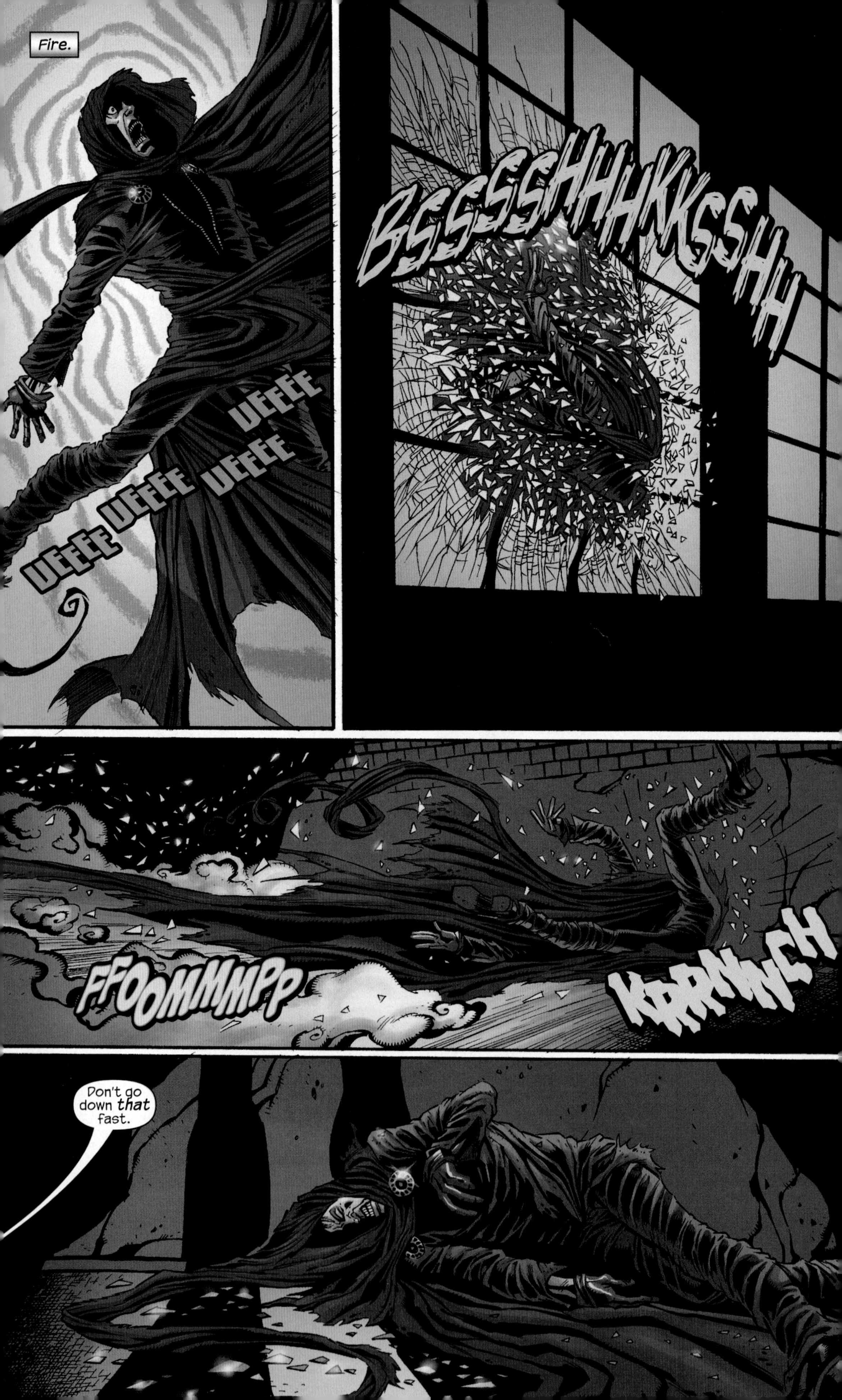

Fire.
VEEEE VEEEE VEEEE VEEEE
BSSSSSHHHKKSSHH
FFOOMMMPP
KRRNNCH
Don't go down *that* fast.

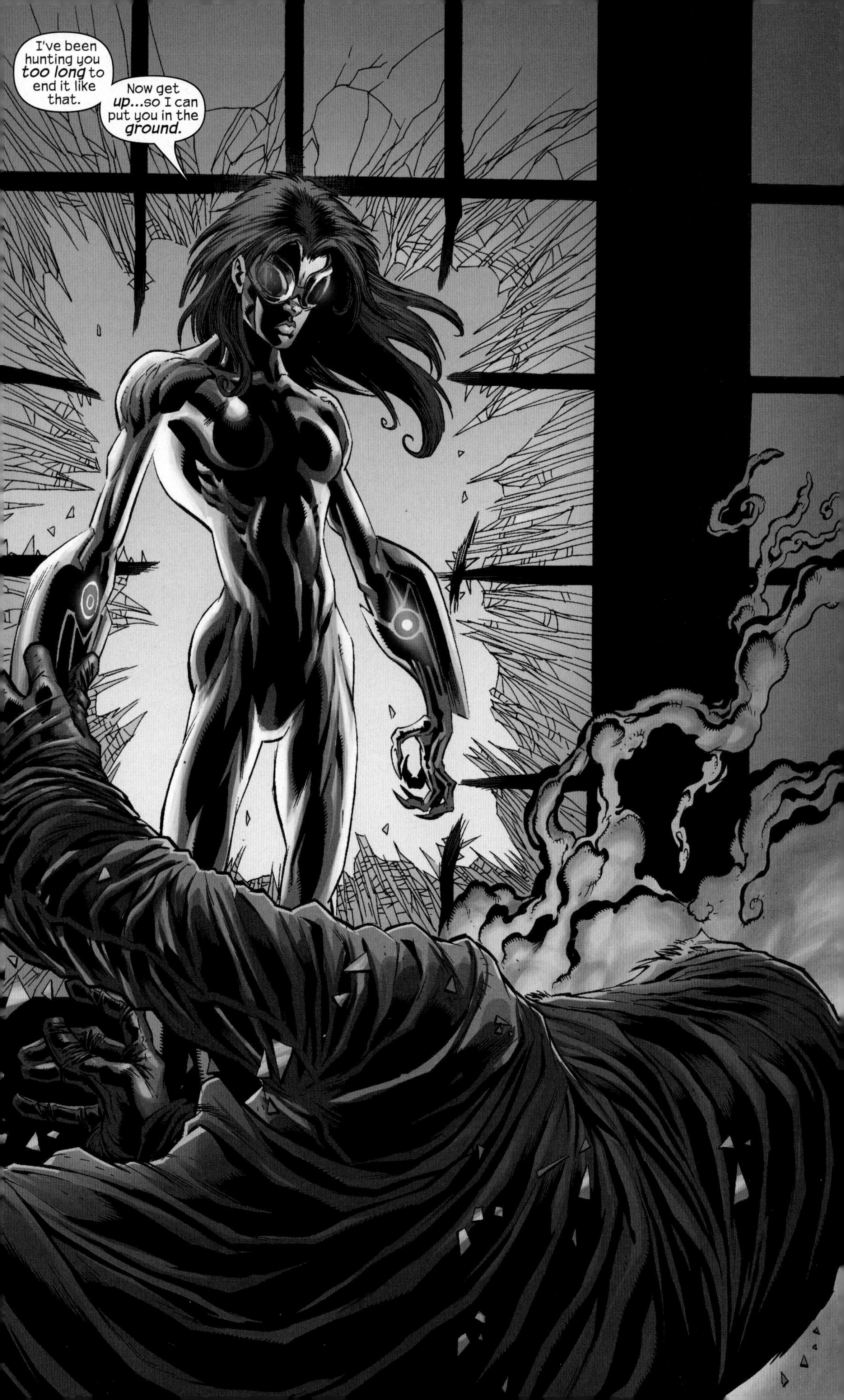
I've been hunting you too long to end it like that.
Now get up...so I can put you in the ground.

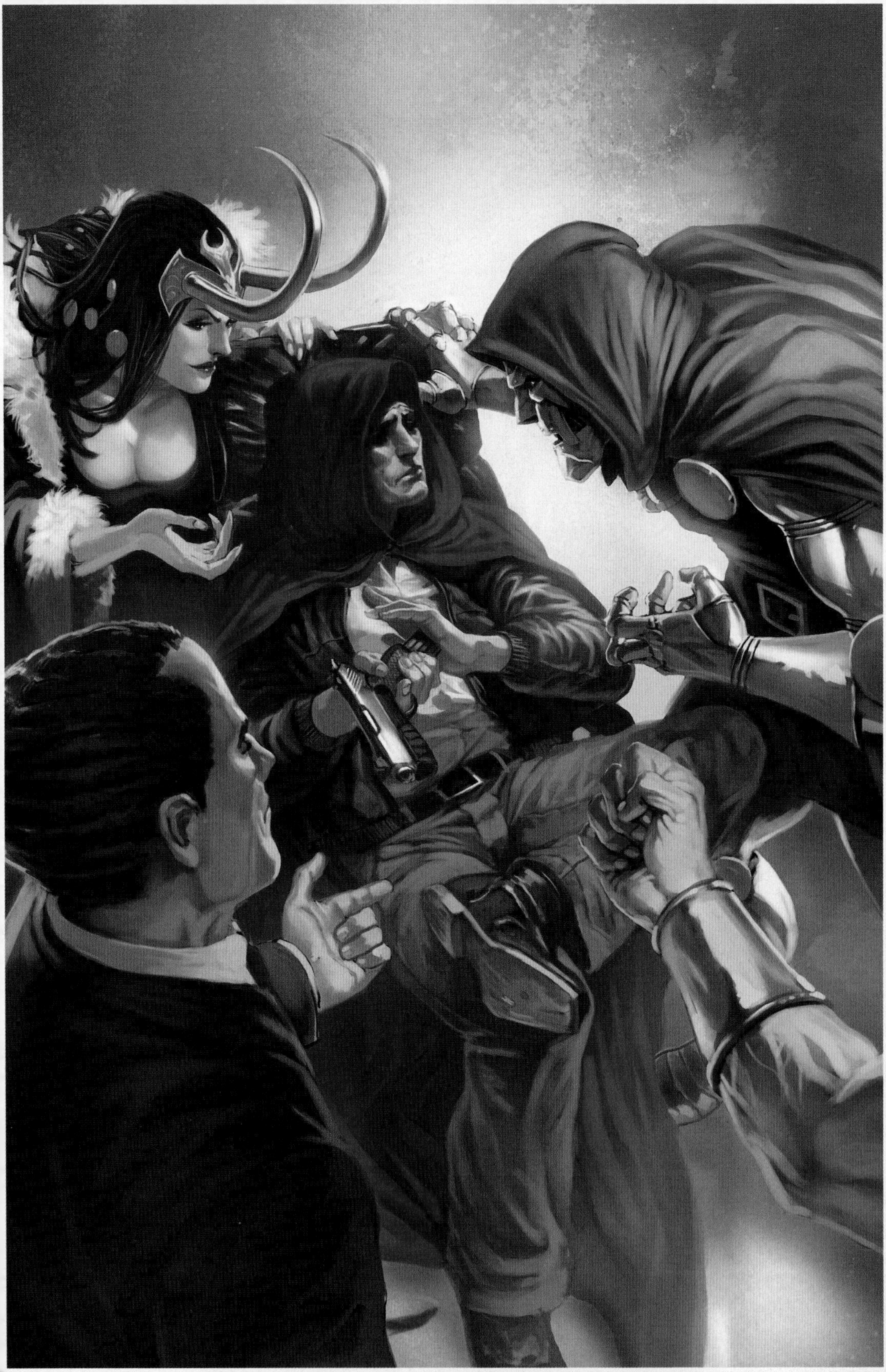

YAAHHHHHH!!

HAUNTED

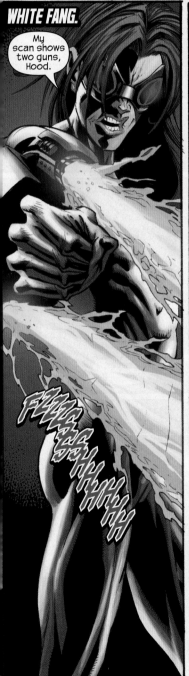

WHITE FANG.

My scan shows two guns, Hood.

FZZZZSSSSHHHHHHH

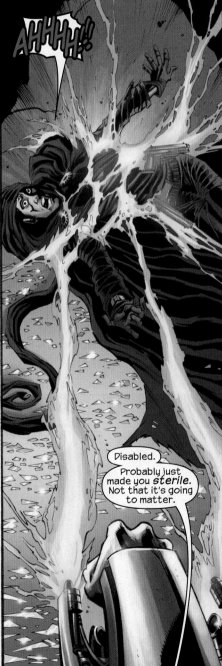

AHHHH!!

Disabled. Probably just made you *sterile*. Not that it's going to matter.

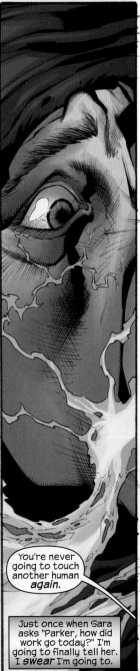

You're never going to touch another human *again*.

Just once when Sara asks "Parker, how did work go today?" I'm going to finally tell her. I *swear* I'm going to.

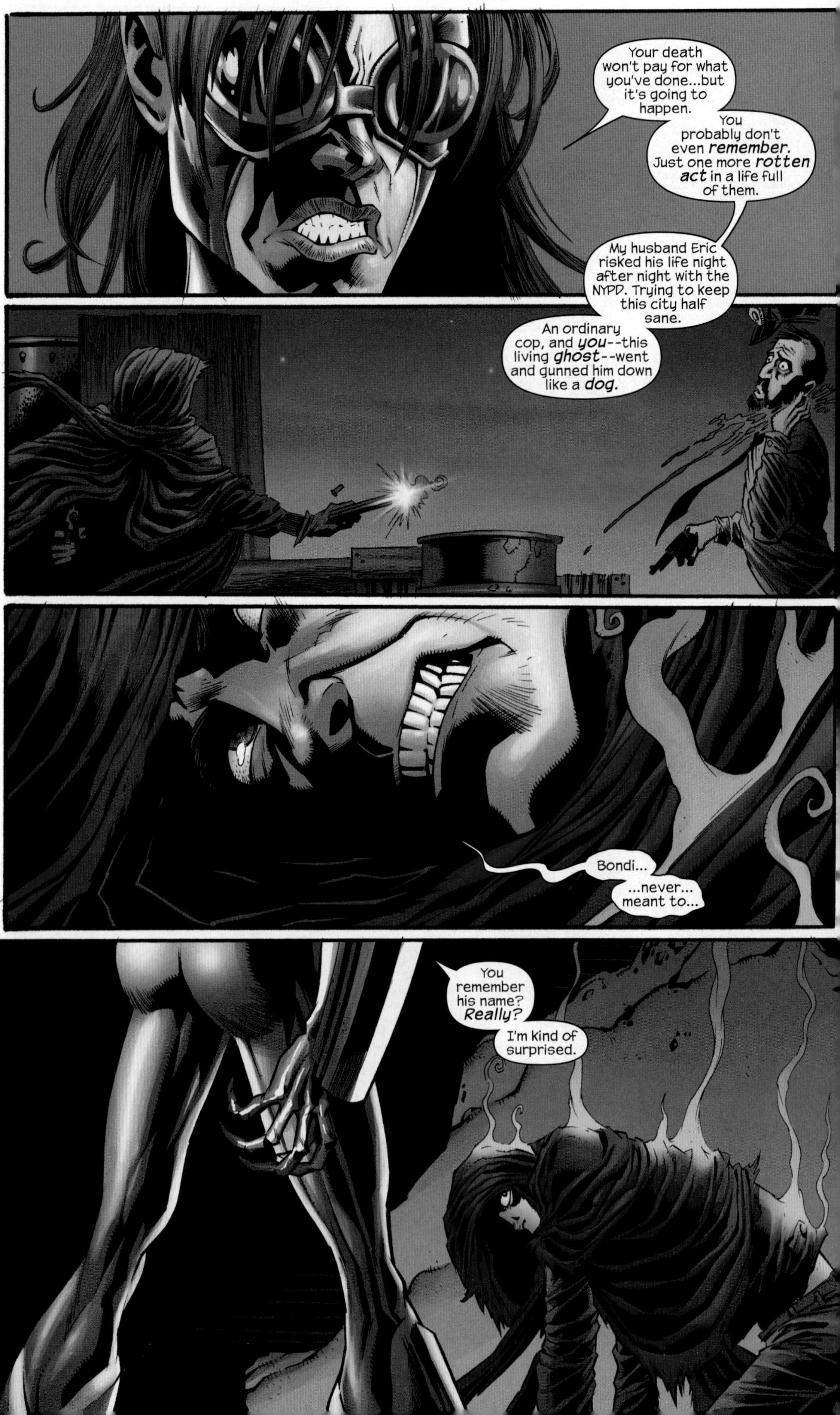

Your death won't pay for what you've done...but it's going to happen.
You probably don't even *remember.* Just one more *rotten act* in a life full of them.
My husband Eric risked his life night after night with the NYPD. Trying to keep this city half sane.
An ordinary cop, and *you*--this living *ghost*--went and gunned him down like a *dog.*
Bondi...
...never... meant to...
You remember his name? *Really?*
I'm kind of surprised.

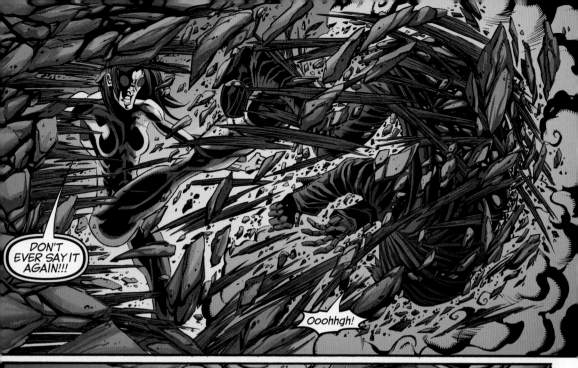

DON'T EVER SAY IT AGAIN!!!

Ooohhgh!

Oh, please.

Fine, be a *coward*. Go invisible.

I can still see you clear as day.

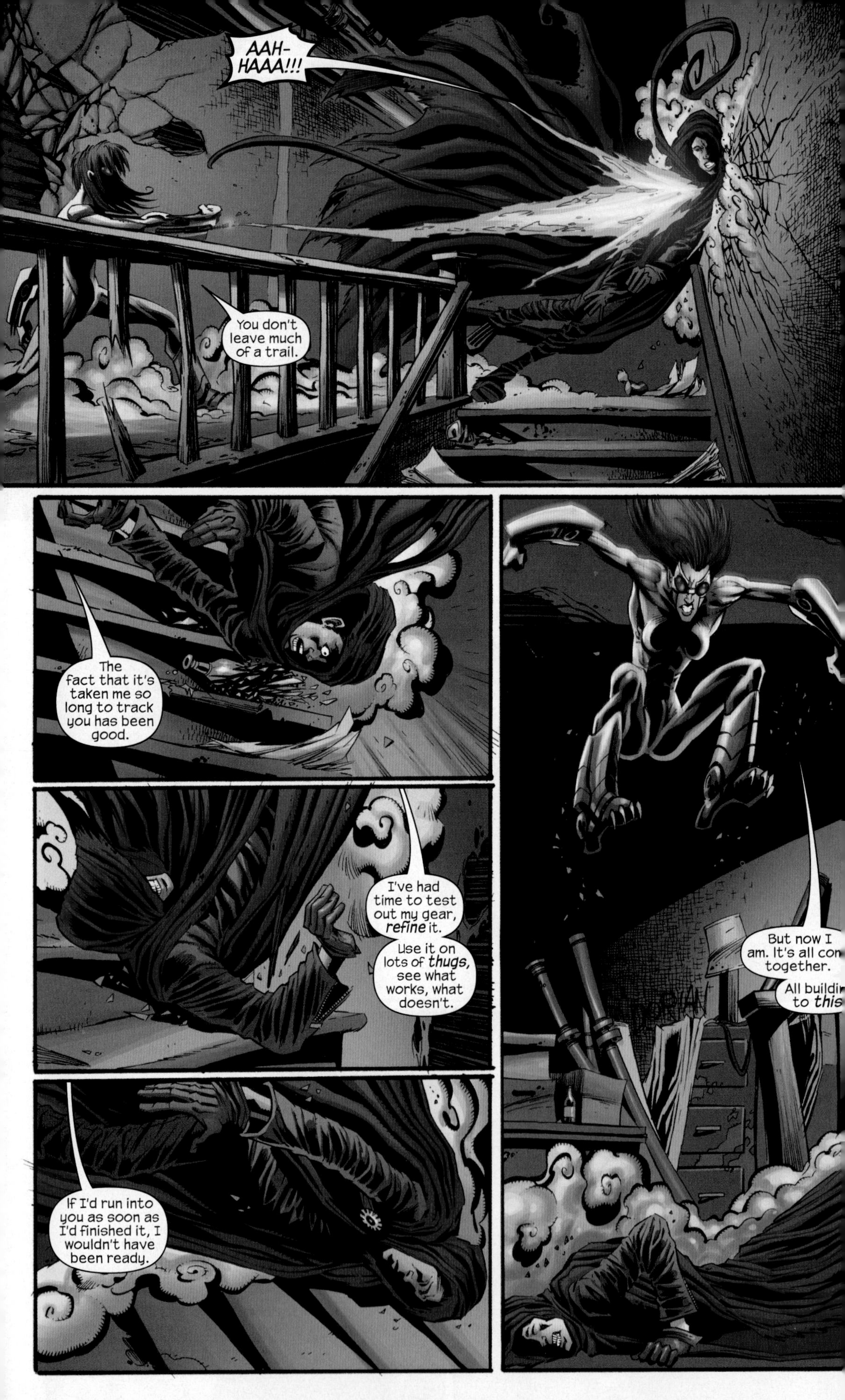
AAH-HAAA!!!
You don't leave much of a trail.
The fact that it's taken me so long to track you has been good.
I've had time to test out my gear, *refine* it.
Use it on lots of *thugs,* see what works, what doesn't.
If I'd run into you as soon as I'd finished it, I wouldn't have been ready.
But now I am. It's all co
together.
All buildi
to *this*

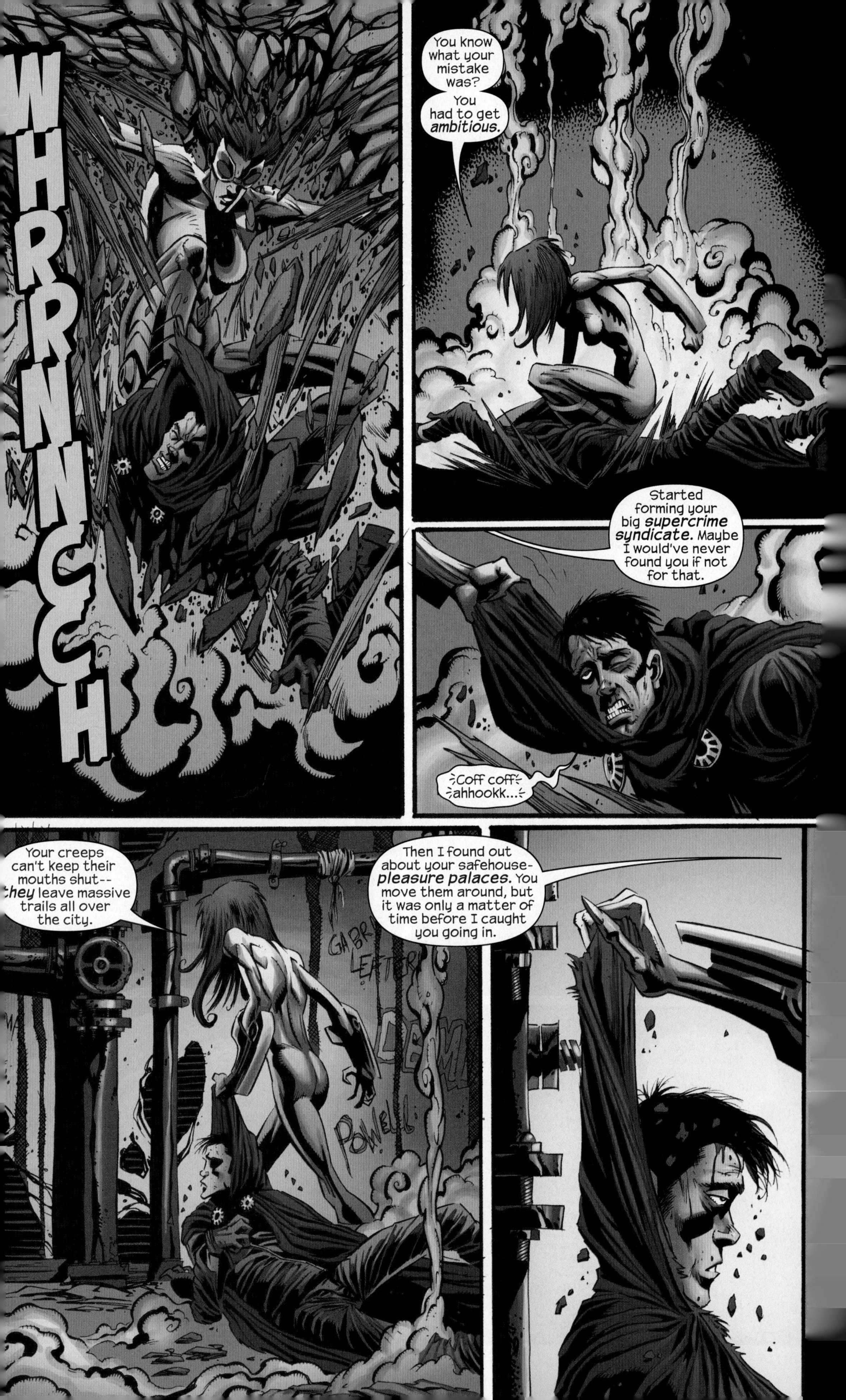

WHRRNNCCH
You know what your mistake was?
You had to get *ambitious.*
Started forming your big *supercrime syndicate.* Maybe I would've never found you if not for that.
Coff coff ahhookk...
Your creeps can't keep their mouths shut-- *they* leave massive trails all over the city.
Then I found out about your safehouse-*pleasure palaces.* You move them around, but it was only a matter of time before I caught you going in.

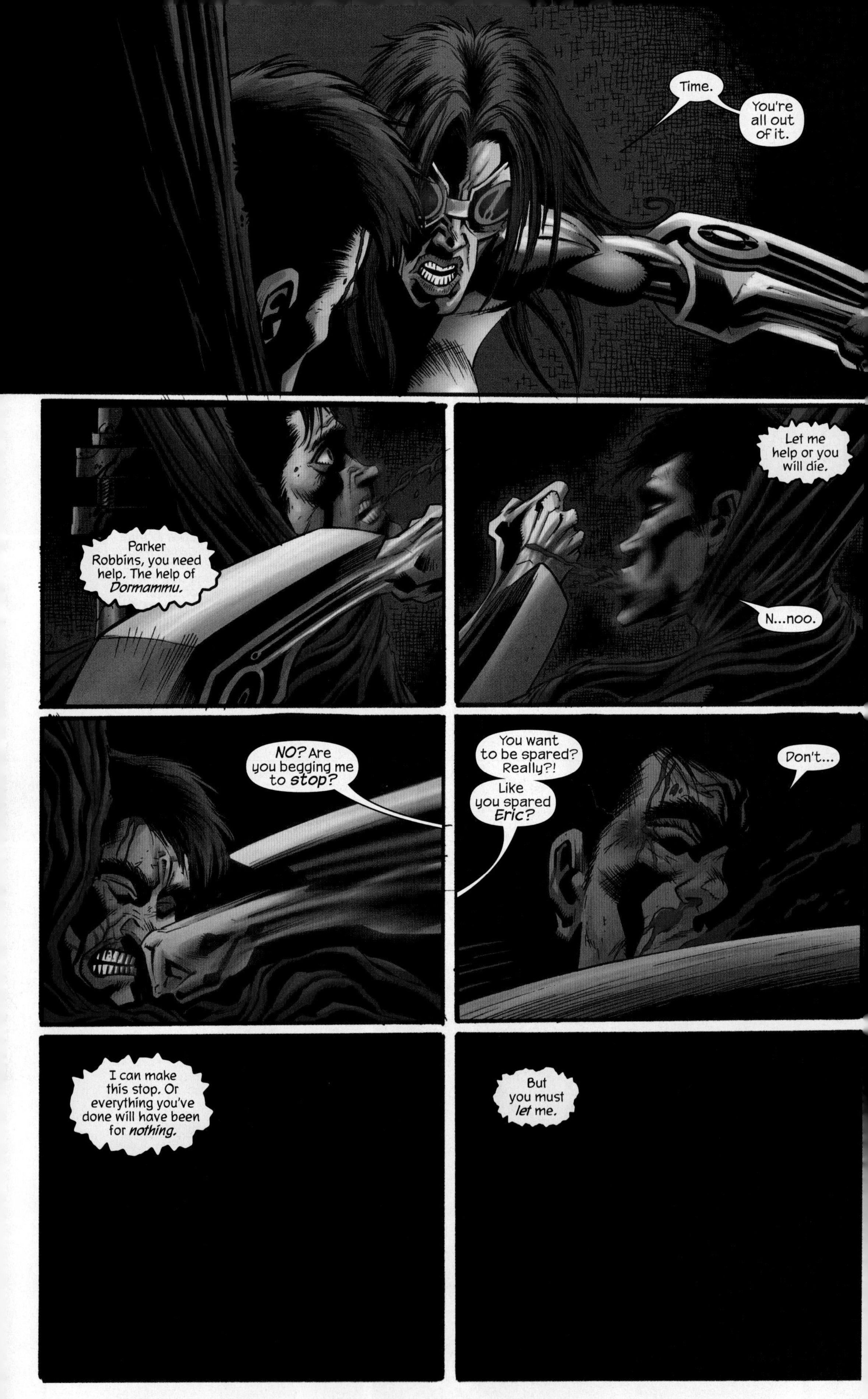
Time.
You're all out of it.
Parker Robbins, you need help. The help of *Dormammu.*
Let me help or you will die.
N...noo.
NO? Are you begging me to ***stop?***
You want to be spared? Really?!
Like you spared ***Eric?***
Don't...
I can make this stop. Or everything you've done will have been for *nothing.*
But you must *let* me.

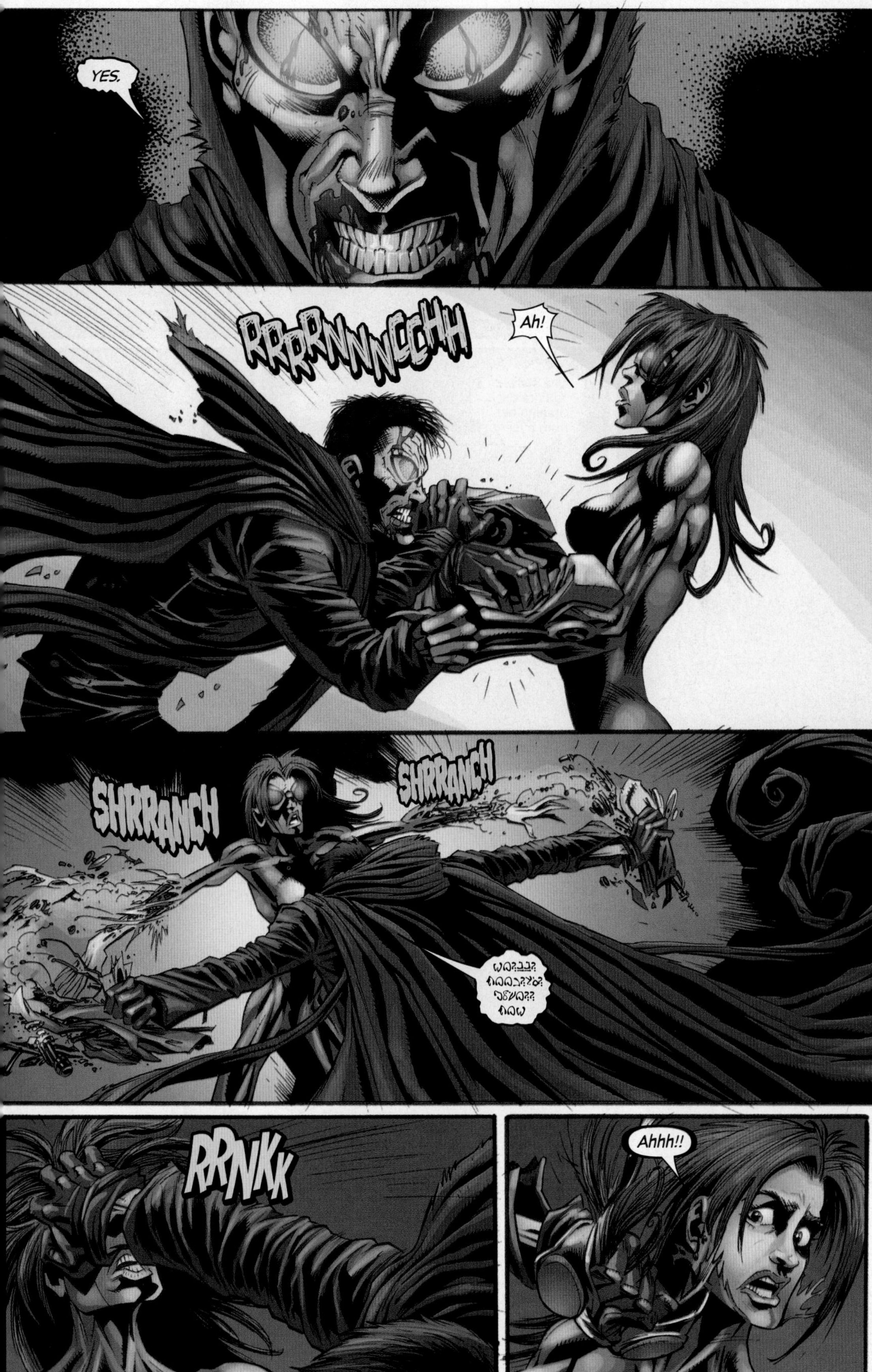
YES.
RRRRNNNCCHH
Ah!
SHRRANCH
SHRRANCH
RRNKK
Ahhh!!

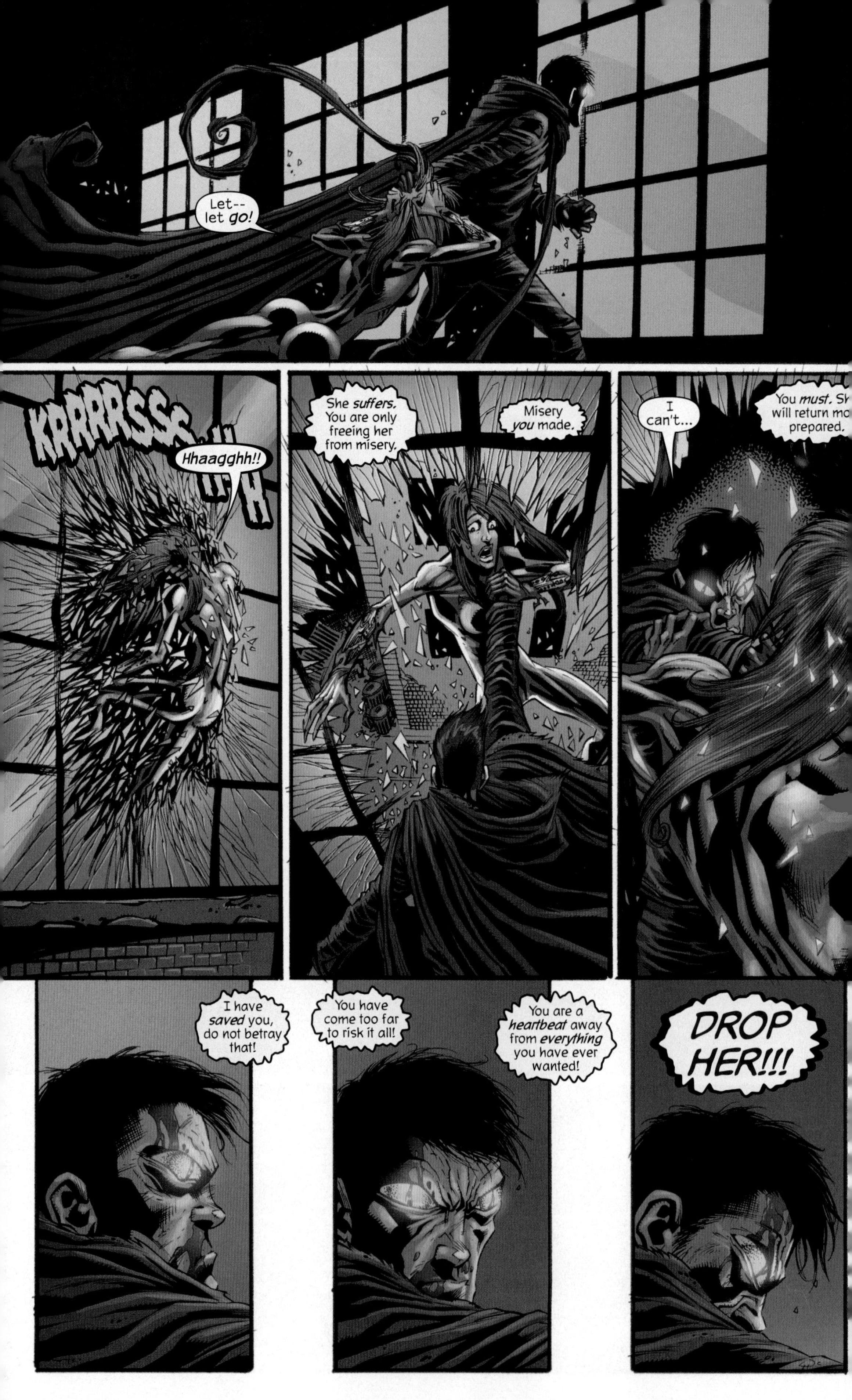
Let--
let go!
KRRRRSSSHH
Hhaaagghh!!
She suffers. You are only freeing her from misery.
Misery you made.
I can't...
You must. Sh will return mo prepared.
I have saved you, do not betray that!
You have come too far to risk it all!
You are a heartbeat away from everything you have ever wanted!
DROP HER!!!

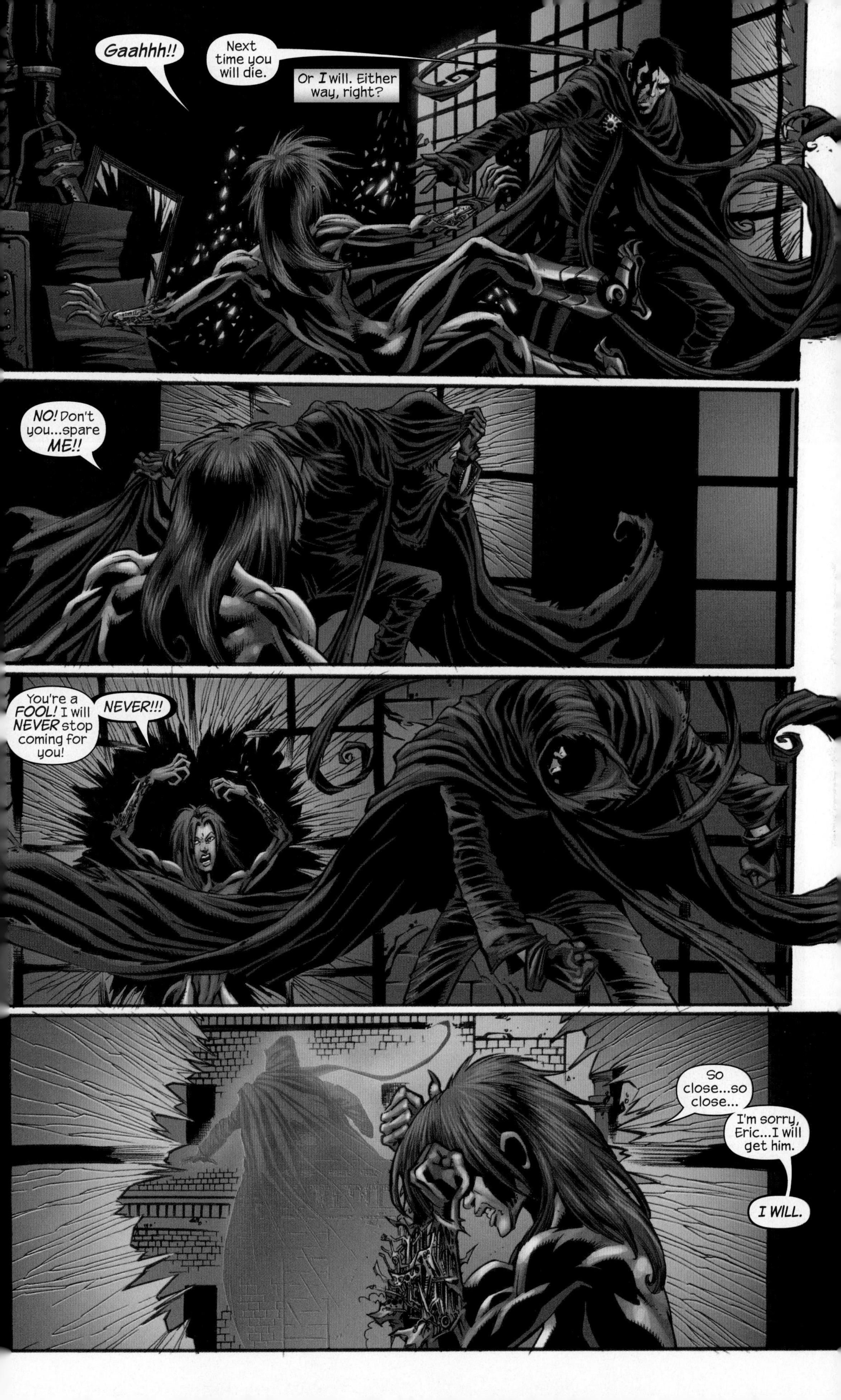
Gaahhh!!
Next time you will die.
Or I will. Either way, right?
NO! Don't you...spare ME!!
You're a FOOL! I will NEVER stop coming for you!
NEVER!!!
So close...so close...
I'm sorry, Eric...I will get him.
I WILL.

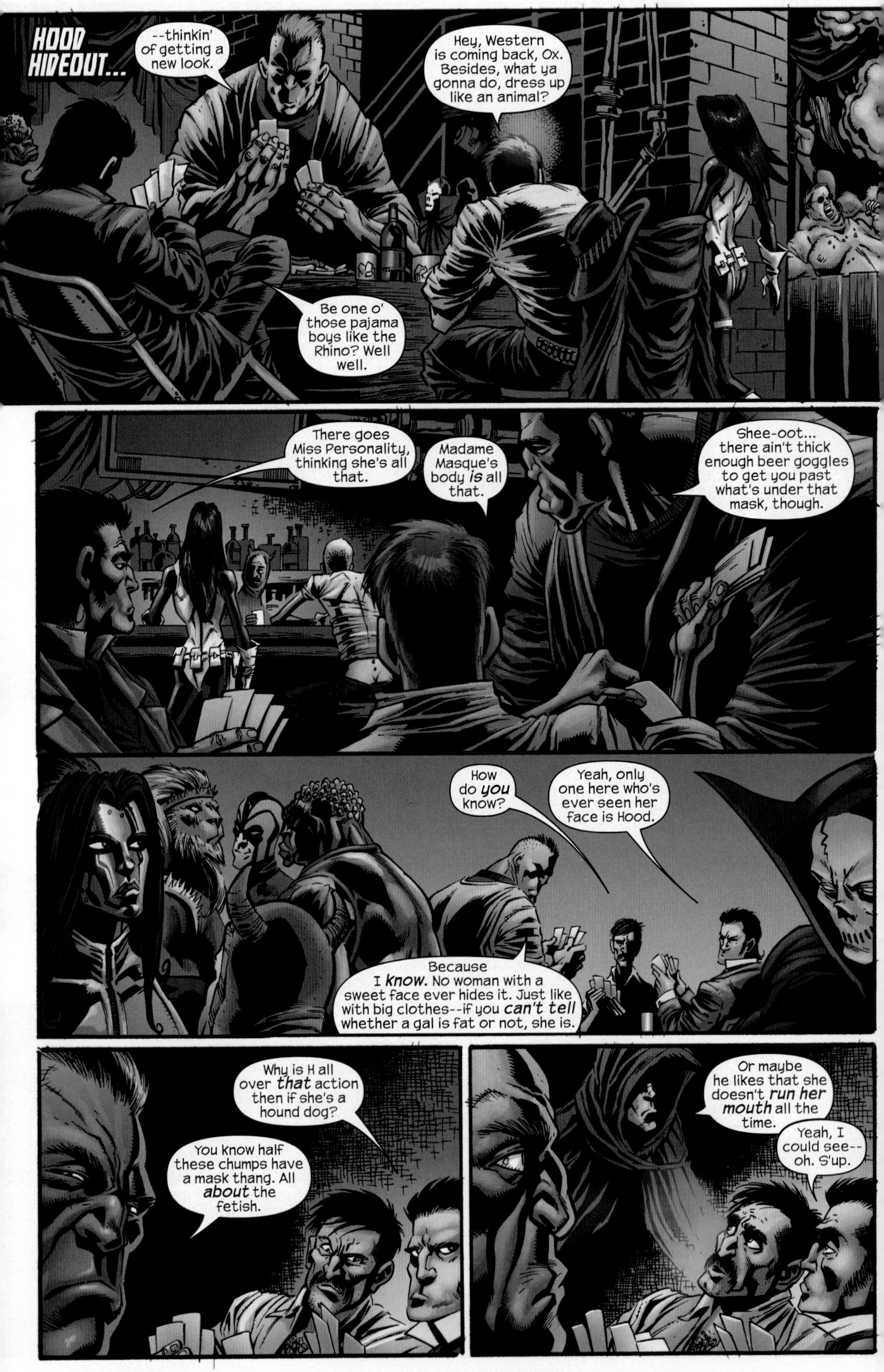
HOOD HIDEOUT...
--thinkin' of getting a new look.
Hey, Western is coming back, Ox. Besides, what ya gonna do, dress up like an animal?
Be one o' those pajama boys like the Rhino? Well well.
There goes Miss Personality, thinking she's all that.
Madame Masque's body *is* all that.
Shee-oot... there ain't thick enough beer goggles to get you past what's under that mask, though.
How do *you* know?
Yeah, only one here who's ever seen her face is Hood.
Because I *know.* No woman with a sweet face ever hides it. Just like with big clothes--if you *can't tell* whether a gal is fat or not, she is.
Why is H all over *that* action then if she's a hound dog?
You know half these chumps have a mask thang. All *about* the fetish.
Or maybe he likes that she doesn't *run her mouth* all the time.
Yeah, I could see--oh. S'up.

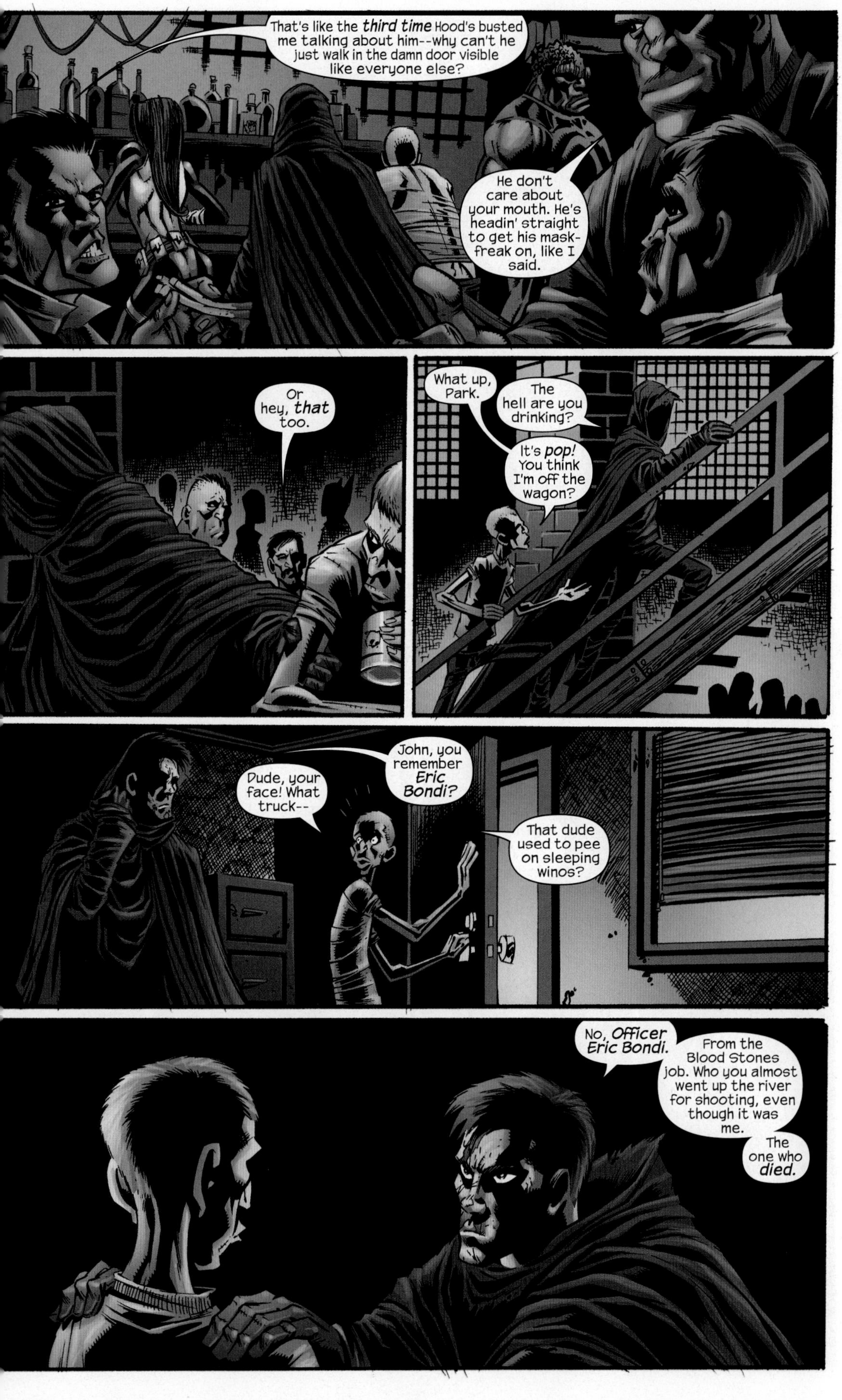
That's like the third time Hood's busted me talking about him--why can't he just walk in the damn door visible like everyone else?
He don't care about your mouth. He's headin' straight to get his mask-freak on, like I said.
Or hey, that too.
What up, Park.
The hell are you drinking?
It's pop! You think I'm off the wagon?
Dude, your face! What truck--
John, you remember Eric Bondi?
That dude used to pee on sleeping winos?
No, Officer Eric Bondi.
From the Blood Stones job. Who you almost went up the river for shooting, even though it was me.
The one who died.

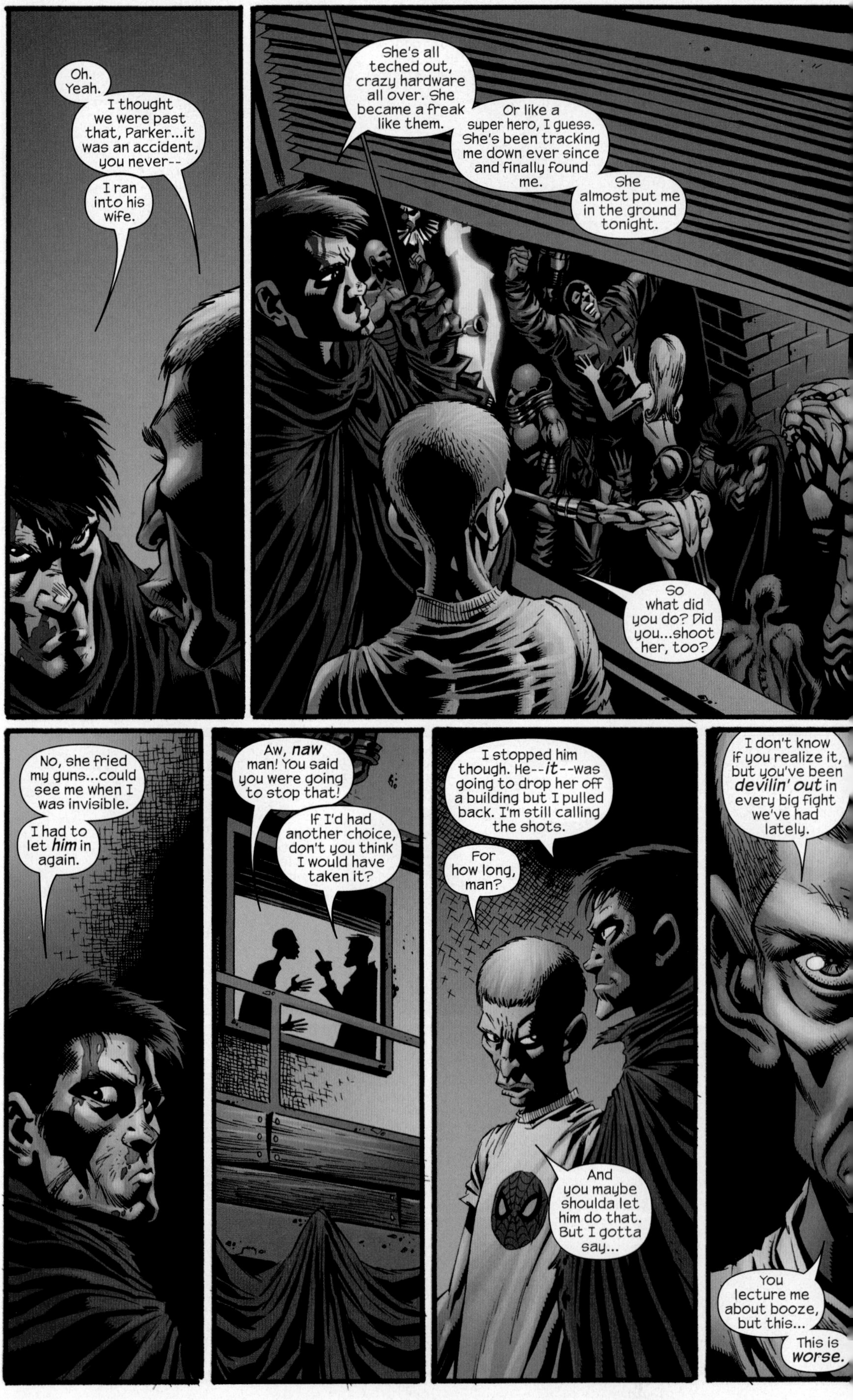

Oh. Yeah.
I thought we were past that, Parker...it was an accident, you never--
I ran into his wife.
She's all teched out, crazy hardware all over. She became a freak like them.
Or like a super hero, I guess. She's been tracking me down ever since and finally found me.
She almost put me in the ground tonight.
So what did you do? Did you...shoot her, too?
No, she fried my guns...could see me when I was invisible.
I had to let *him* in again.
Aw, *naw* man! You said you were going to stop that!
If I'd had another choice, don't you think I would have taken it?
I stopped him though. He--*it*--was going to drop her off a building but I pulled back. I'm still calling the shots.
For how long, man?
And you maybe shoulda let him do that. But I gotta say...
I don't know if you realize it, but you've been *devilin' out* in every big fight we've had lately.
You lecture me about booze, but this...
This is *worse.*

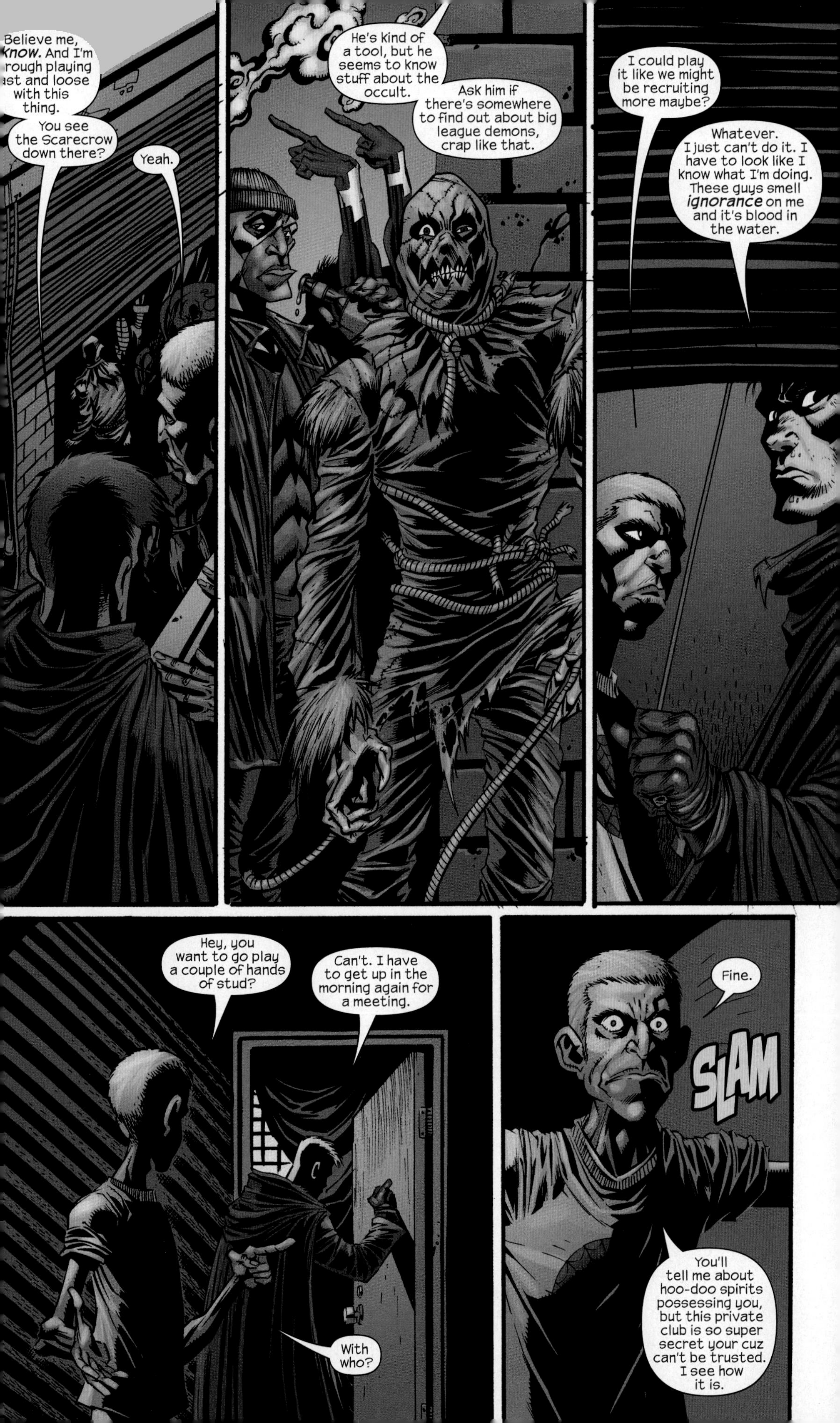
Believe me, know. And I'm rough playing ast and loose with this thing.
You see the Scarecrow down there?
Yeah.
He's kind of a tool, but he seems to know stuff about the occult.
Ask him if there's somewhere to find out about big league demons, crap like that.
I could play it like we might be recruiting more maybe?
Whatever. I just can't do it. I have to look like I know what I'm doing. These guys smell *ignorance* on me and it's blood in the water.
Hey, you want to go play a couple of hands of stud?
Can't. I have to get up in the morning again for a meeting.
With who?
Fine.
SLAM
You'll tell me about hoo-doo spirits possessing you, but this private club is so super secret your cuz can't be trusted. I see how it is.

BRRRRRRRRNNNGGG

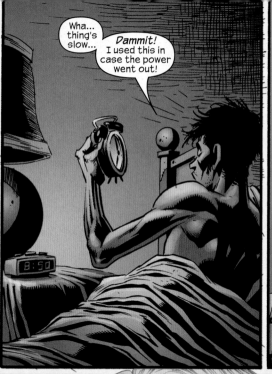

Wha... thing's slow... *Dammit!* I used this in case the power went out!

Don't even have time to get coffee--

Good morning.

You didn't forget our *meeting* this morning, did you?

No...late night.

I can imagine. Come, the alliance doesn't like to wait.

White Queen, wait. One thing...

My mental image...I can make myself look...*better*, right?

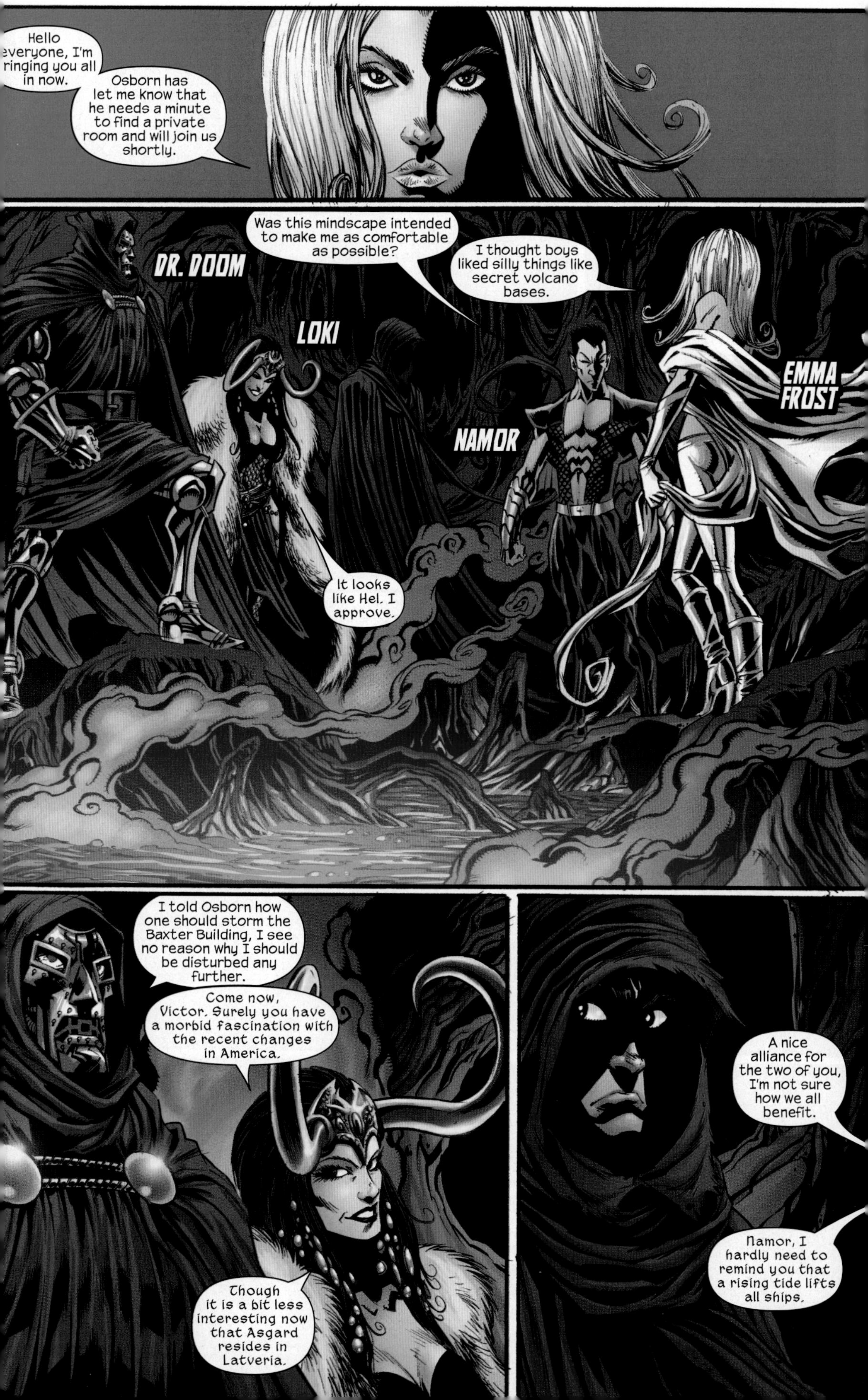

Hello everyone, I'm ringing you all in now.
Osborn has let me know that he needs a minute to find a private room and will join us shortly.
Was this mindscape intended to make me as comfortable as possible?
I thought boys liked silly things like secret volcano bases.
DR. DOOM
LOKI
NAMOR
EMMA FROST
It looks like Hel. I approve.
I told Osborn how one should storm the Baxter Building, I see no reason why I should be disturbed any further.
Come now, Victor. Surely you have a morbid fascination with the recent changes in America.
Though it is a bit less interesting now that Asgard resides in Latveria.
A nice alliance for the two of you, I'm not sure how we all benefit.
Namor, I hardly need to remind you that a rising tide lifts all ships.

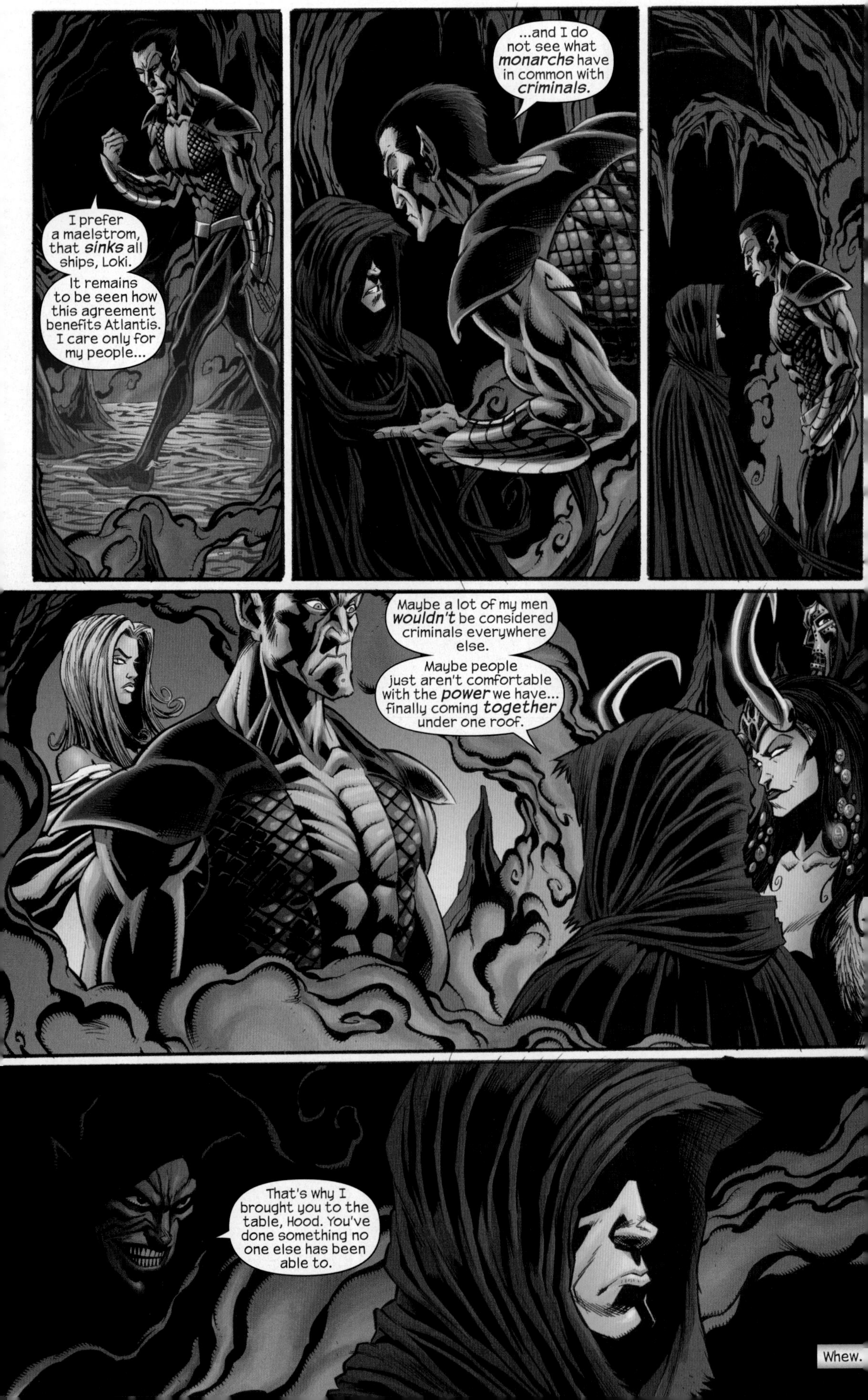
I prefer a maelstrom, that sinks all ships, Loki.
It remains to be seen how this agreement benefits Atlantis. I care only for my people...
...and I do not see what monarchs have in common with criminals.
Maybe a lot of my men wouldn't be considered criminals everywhere else.
Maybe people just aren't comfortable with the power we have... finally coming together under one roof.
That's why I brought you to the table, Hood. You've done something no one else has been able to.
Whew.

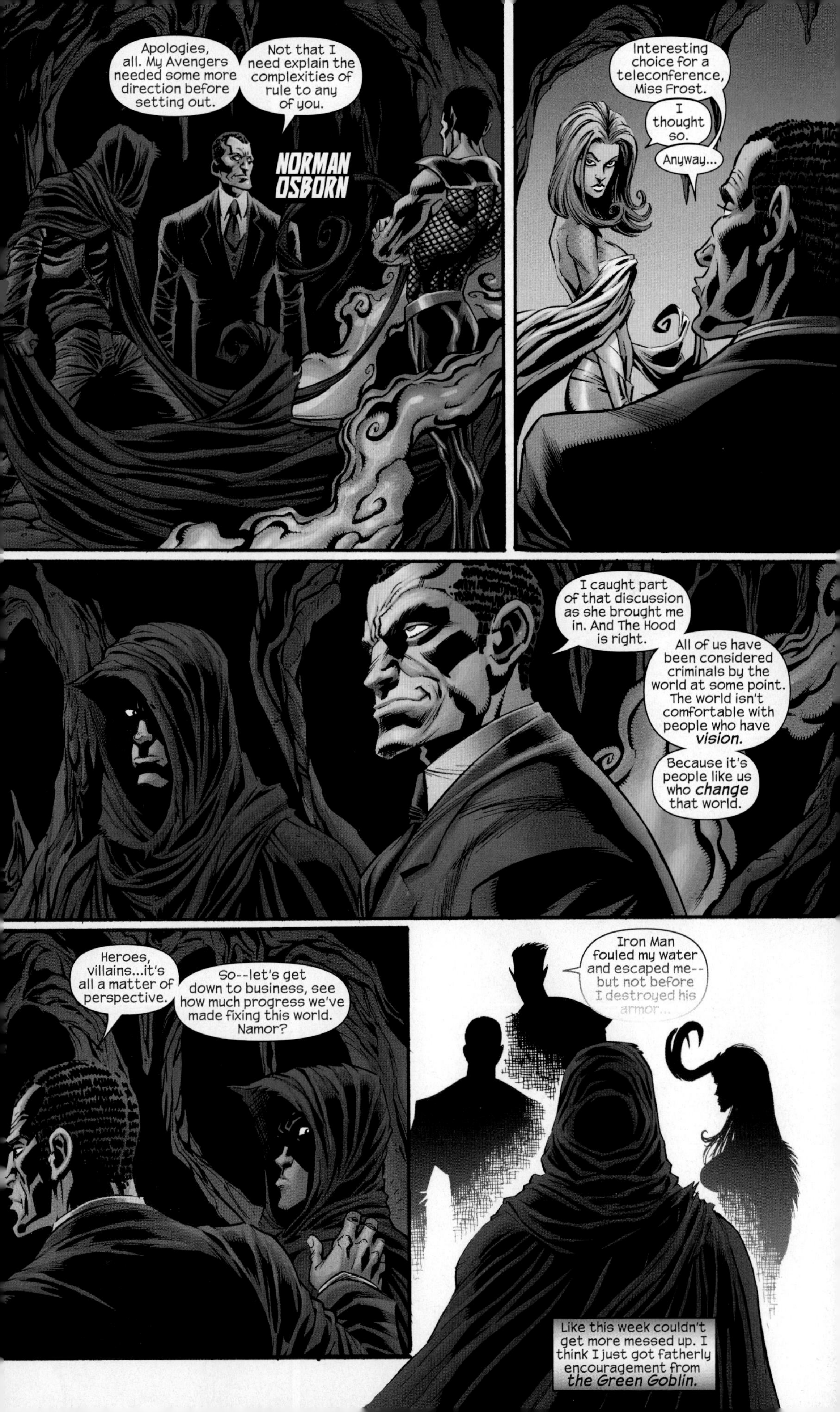
Apologies, all. My Avengers needed some more direction before setting out.
Not that I need explain the complexities of rule to any of you.
NORMAN OSBORN
Interesting choice for a teleconference, Miss Frost.
I thought so.
Anyway...
I caught part of that discussion as she brought me in. And The Hood is right.
All of us have been considered criminals by the world at some point. The world isn't comfortable with people who have *vision.*
Because it's people like us who *change* that world.
Heroes, villains...it's all a matter of perspective.
So--let's get down to business, see how much progress we've made fixing this world. Namor?
Iron Man fouled my water and escaped me--but not before I destroyed his armor...
Like this week couldn't get more messed up. I think I just got fatherly encouragement from *the Green Goblin.*

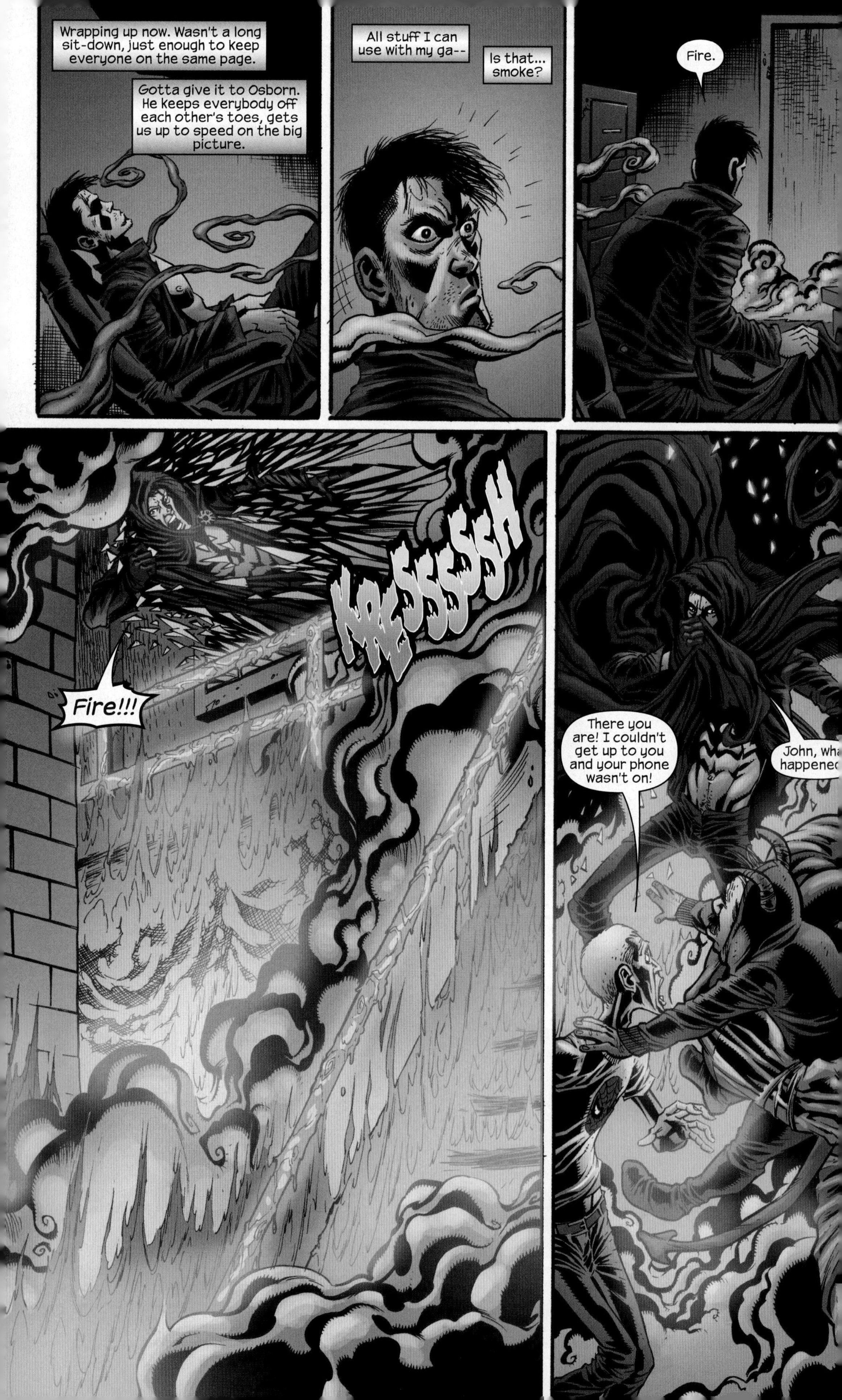
Wrapping up now. Wasn't a long sit-down, just enough to keep everyone on the same page.
Gotta give it to Osborn. He keeps everybody off each other's toes, gets us up to speed on the big picture.
All stuff I can use with my ga--
Is that... smoke?
Fire.
KRESSSSSH
Fire!!!
There you are! I couldn't get up to you and your phone wasn't on!
John, wha happene

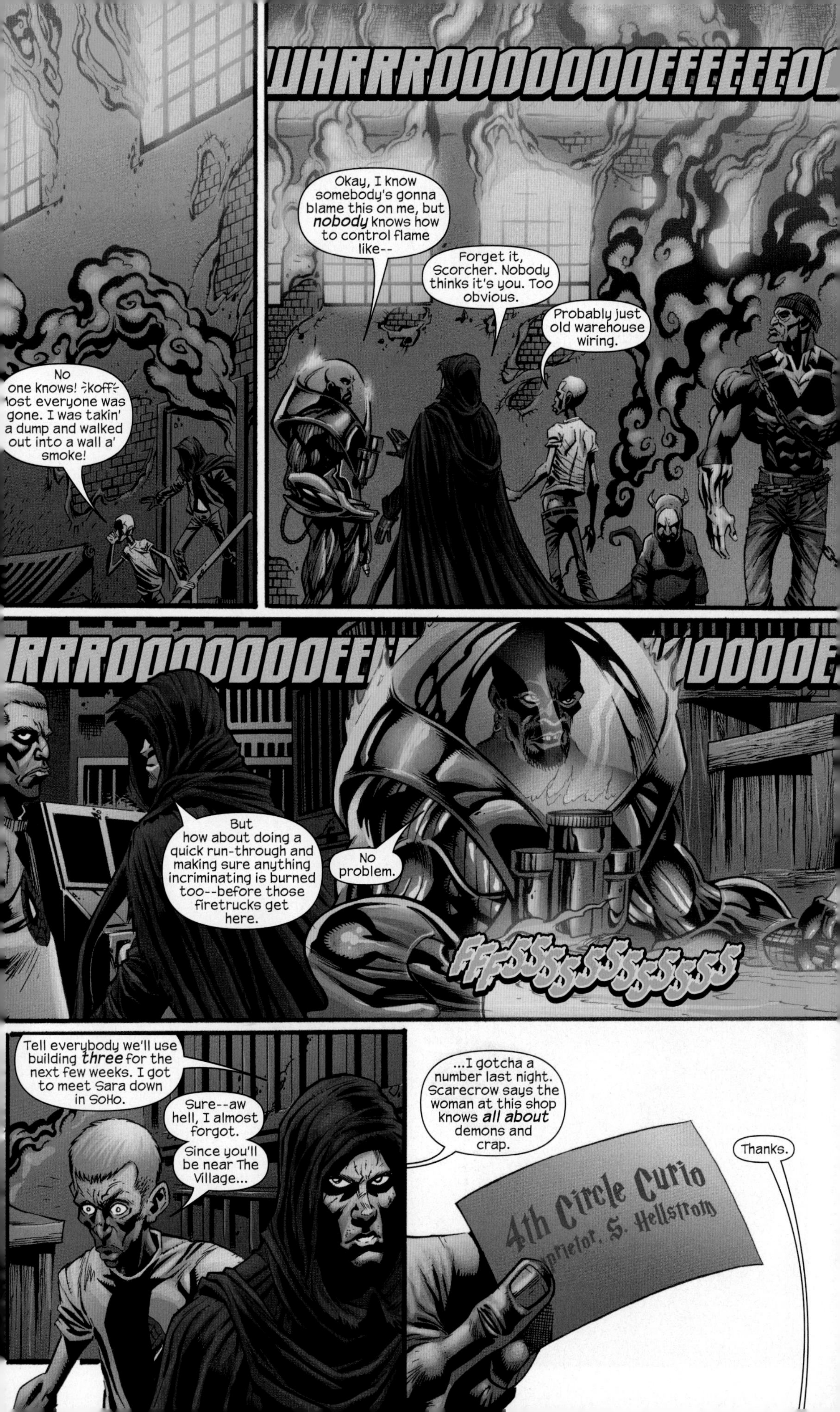
No one knows! ⁂koff⁂ Most everyone was gone. I was takin' a dump and walked out into a wall a' smoke!
UHRRROOOOOOOEEEEEOO
Okay, I know somebody's gonna blame this on me, but *nobody* knows how to control flame like--
Forget it, Scorcher. Nobody thinks it's you. Too obvious.
Probably just old warehouse wiring.
RRROOOOOOOEE
OOOOE
But how about doing a quick run-through and making sure anything incriminating is burned too--before those firetrucks get here.
No problem.
FFFSSSSSSSSSSSS
Tell everybody we'll use building *three* for the next few weeks. I got to meet Sara down in SoHo.
Sure--aw hell, I almost forgot.
Since you'll be near The Village...
...I gotcha a number last night. Scarecrow says the woman at this shop knows *all about* demons and crap.
4th Circle Curio
prietor, S. Hellstrom
Thanks.

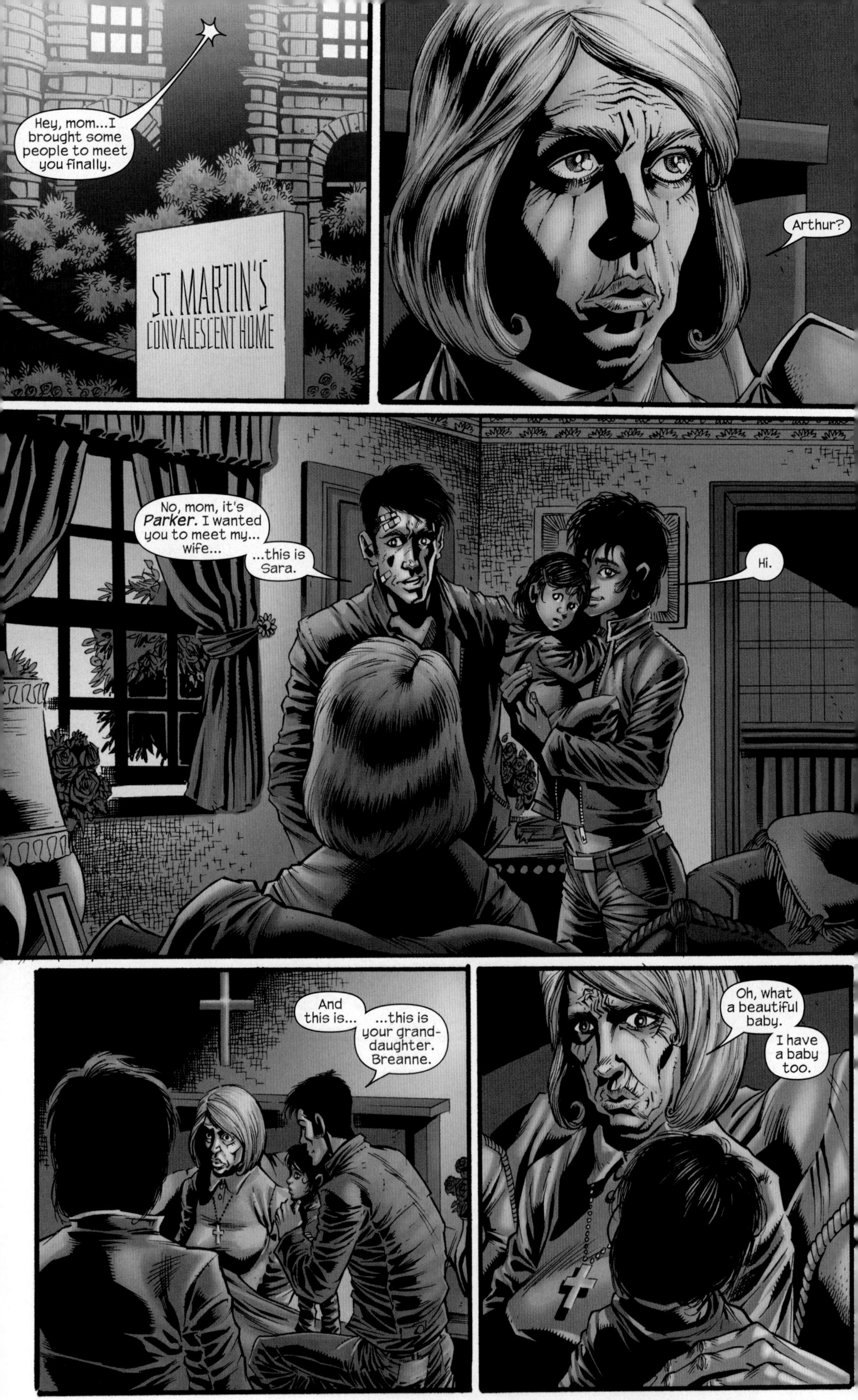
Hey, mom...I brought some people to meet you finally.
ST. MARTIN'S CONVALESCENT HOME
Arthur?
No, mom, it's *Parker.* I wanted you to meet my... wife...
...this is Sara.
Hi.
And this is...
...this is your grand-daughter. Breanne.
Oh, what a beautiful baby.
I have a baby too.

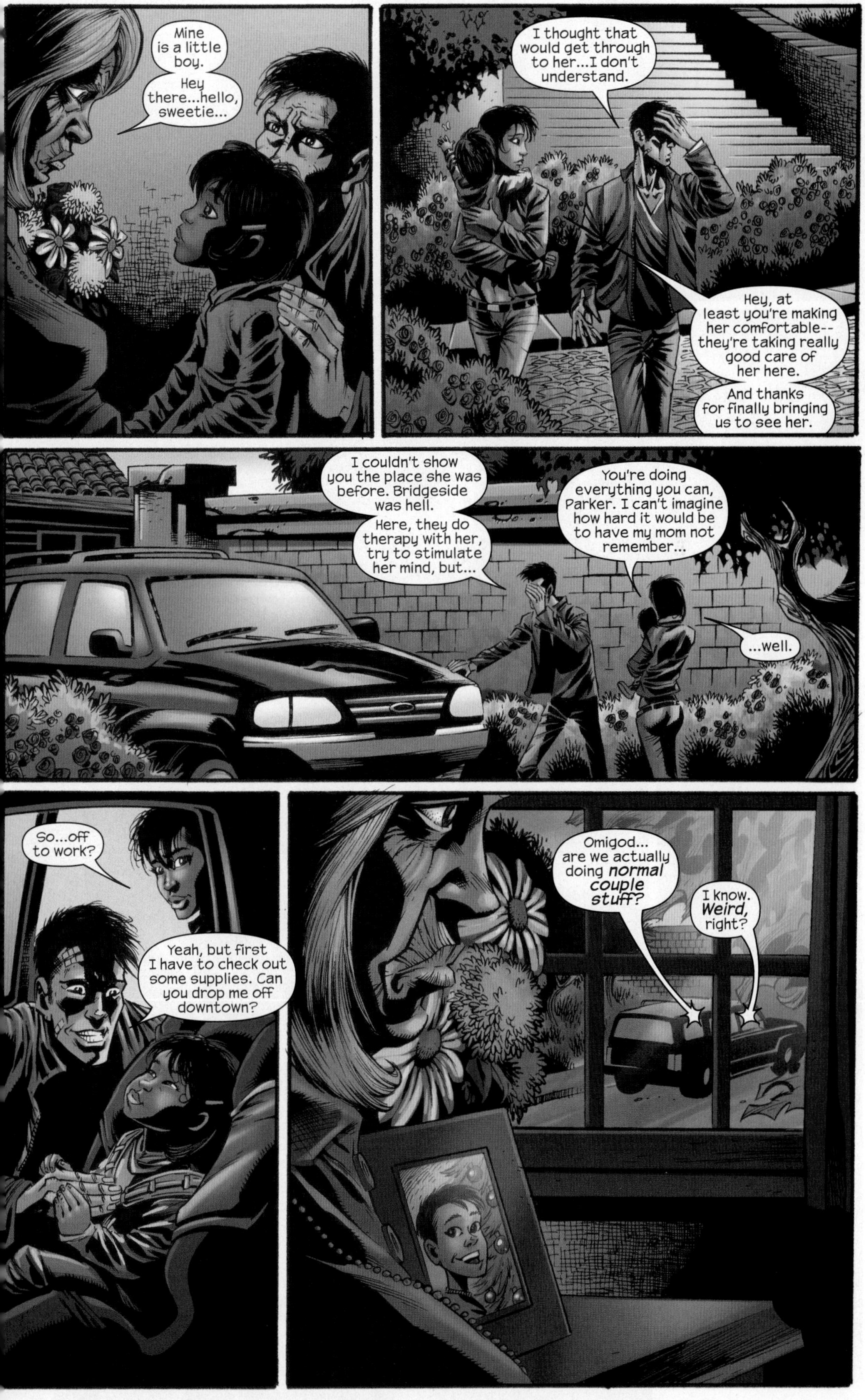
Mine is a little boy.
Hey there...hello, sweetie...
I thought that would get through to her...I don't understand.
Hey, at least you're making her comfortable-- they're taking really good care of her here.
And thanks for finally bringing us to see her.
I couldn't show you the place she was before. Bridgeside was hell.
Here, they do therapy with her, try to stimulate her mind, but...
You're doing everything you can, Parker. I can't imagine how hard it would be to have my mom not remember...
...well.
So...off to work?
Yeah, but first I have to check out some supplies. Can you drop me off downtown?
Omigod... are we actually doing *normal couple stuff?*
I know. *Weird,* right?

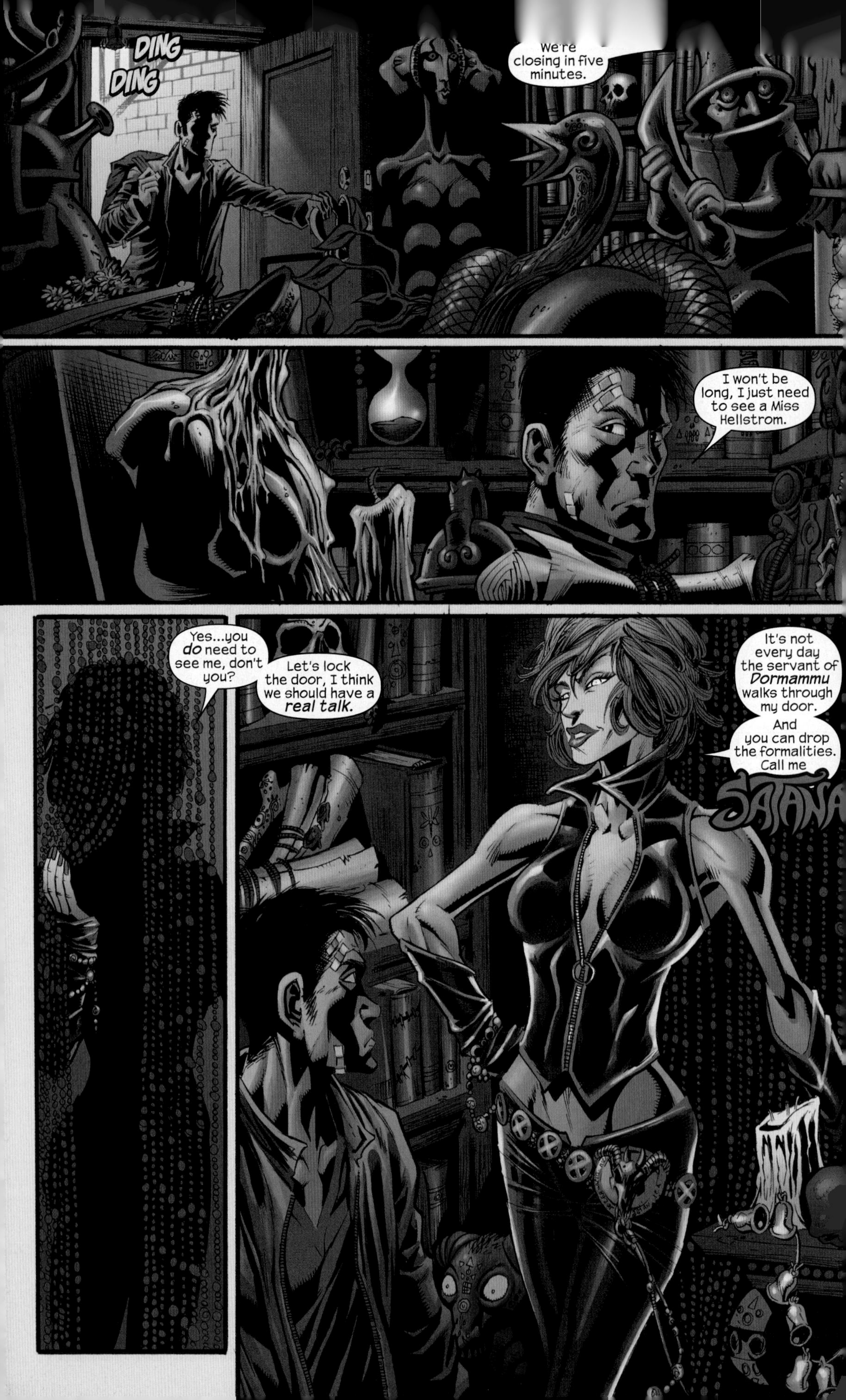
DING
DING
We're closing in five minutes.
I won't be long, I just need to see a Miss Hellstrom.
Yes...you do need to see me, don't you?
Let's lock the door, I think we should have a real talk.
It's not every day the servant of Dormammu walks through my door.
And you can drop the formalities. Call me
SATANA

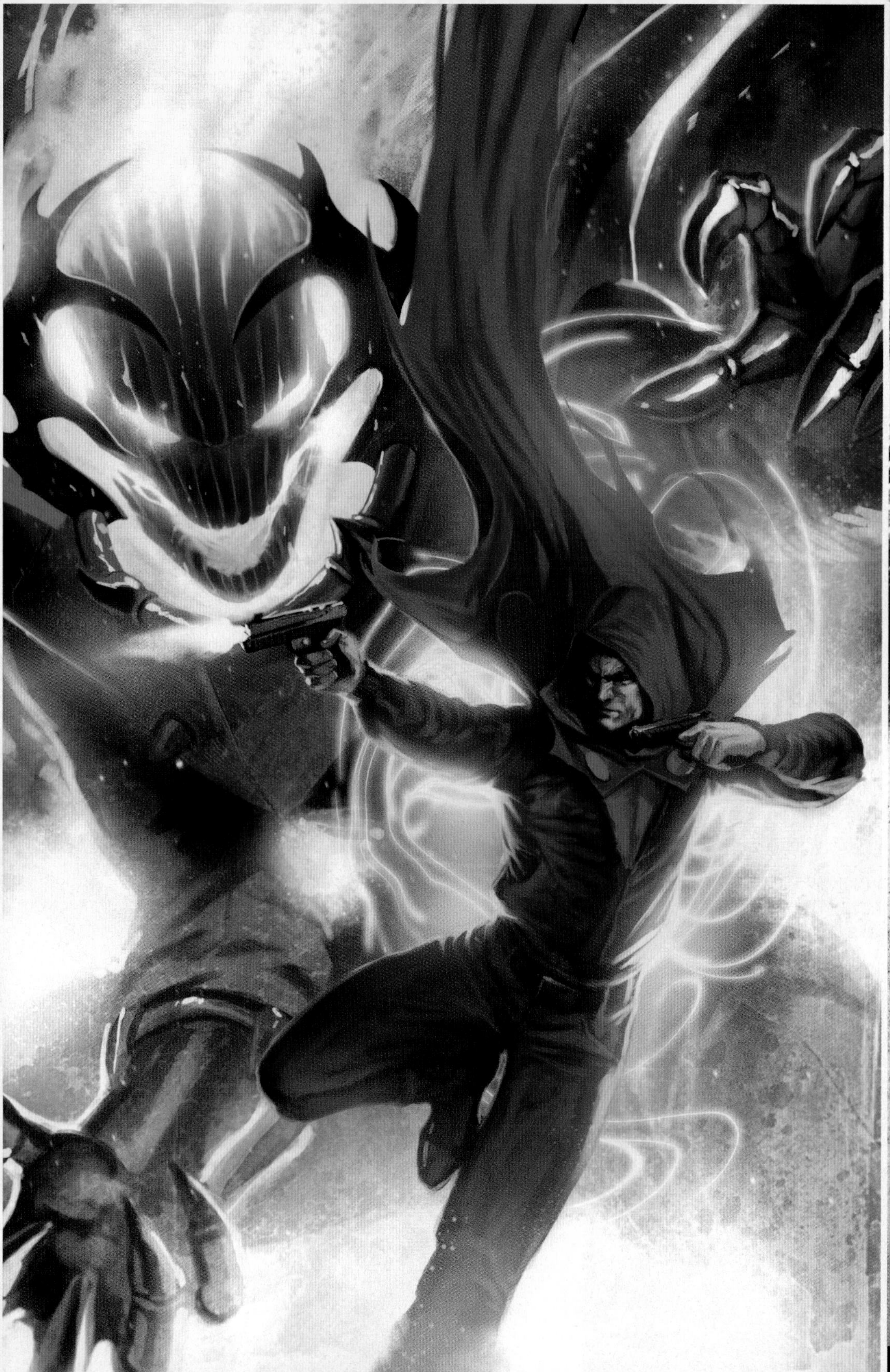

DARK REIGN: THE HOOD #3

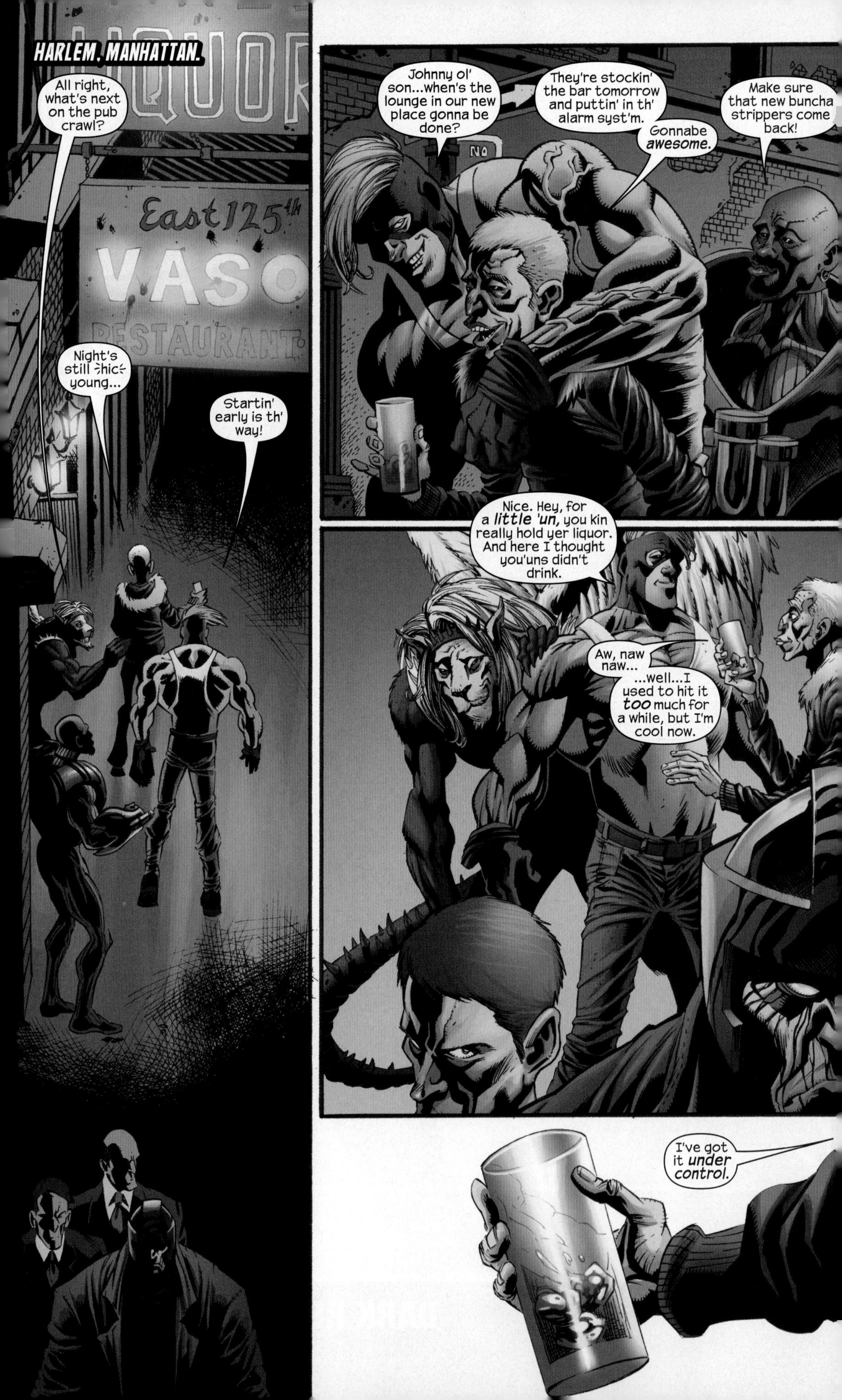

HARLEM, MANHATTAN.
All right, what's next on the pub crawl?
Night's still -hic- young...
Startin' early is th' way!
Johnny ol' son...when's the lounge in our new place gonna be done?
They're stockin' the bar tomorrow and puttin' in th' alarm syst'm.
Gonnabe awesome.
Make sure that new buncha strippers come back!
Nice. Hey, for a little 'un, you kin really hold yer liquor. And here I thought you'uns didn't drink.
Aw, naw naw...
...well...I used to hit it too much for a while, but I'm cool now.
I've got it under control.

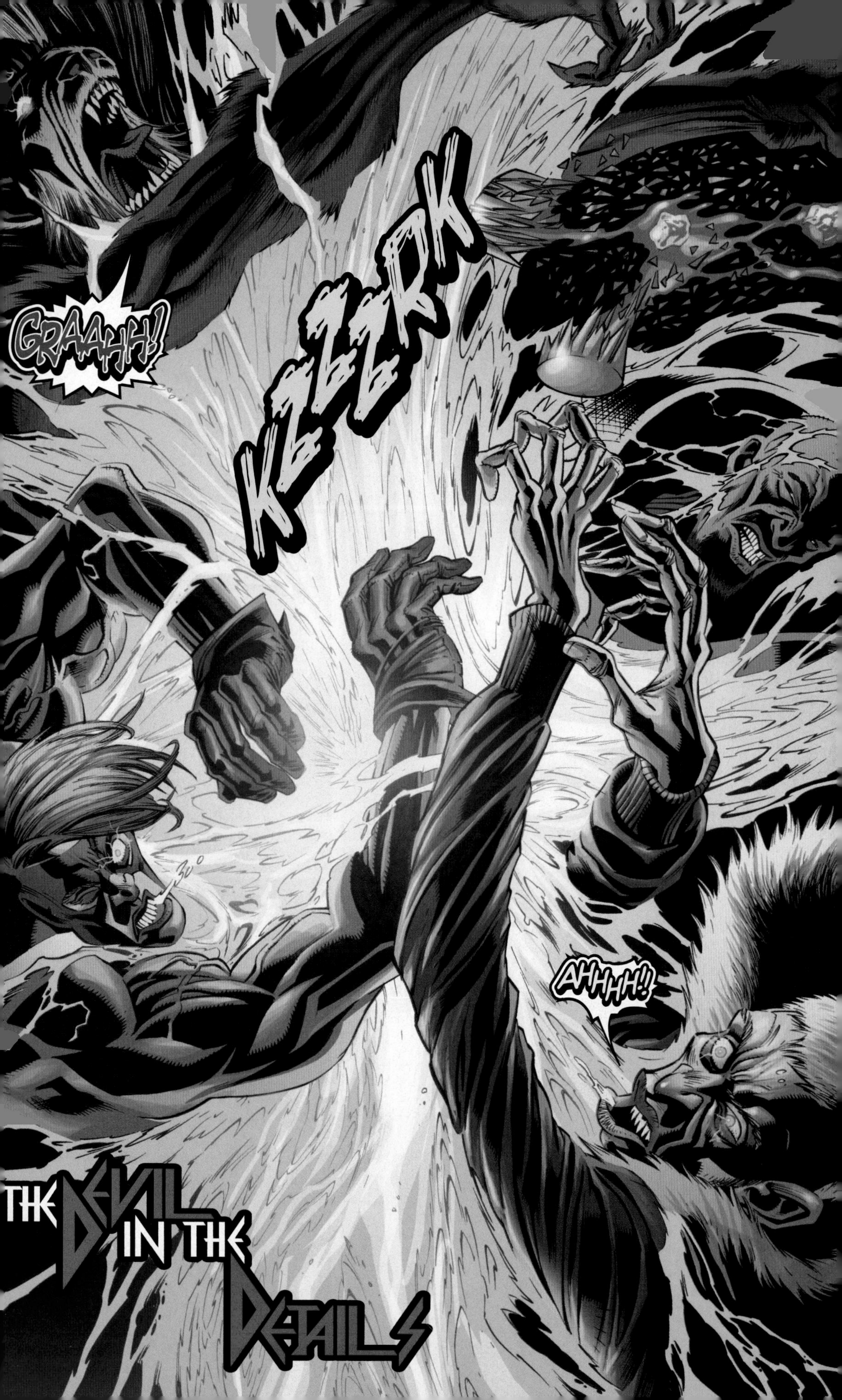
GRAAHH!
KZZZRK
AHHHH!!
THE DEVIL IN THE DETAILS

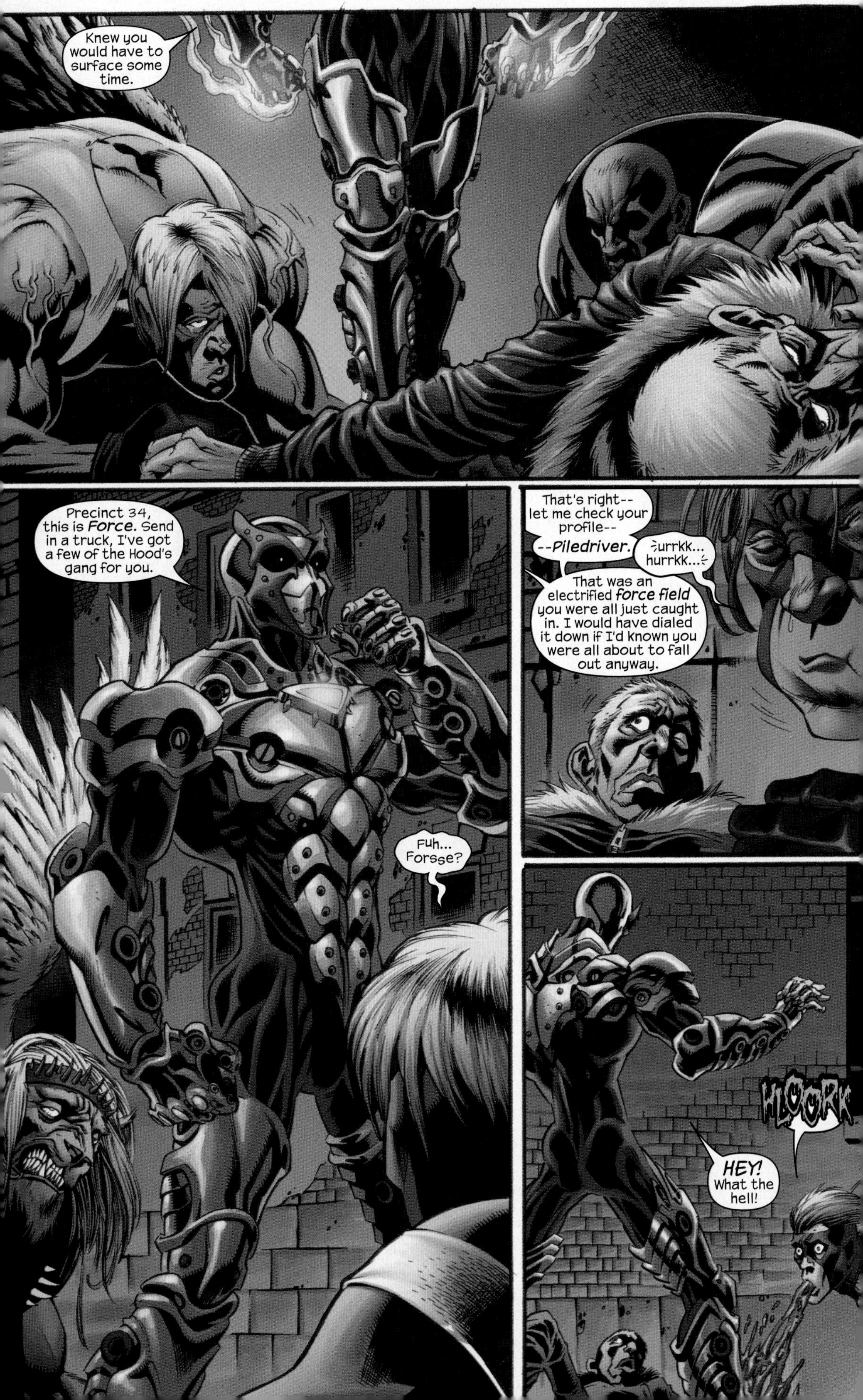

Knew you would have to surface some time.
Precinct 34, this is *Force.* Send in a truck, I've got a few of the Hood's gang for you.
Fuh... Forsse?
That's right-- let me check your profile--
--*Piledriver.*
urrkk... hurrkk...
That was an electrified *force field* you were all just caught in. I would have dialed it down if I'd known you were all about to fall out anyway.
HLOORK
HEY! What the hell!

Dammit!

Ummp--

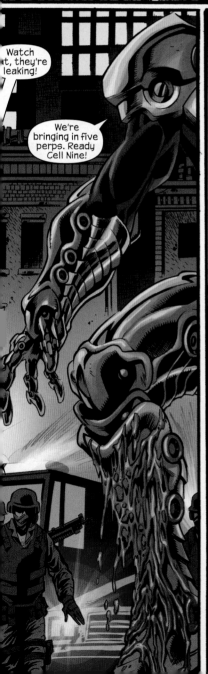

Watch it, they're leaking!

We're bringing in five perps. Ready Cell Nine!

Freaking *lowlifes.*

Thanks a lot, Force. The NYPD appreciates it.

You have the right to remain *silent.* Anything you say *can* and *will be* used against you in a court of law...

You have the right to an *attorney* present during questioning. If you do *not* have an attorney, one will be appointed for you--

...I'm in control...

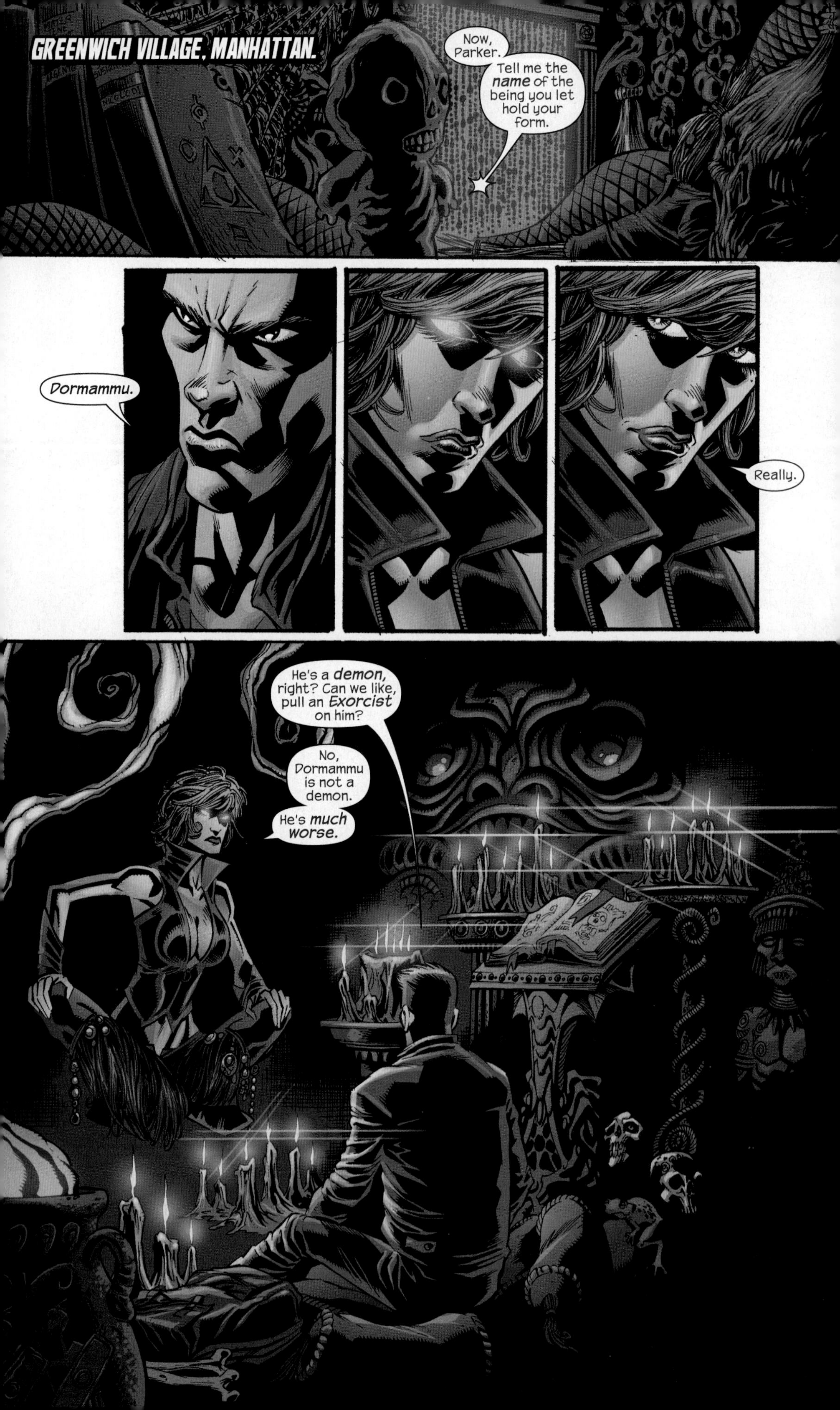

GREENWICH VILLAGE, MANHATTAN.
Now, Parker.
Tell me the name of the being you let hold your form.
Dormammu.
Really.
He's a demon, right? Can we like, pull an Exorcist on him?
No, Dormammu is not a demon.
He's much worse.

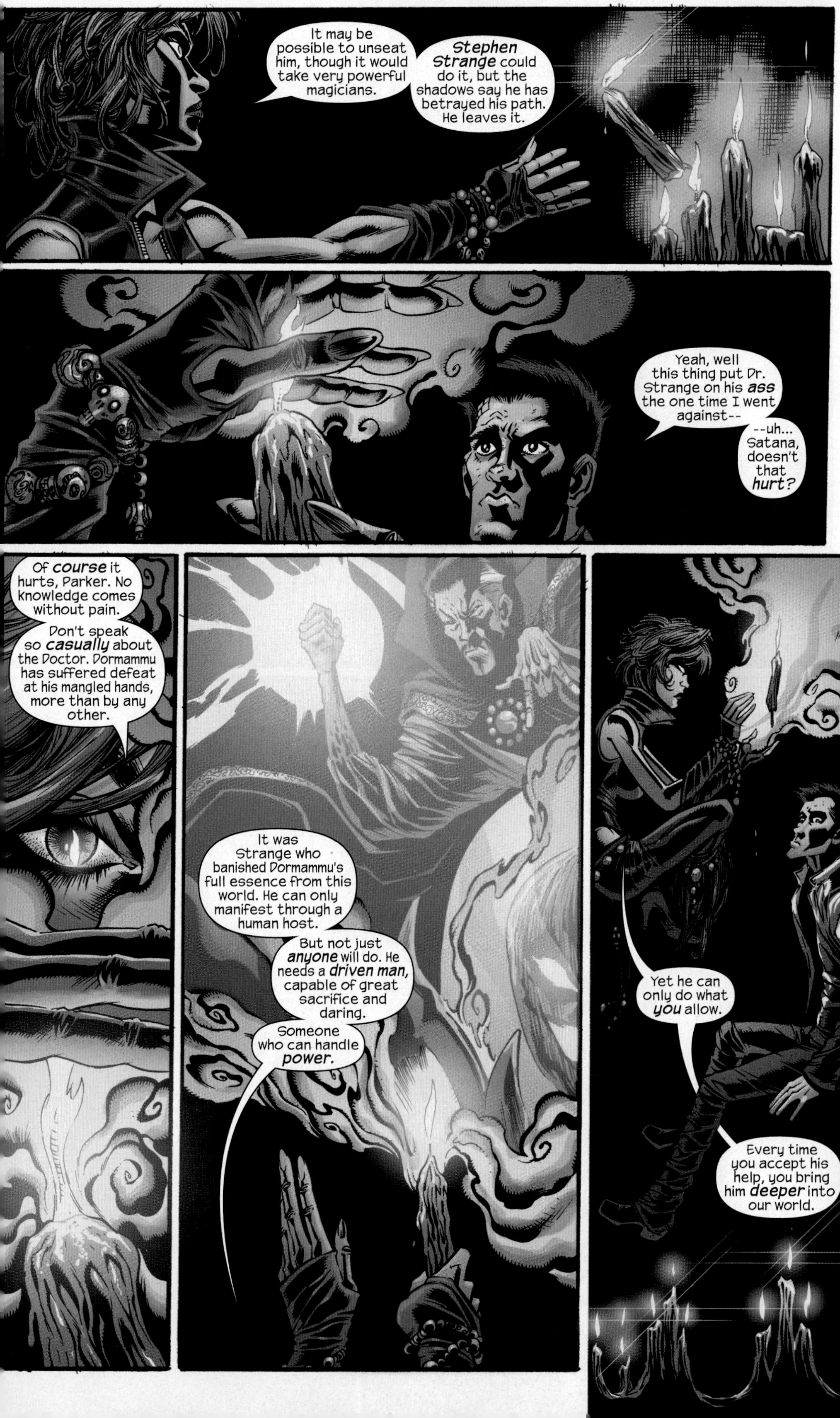
It may be possible to unseat him, though it would take very powerful magicians.
Stephen Strange could do it, but the shadows say he has betrayed his path. He leaves it.
Yeah, well this thing put Dr. Strange on his ass the one time I went against--
--uh... Satana, doesn't that hurt?
Of course it hurts, Parker. No knowledge comes without pain.
Don't speak so casually about the Doctor. Dormammu has suffered defeat at his mangled hands, more than by any other.
It was Strange who banished Dormammu's full essence from this world. He can only manifest through a human host.
But not just anyone will do. He needs a driven man, capable of great sacrifice and daring.
Someone who can handle power.
Yet he can only do what you allow.
Every time you accept his help, you bring him deeper into our world.

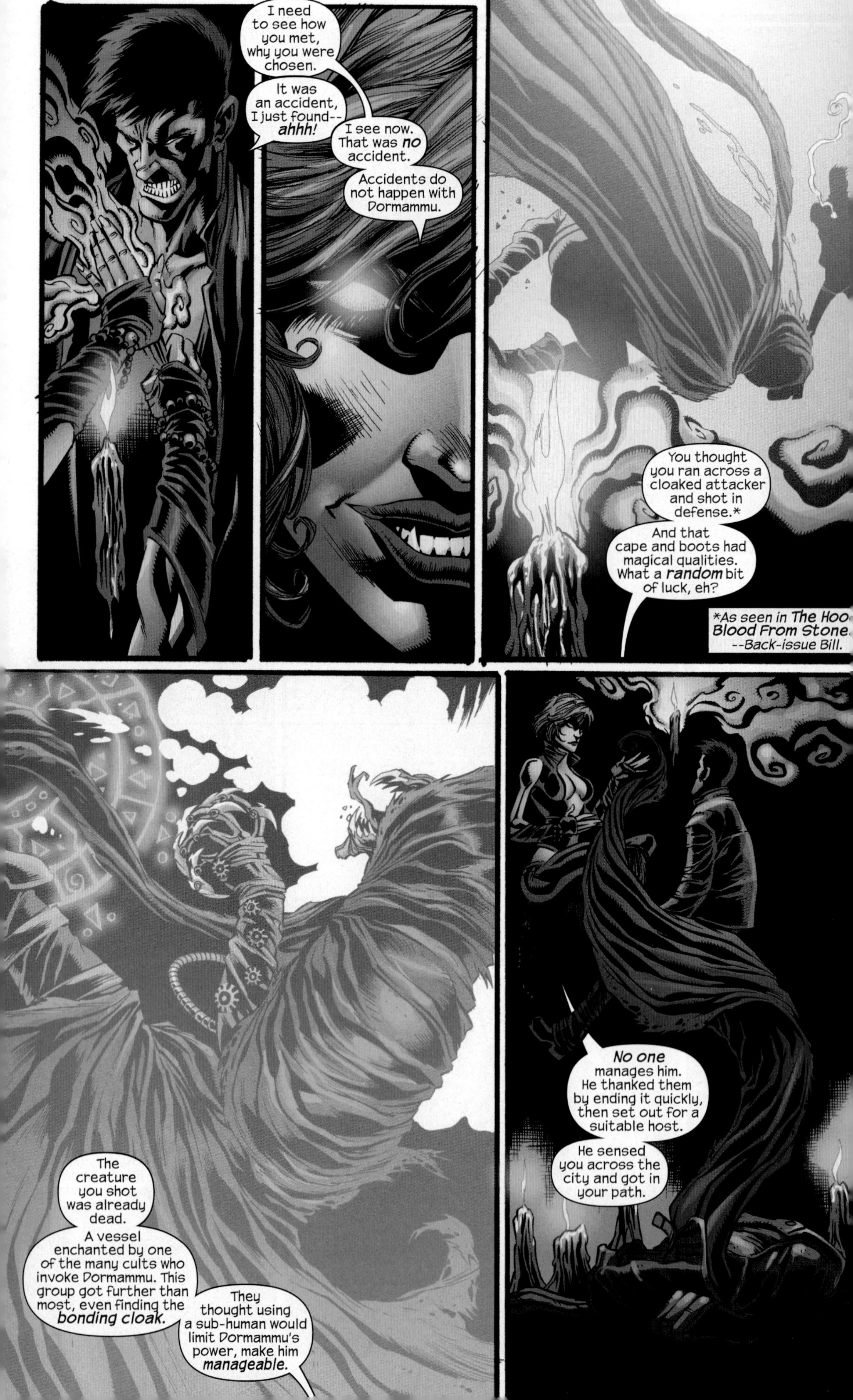
I need to see how you met, why you were chosen.
It was an accident, I just found-- *ahhh!*
I see now. That was **no** accident.
Accidents do not happen with Dormammu.
You thought you ran across a cloaked attacker and shot in defense.*
And that cape and boots had magical qualities. What a ***random*** bit of luck, eh?
*As seen in The Hoo Blood From Stone --Back-issue Bill.
The creature you shot was already dead.
A vessel enchanted by one of the many cults who invoke Dormammu. This group got further than most, even finding the ***bonding cloak.***
They thought using a sub-human would limit Dormammu's power, make him *manageable.*
No one manages him. He thanked them by ending it quickly, then set out for a suitable host.
He sensed you across the city and got in your path.

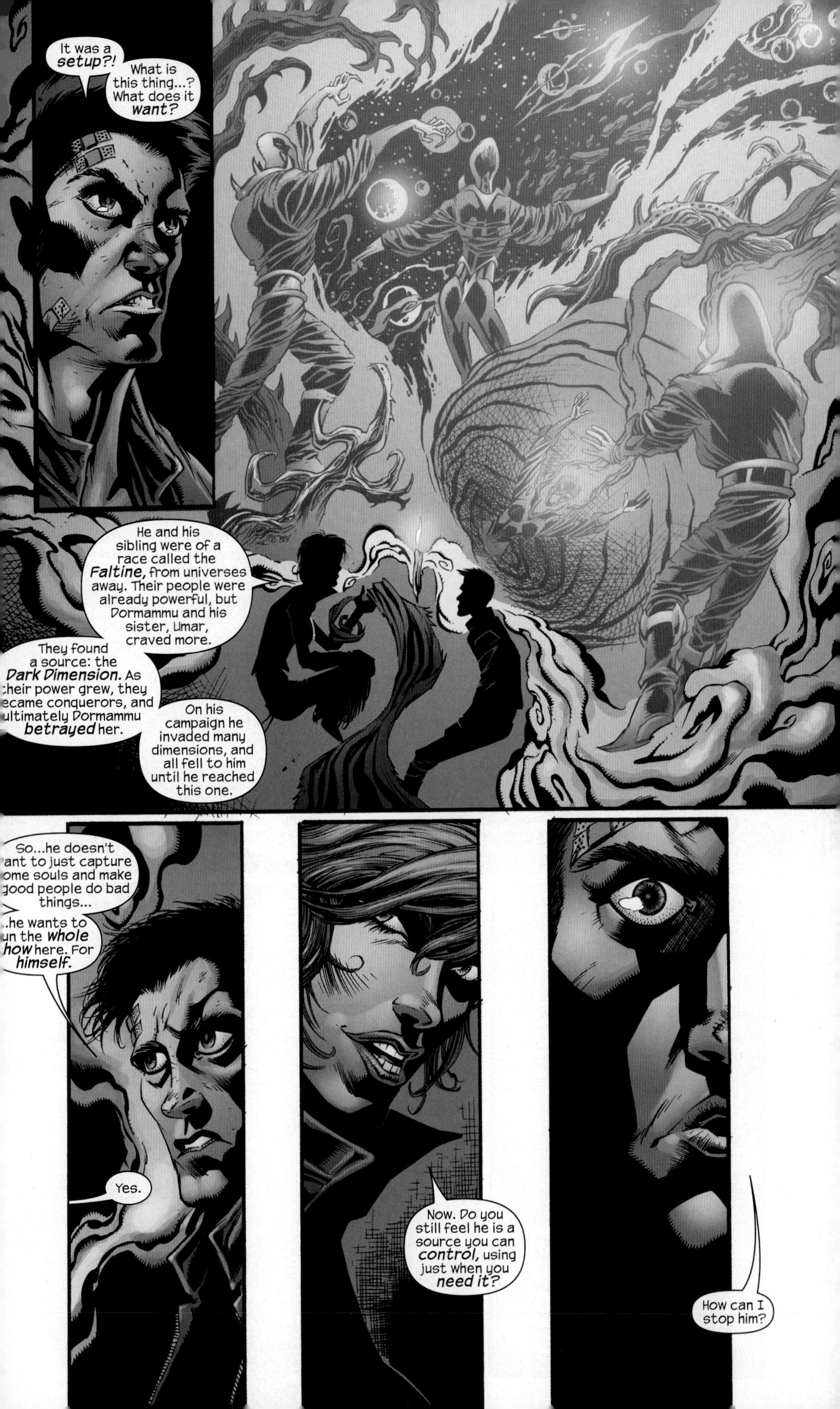

It was a setup?!
What is this thing...? What does it want?
He and his sibling were of a race called the Faltine, from universes away. Their people were already powerful, but Dormammu and his sister, Umar, craved more.
They found a source: the Dark Dimension. As their power grew, they became conquerors, and ultimately Dormammu betrayed her.
On his campaign he invaded many dimensions, and all fell to him until he reached this one.
So...he doesn't want to just capture some souls and make good people do bad things...
...he wants to run the whole show here. For himself.
Yes.
Now. Do you still feel he is a source you can control, using just when you need it?
How can I stop him?

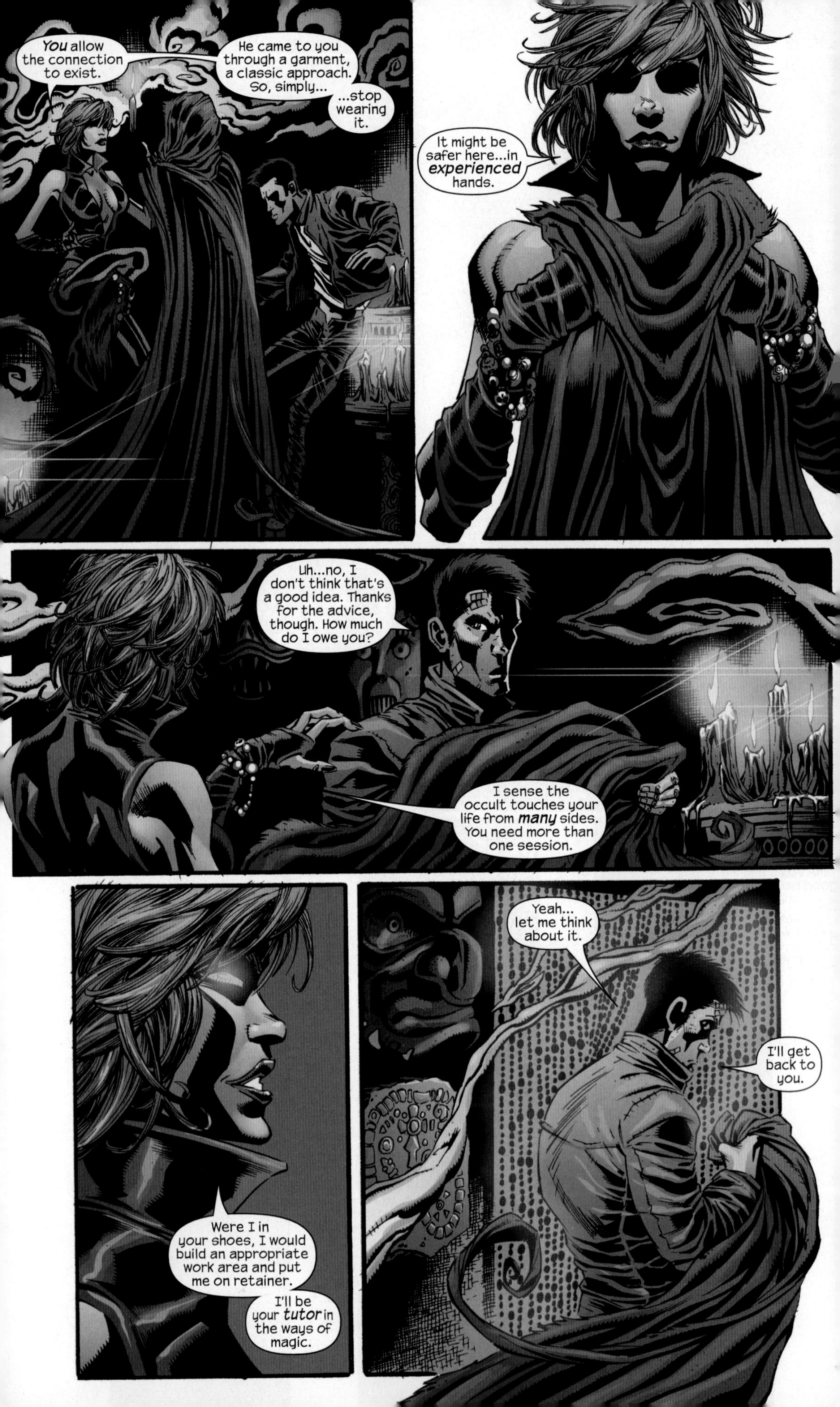

You allow the connection to exist.
He came to you through a garment, a classic approach. So, simply...
...stop wearing it.
It might be safer here...in experienced hands.
Uh...no, I don't think that's a good idea. Thanks for the advice, though. How much do I owe you?
I sense the occult touches your life from many sides. You need more than one session.
Were I in your shoes, I would build an appropriate work area and put me on retainer.
I'll be your tutor in the ways of magic.
Yeah... let me think about it.
I'll get back to you.

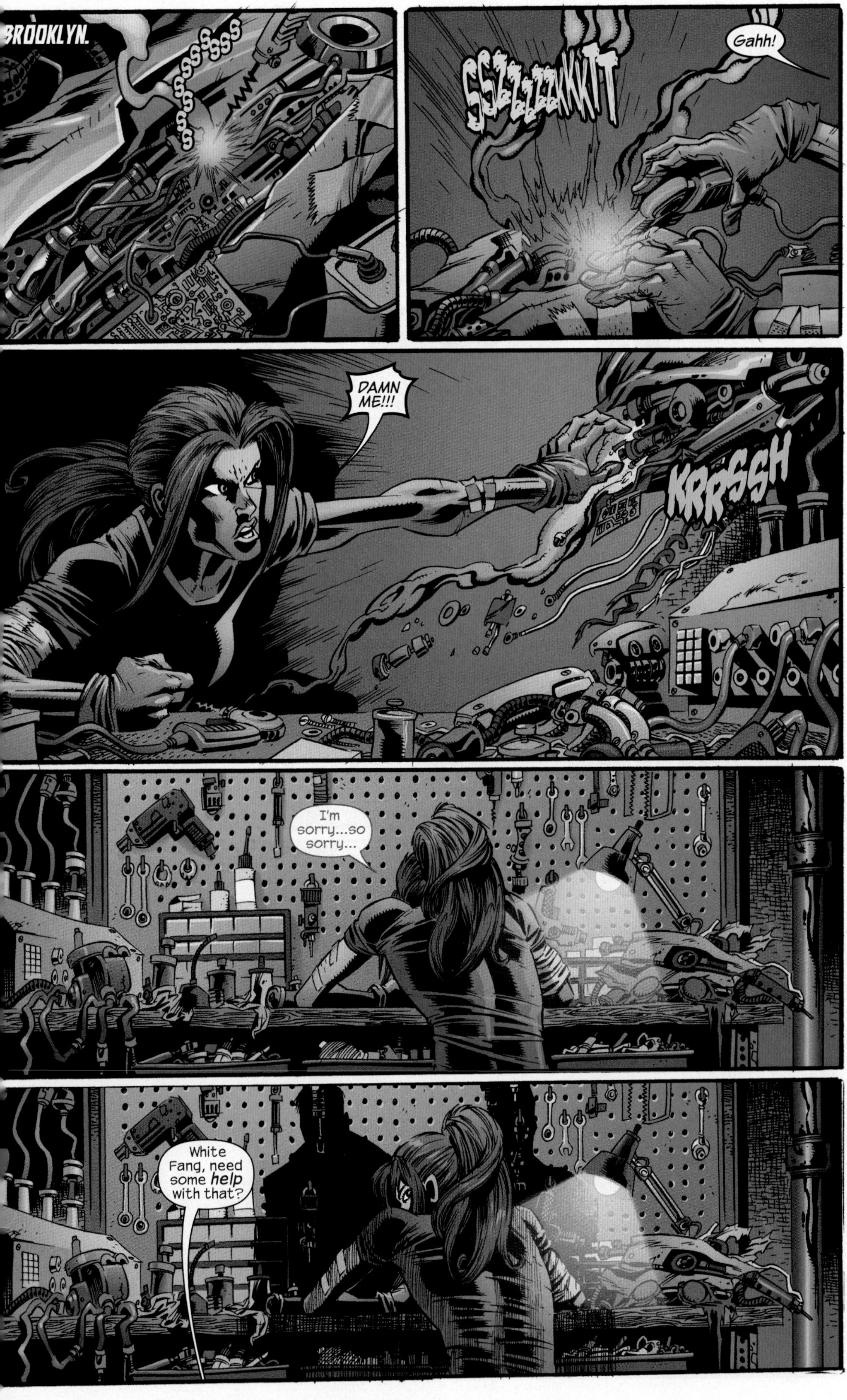
BROOKLYN.
SSSSSSSSS
SSZZzzzzKKKTT
Gahh!
DAMN ME!!!
KRRSSH
I'm sorry...so sorry...
White Fang, need some *help* with that?

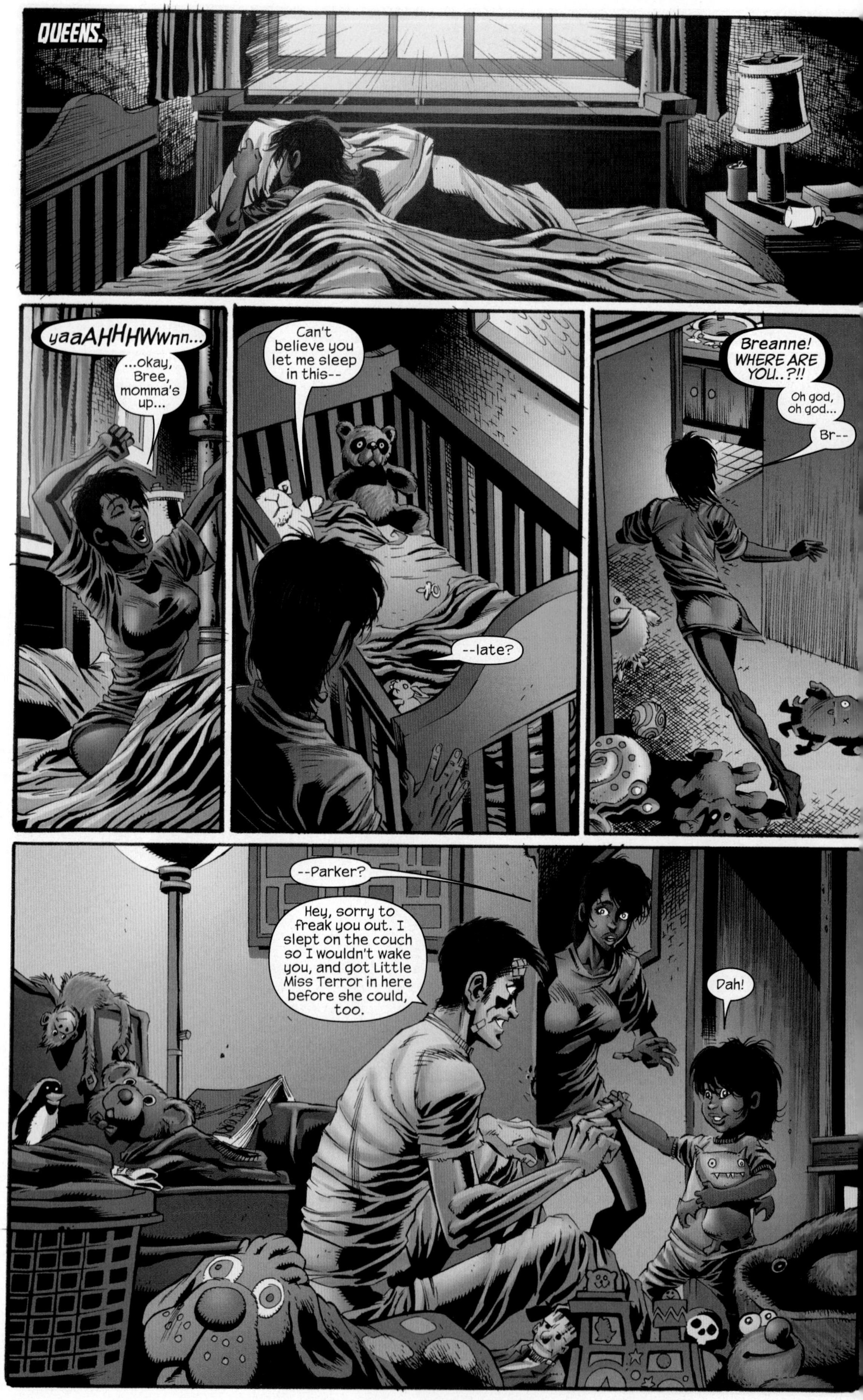
QUEENS.
yaaAHHHWwnn...
...okay, Bree, momma's up...
Can't believe you let me sleep in this--
--late?
Breanne! WHERE ARE YOU..?!!
Oh god, oh god...
Br--
--Parker?
Hey, sorry to freak you out. I slept on the couch so I wouldn't wake you, and got Little Miss Terror in here before she could, too.
Dah!

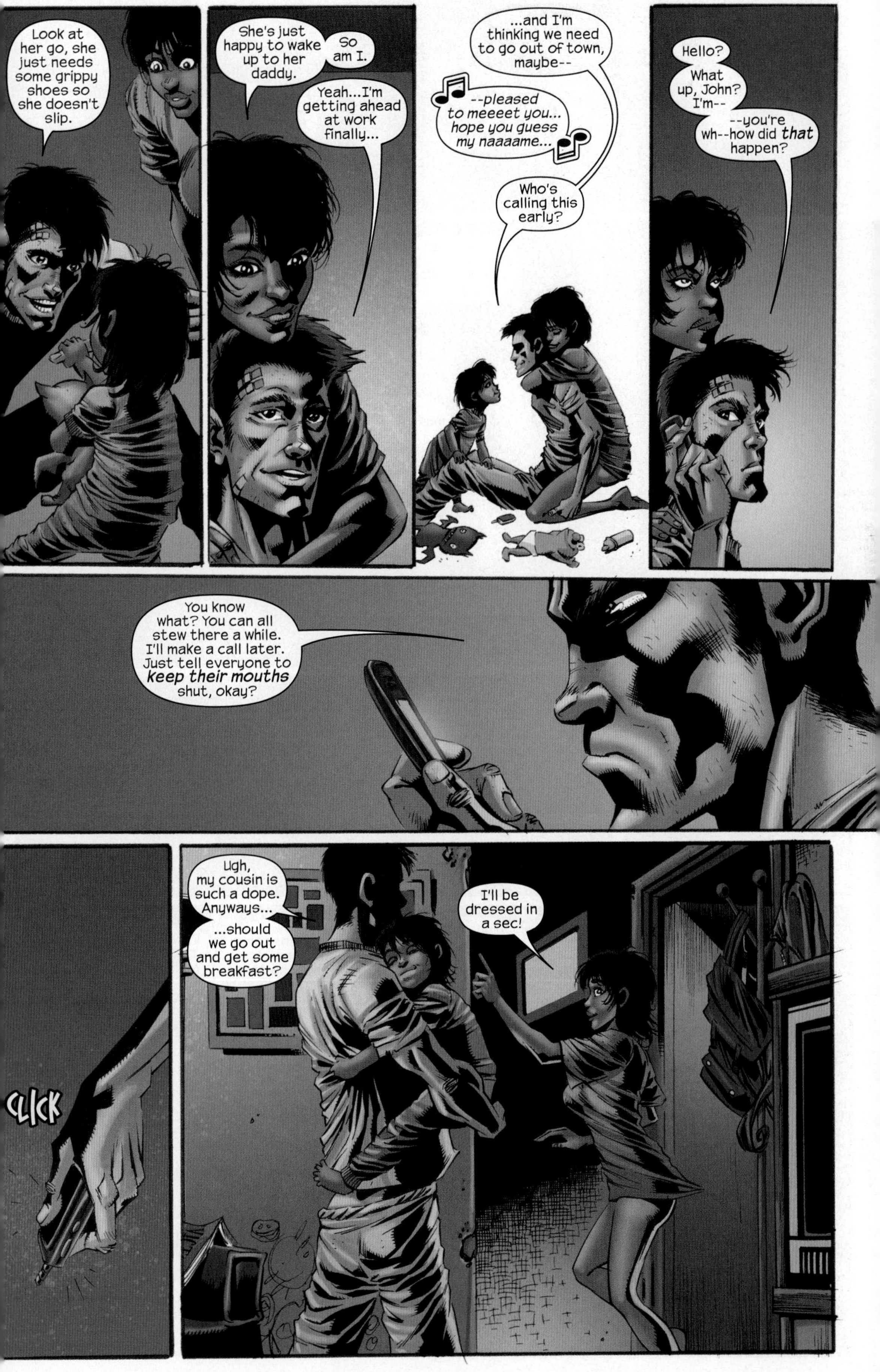

Look at her go, she just needs some grippy shoes so she doesn't slip.
She's just happy to wake up to her daddy.
So am I.
Yeah...I'm getting ahead at work finally...
...and I'm thinking we need to go out of town, maybe--
--pleased to meeeet you... hope you guess my naaaame...
Who's calling this early?
Hello?
What up, John? I'm--
--you're wh--how did *that* happen?
You know what? You can all stew there a while. I'll make a call later. Just tell everyone to ***keep their mouths*** shut, okay?
CLICK
Ugh, my cousin is such a dope. Anyways...
...should we go out and get some breakfast?
I'll be dressed in a sec!

PRECINCT 34.

Where'm I at?

Like you never seen the inside of a cell before, Piledriver.

I'd smash us out, but I got the worst dang hangover...

Yo, John, what about our one phone call?

I already made it, Scorcher. Didn't help.

All right, all of you out. You're being *transferred*.

You're now under confinement with H.A.M.M.E.R.

Put your arms forward to be cuffed or you will receive a neural shock.

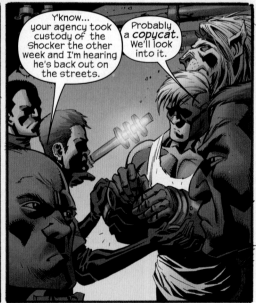

Y'know... your agency took custody of the Shocker the other week and I'm hearing he's back out on the streets.

Probably a *copycat*. We'll look into it.

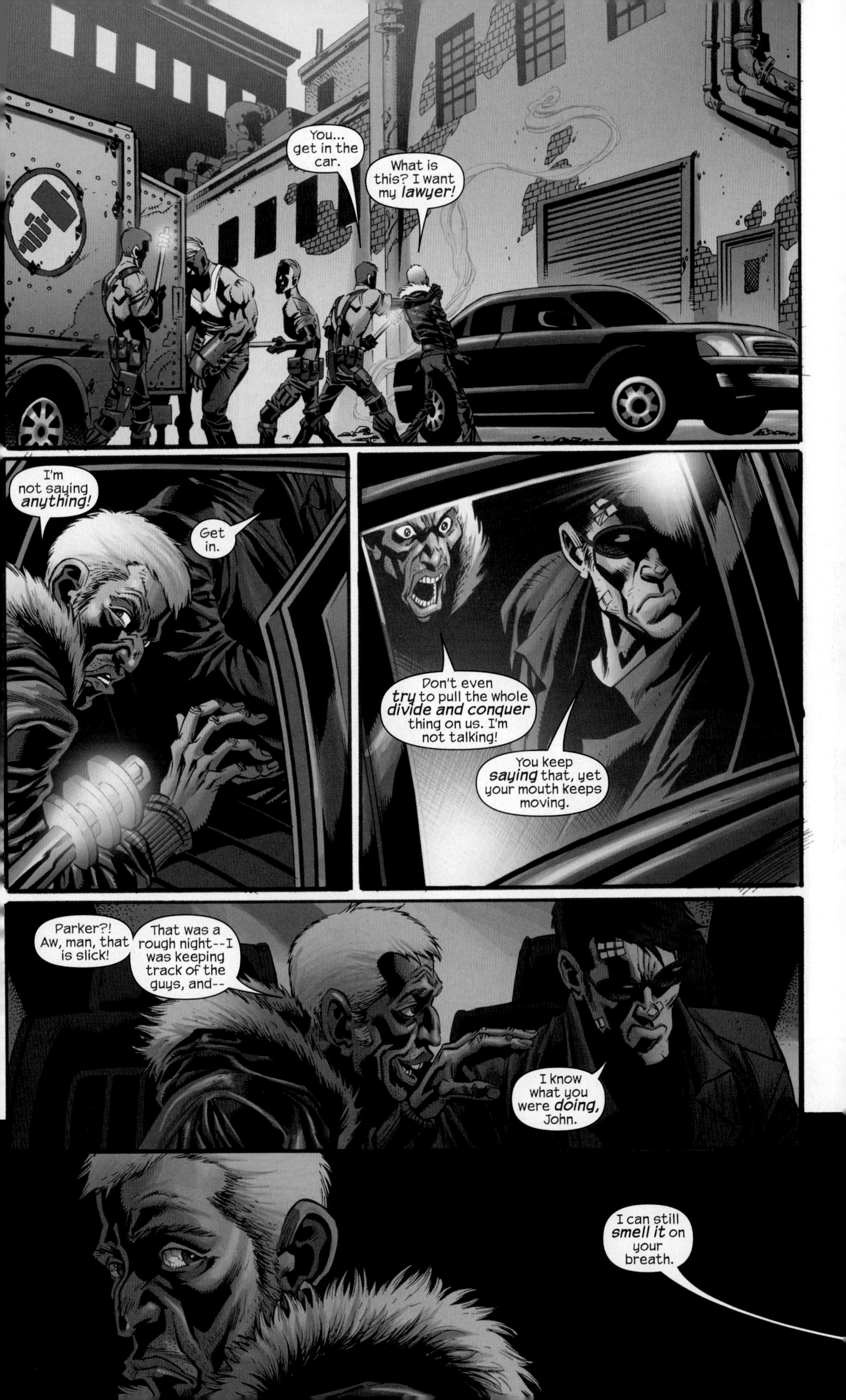
You... get in the car.
What is this? I want my *lawyer!*
I'm not saying *anything!*
Get in.
Don't even *try* to pull the whole *divide and conquer* thing on us. I'm not talking!
You keep *saying* that, yet your mouth keeps moving.
Parker?! Aw, man, that is slick!
That was a rough night--I was keeping track of the guys, and--
I know what you were *doing,* John.
I can still *smell it* on your breath.

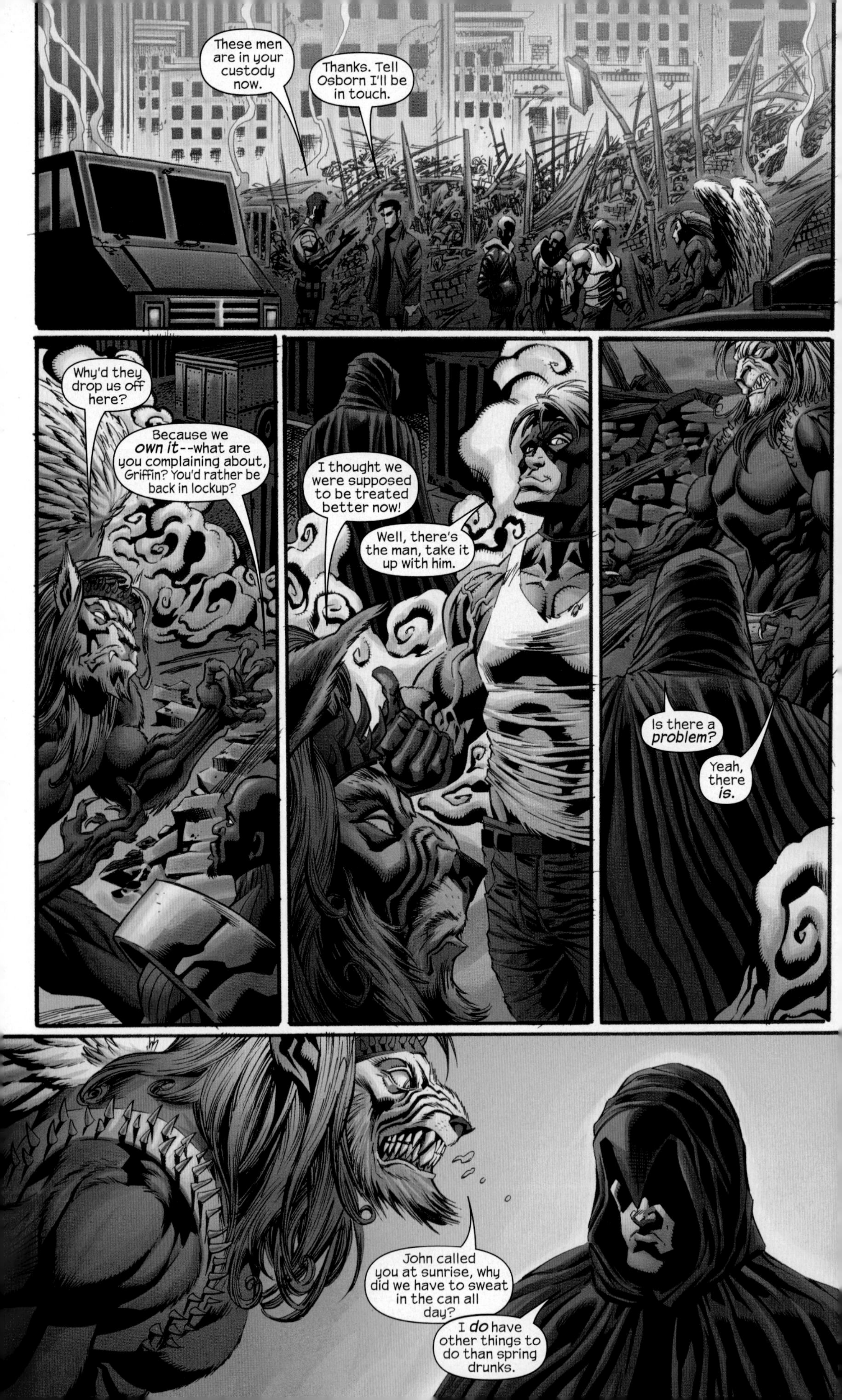
These men are in your custody now.
Thanks. Tell Osborn I'll be in touch.
Why'd they drop us off here?
Because we own it--what are you complaining about, Griffin? You'd rather be back in lockup?
I thought we were supposed to be treated better now!
Well, there's the man, take it up with him.
Is there a problem?
Yeah, there is.
John called you at sunrise, why did we have to sweat in the can all day?
I do have other things to do than spring drunks.

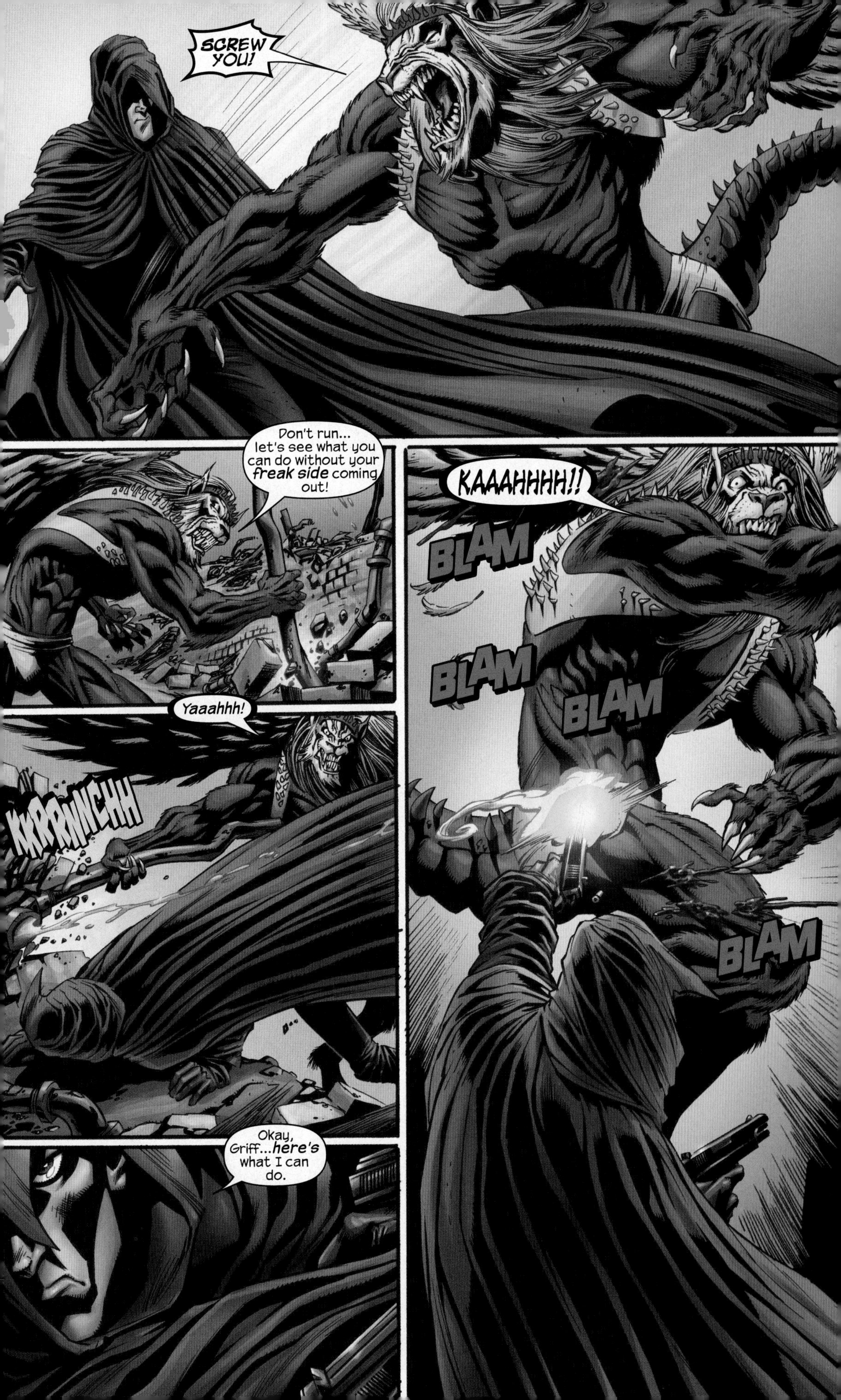
SCREW YOU!
Don't run... let's see what you can do without your freak side coming out!
Yaaahhh!
KKRRNNCHH
Okay, Griff...here's what I can do.
KAAAHHHH!!
BLAM
BLAM
BLAM
BLAM

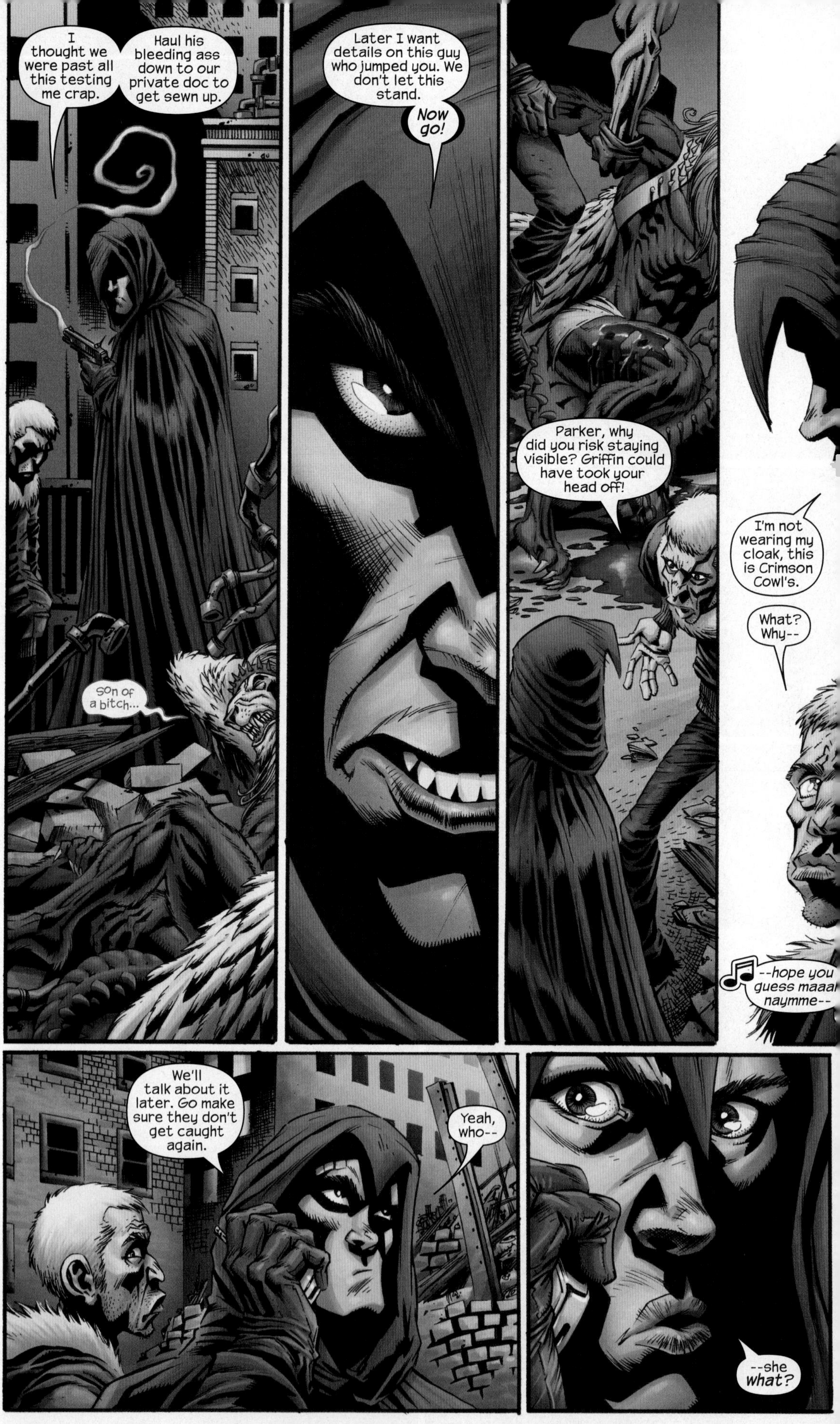

I thought we were past all this testing me crap.
Haul his bleeding ass down to our private doc to get sewn up.
Son of a bitch...
Later I want details on this guy who jumped you. We don't let this stand.
Now go!
Parker, why did you risk staying visible? Griffin could have took your head off!
I'm not wearing my cloak, this is Crimson Cowl's.
What? Why--
--hope you guess maaa naymme--
We'll talk about it later. Go make sure they don't get caught again.
Yeah, who--
--she what?

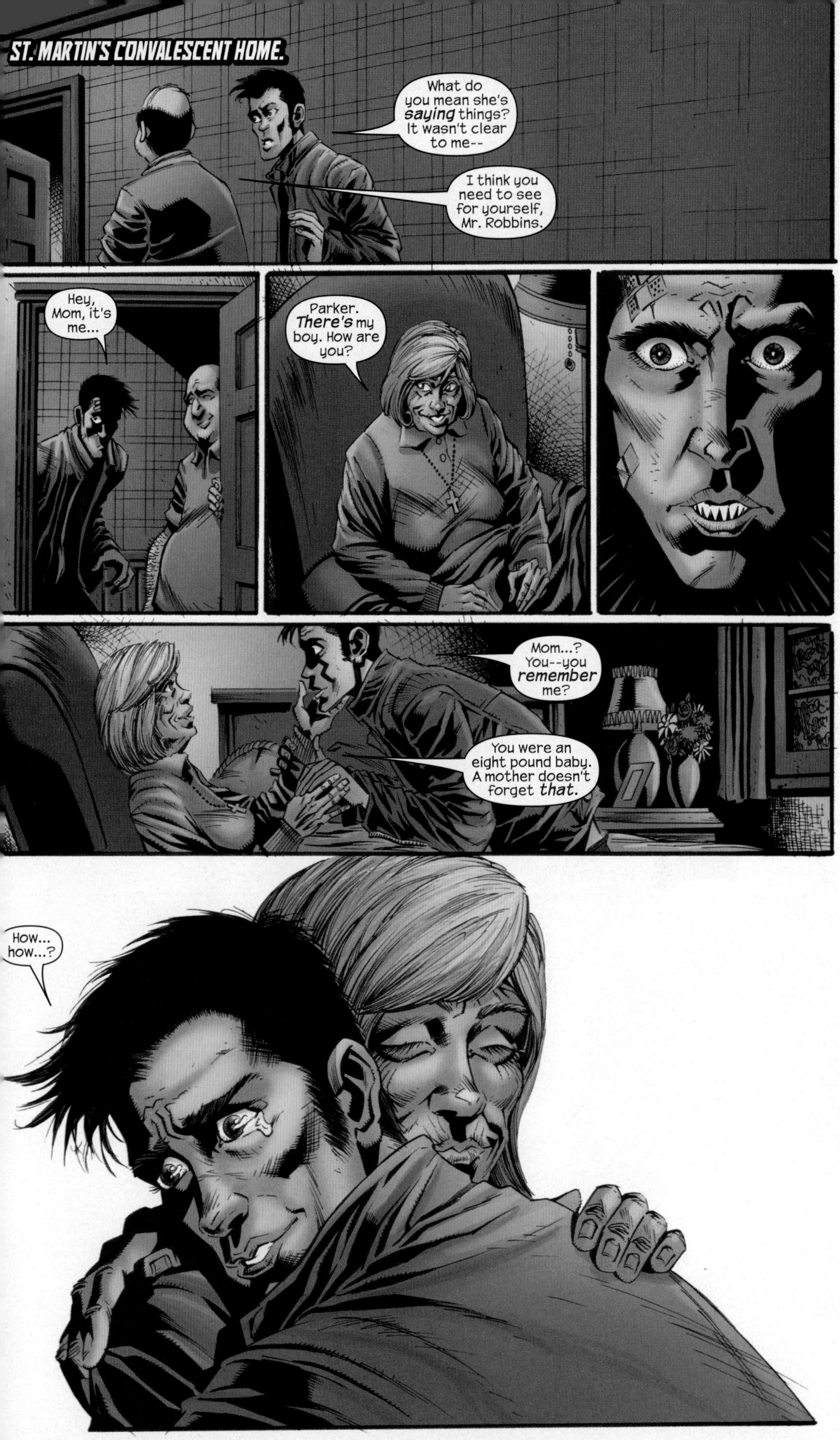
ST. MARTIN'S CONVALESCENT HOME.
What do you mean she's *saying* things? It wasn't clear to me--
I think you need to see for yourself, Mr. Robbins.
Hey, Mom, it's me...
Parker. *There's* my boy. How are you?
Mom...? You--you *remember* me?
You were an eight pound baby. A mother doesn't forget *that.*
How... how...?

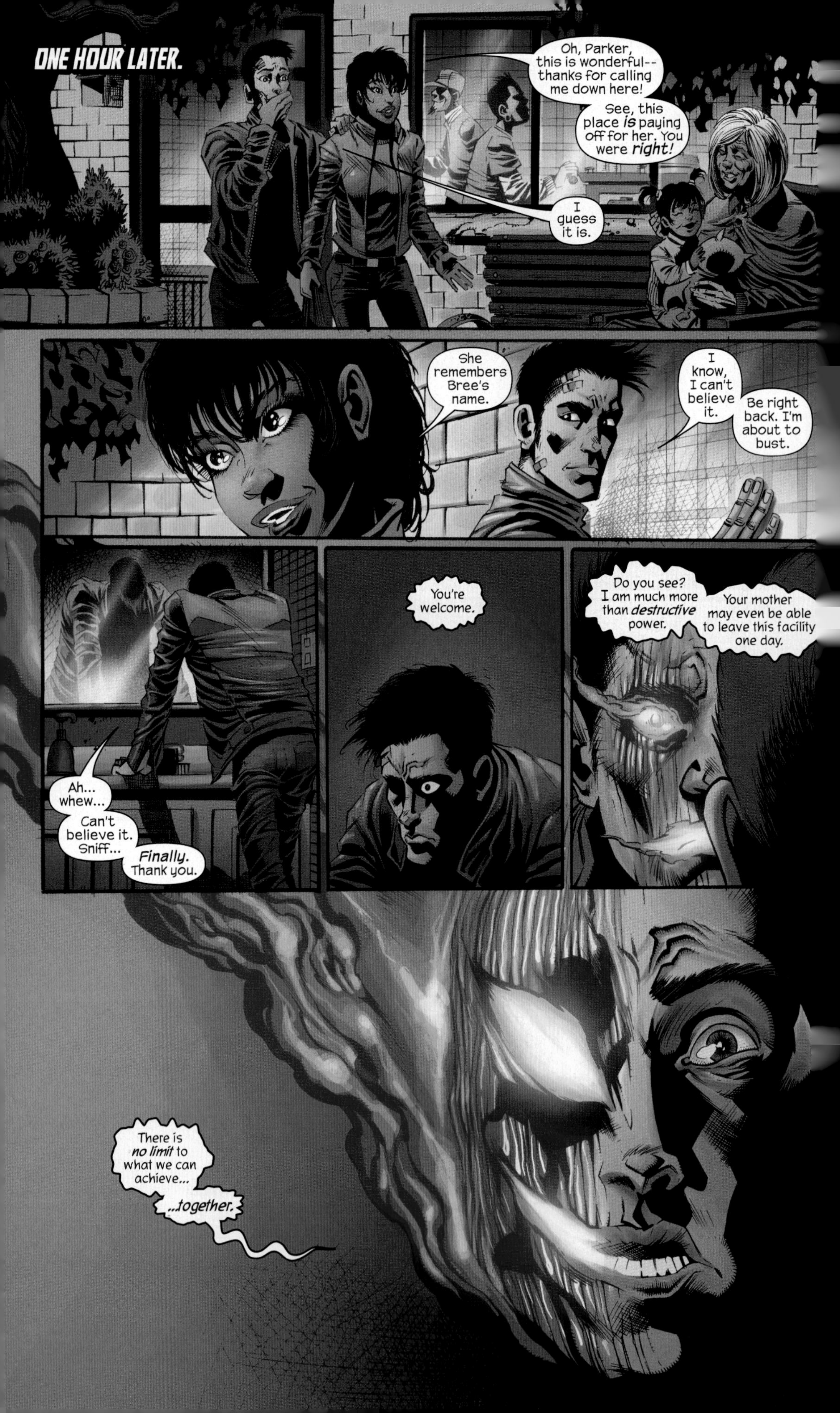
ONE HOUR LATER.
Oh, Parker, this is wonderful--thanks for calling me down here!
See, this place *is* paying off for her. You were *right!*
I guess it is.
She remembers Bree's name.
I know, I can't believe it.
Be right back. I'm about to bust.
Ah... whew...
Can't believe it. Sniff...
Finally. Thank you.
You're welcome.
Do you see? I am much more than *destructive* power.
Your mother may even be able to leave this facility one day.
There is *no limit* to what we can achieve...
...*together.*

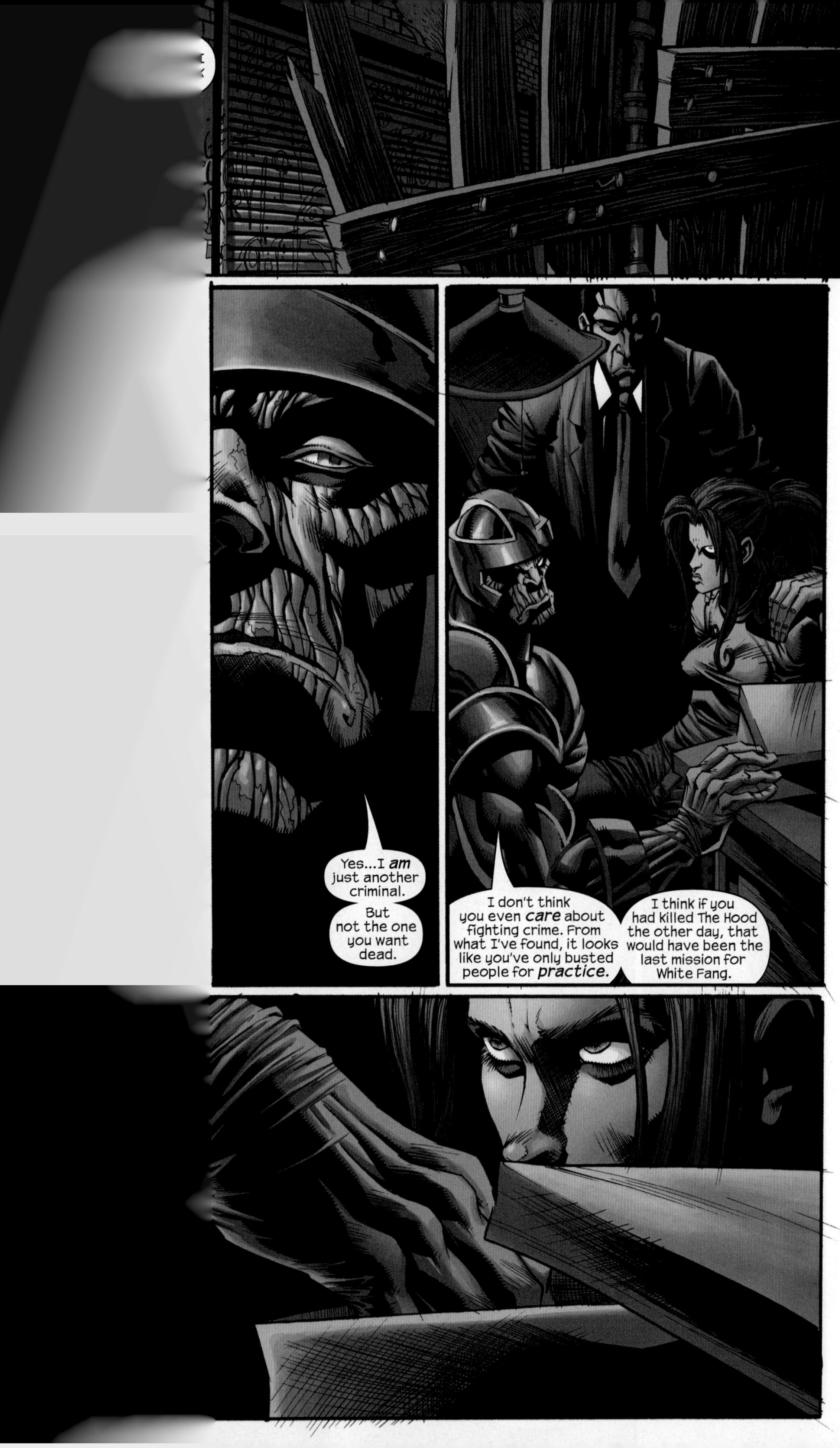
Yes...I am just another criminal.
But not the one you want dead.
I don't think you even care about fighting crime. From what I've found, it looks like you've only busted people for practice.
I think if you had killed The Hood the other day, that would have been the last mission for White Fang.

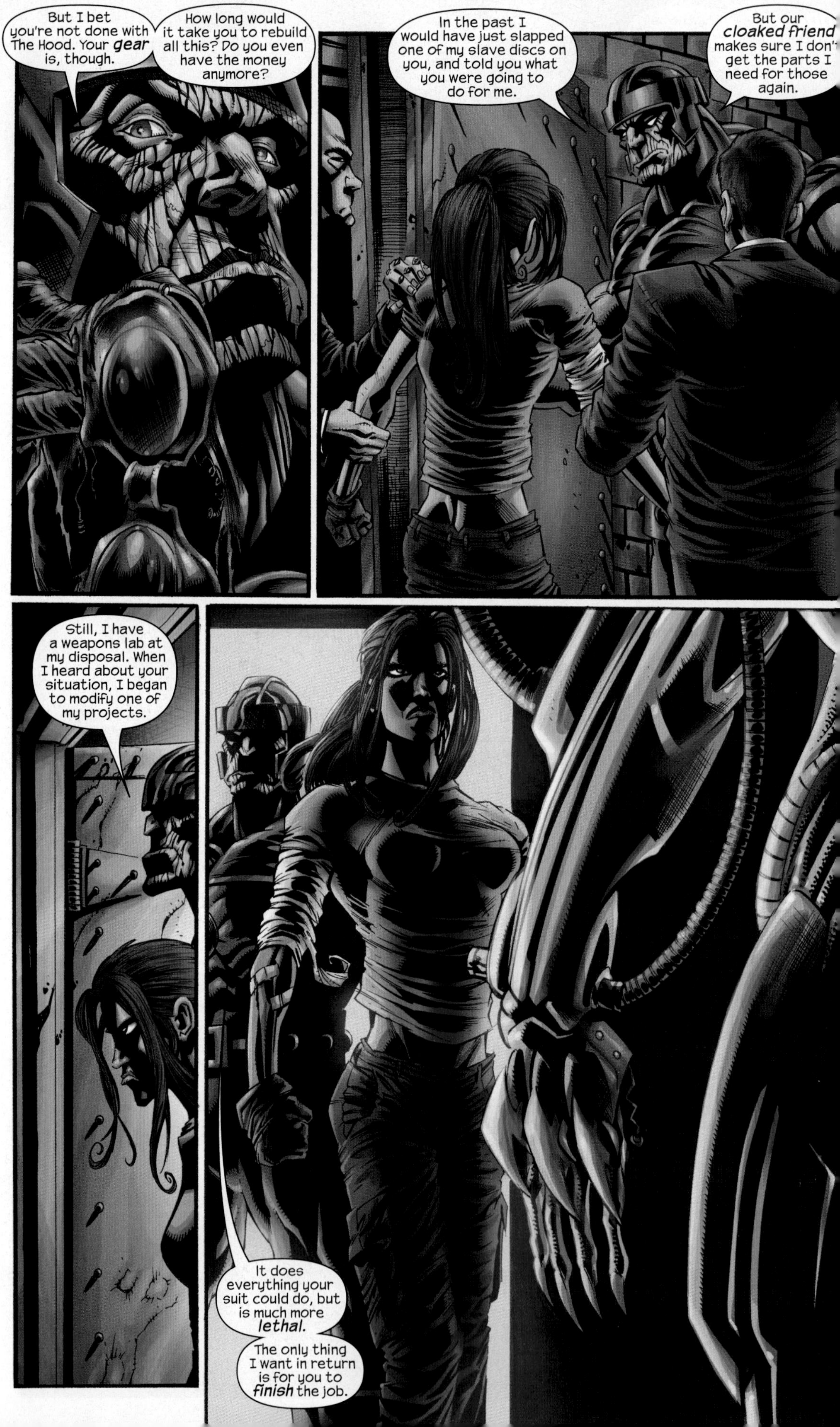
But I bet you're not done with The Hood. Your *gear* is, though.
How long would it take you to rebuild all this? Do you even have the money anymore?
In the past I would have just slapped one of my slave discs on you, and told you what you were going to do for me.
But our *cloaked friend* makes sure I don't get the parts I need for those again.
Still, I have a weapons lab at my disposal. When I heard about your situation, I began to modify one of my projects.
It does everything your suit could do, but is much more *lethal.*
The only thing I want in return is for you to *finish* the job.

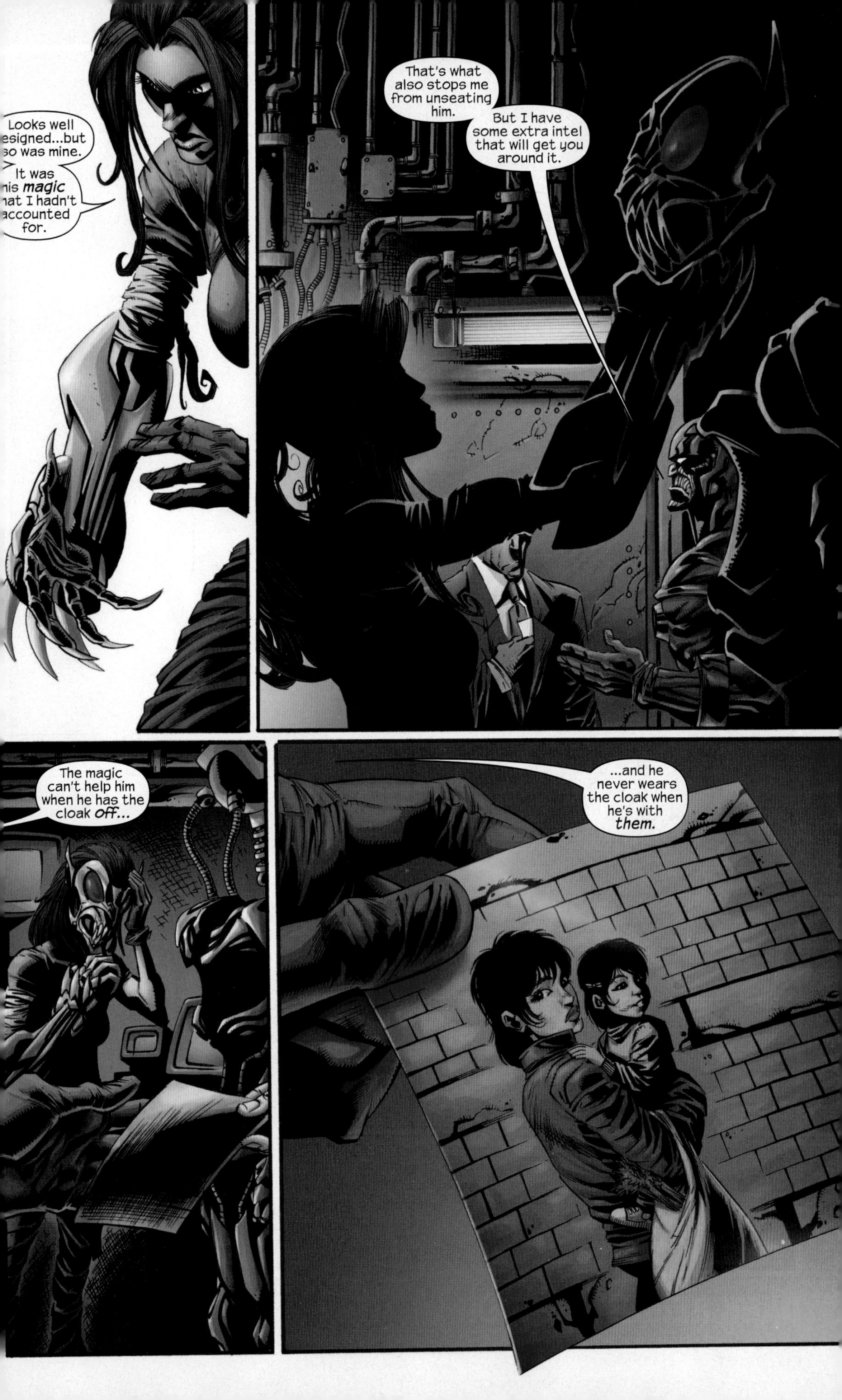

Looks well esigned...but so was mine.
It was his *magic* hat I hadn't accounted for.
That's what also stops me from unseating him.
But I have some extra intel that will get you around it.
The magic can't help him when he has the cloak *off*...
...and he never wears the cloak when he's with *them.*

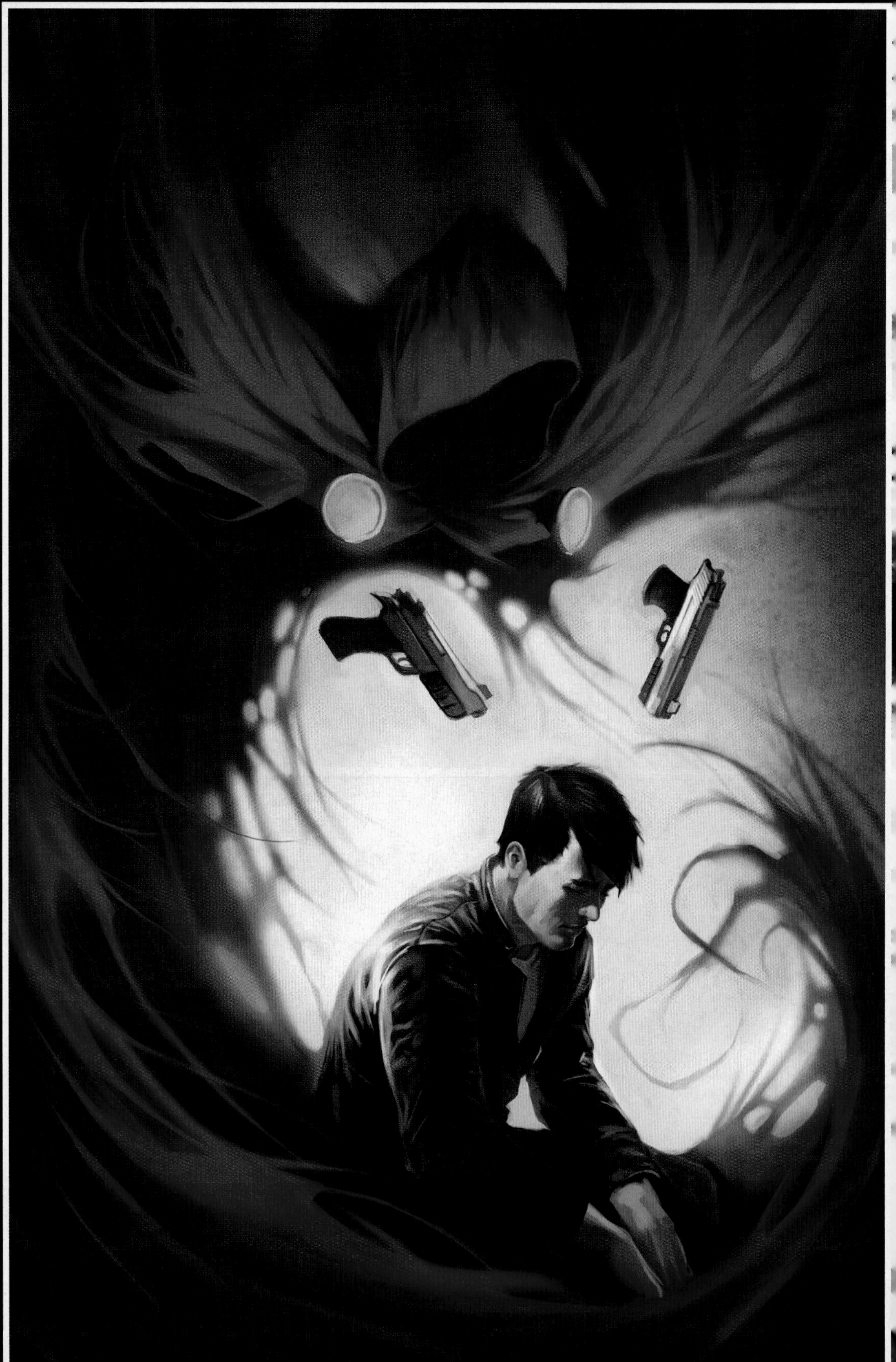

DARK REIGN: THE HOOD #4

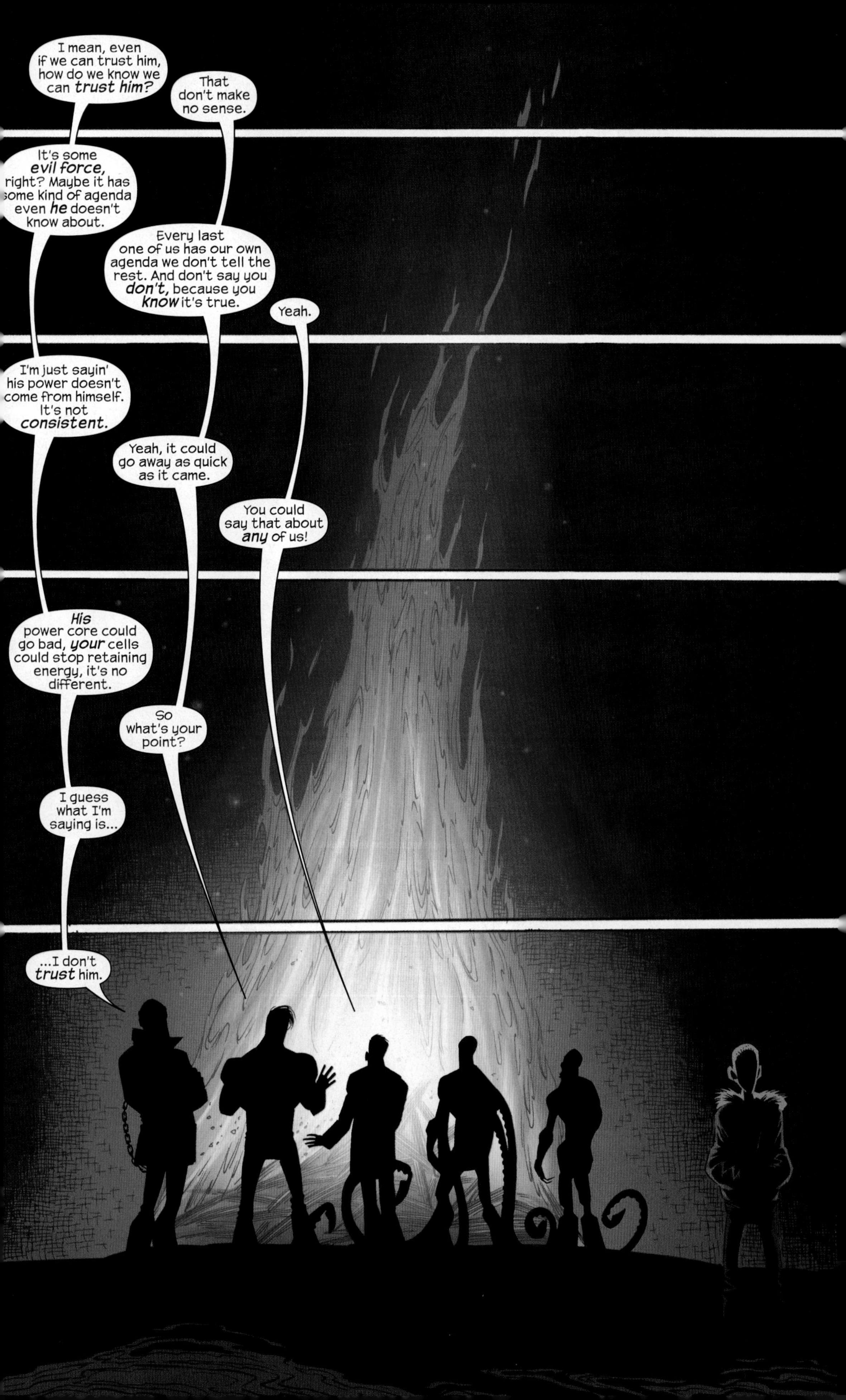
I mean, even if we can trust him, how do we know we can trust him?
That don't make no sense.
It's some evil force, right? Maybe it has some kind of agenda even he doesn't know about.
Every last one of us has our own agenda we don't tell the rest. And don't say you don't, because you know it's true.
Yeah.
I'm just sayin' his power doesn't come from himself. It's not consistent.
Yeah, it could go away as quick as it came.
You could say that about any of us!
His power core could go bad, your cells could stop retaining energy, it's no different.
So what's your point?
I guess what I'm saying is...
...I don't trust him.

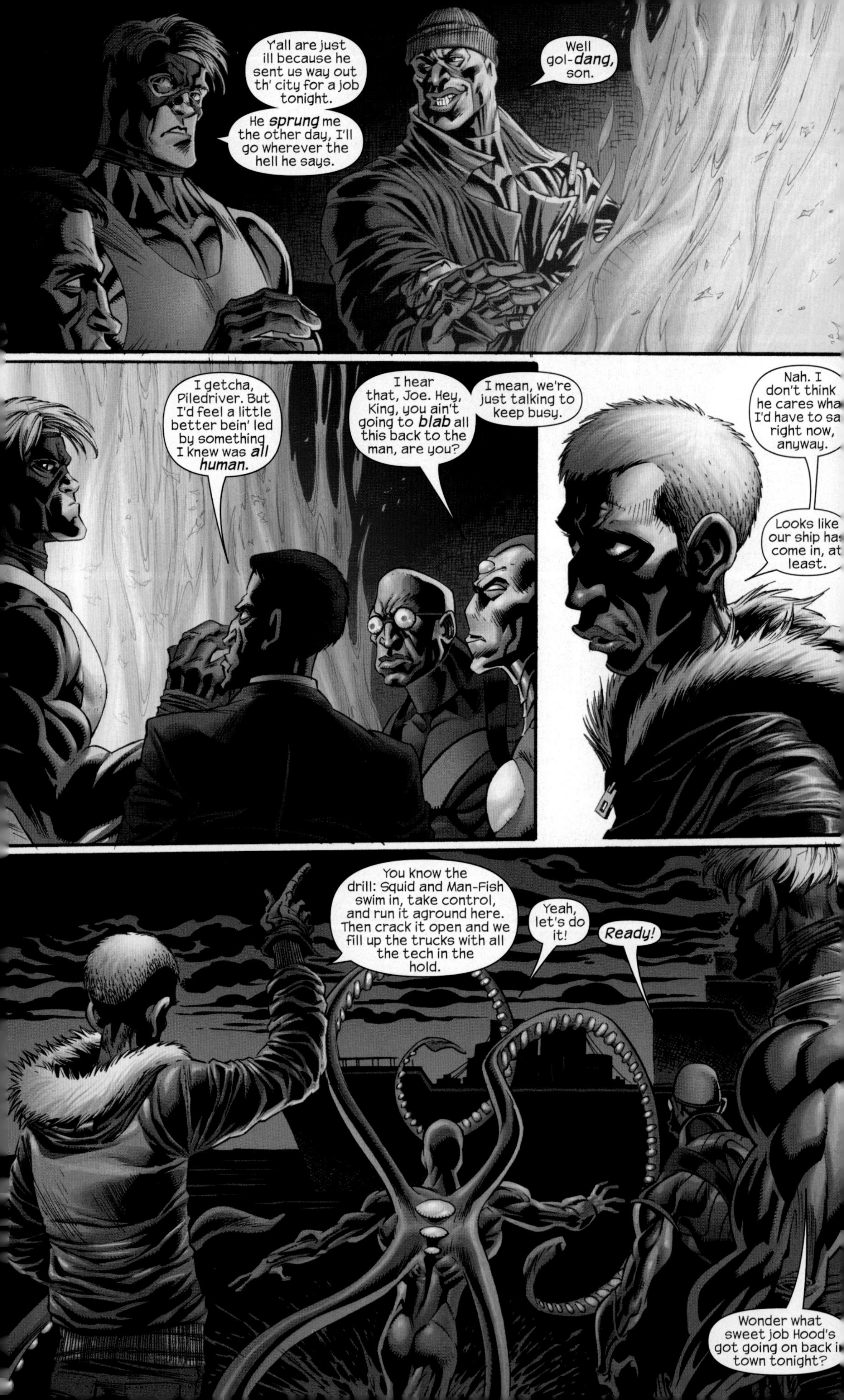
Y'all are just ill because he sent us way out th' city for a job tonight.
He sprung me the other day, I'll go wherever the hell he says.
Well gol-dang, son.
I getcha, Piledriver. But I'd feel a little better bein' led by something I knew was all human.
I hear that, Joe. Hey, King, you ain't going to blab all this back to the man, are you?
I mean, we're just talking to keep busy.
Nah. I don't think he cares wha I'd have to sa right now, anyway.
Looks like our ship ha come in, at least.
You know the drill: Squid and Man-Fish swim in, take control, and run it aground here. Then crack it open and we fill up the trucks with all the tech in the hold.
Yeah, let's do it!
Ready!
Wonder what sweet job Hood's got going on back i town tonight?

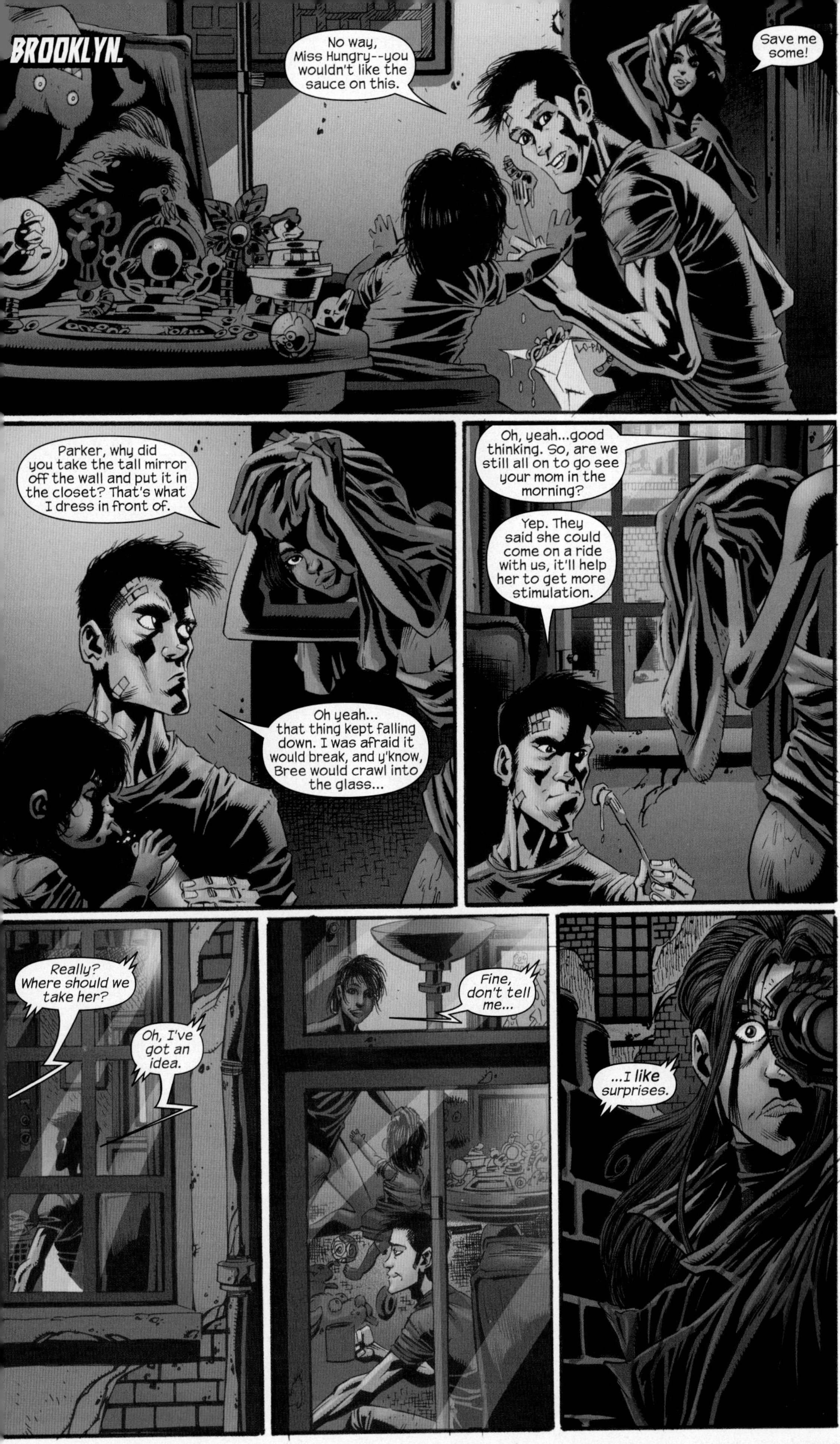
BROOKLYN.
No way, Miss Hungry--you wouldn't like the sauce on this.
Save me some!
Parker, why did you take the tall mirror off the wall and put it in the closet? That's what I dress in front of.
Oh yeah... that thing kept falling down. I was afraid it would break, and y'know, Bree would crawl into the glass...
Oh, yeah...good thinking. So, are we still all on to go see your mom in the morning?
Yep. They said she could come on a ride with us, it'll help her to get more stimulation.
Really? Where should we take her?
Oh, I've got an idea.
Fine, don't tell me...
...I like surprises.

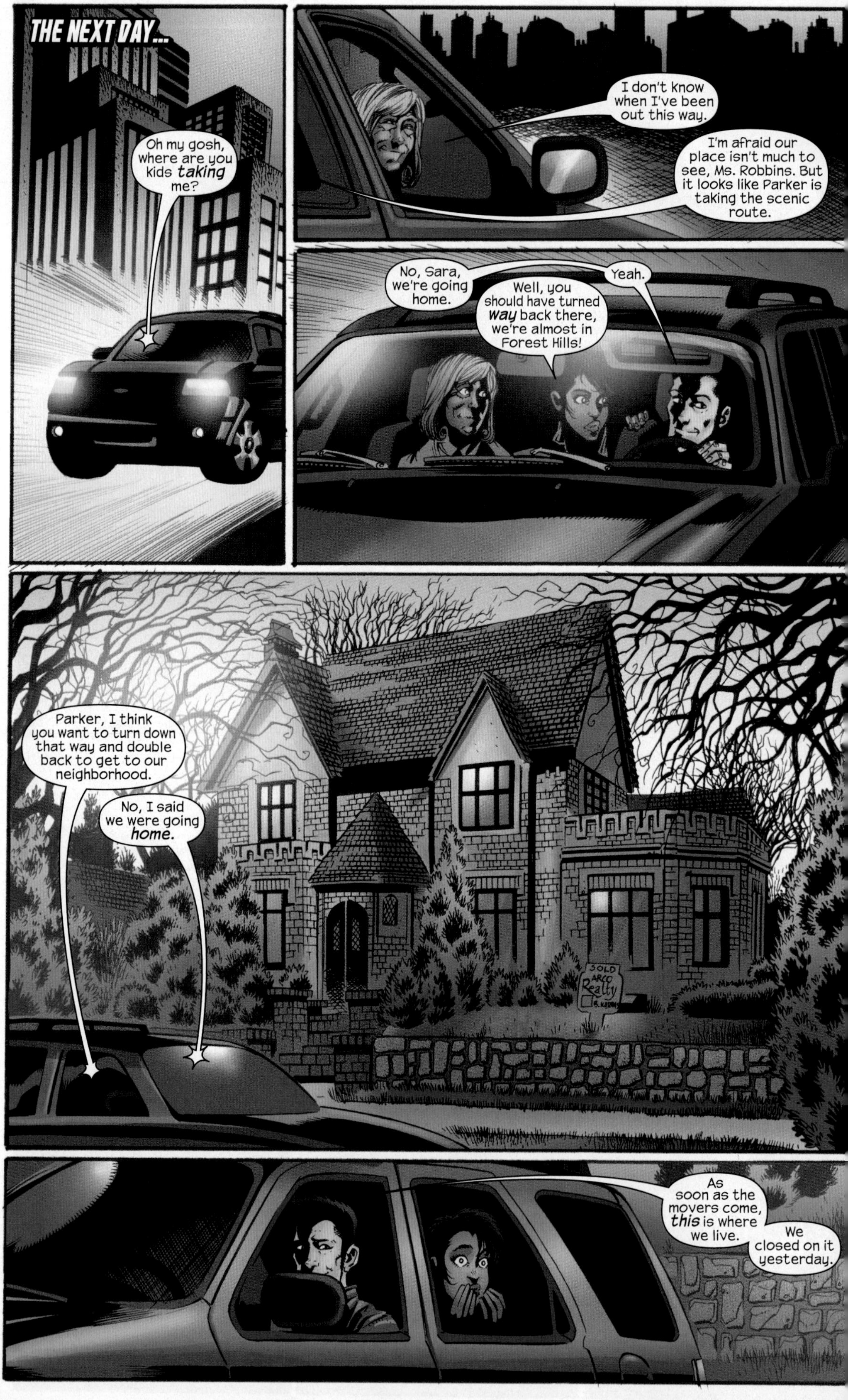
THE NEXT DAY...
Oh my gosh, where are you kids taking me?
I don't know when I've been out this way.
I'm afraid our place isn't much to see, Ms. Robbins. But it looks like Parker is taking the scenic route.
No, Sara, we're going home.
Yeah.
Well, you should have turned way back there, we're almost in Forest Hills!
SOLD
Realty
Parker, I think you want to turn down that way and double back to get to our neighborhood.
No, I said we were going home.
As soon as the movers come, this is where we live.
We closed on it yesterday.

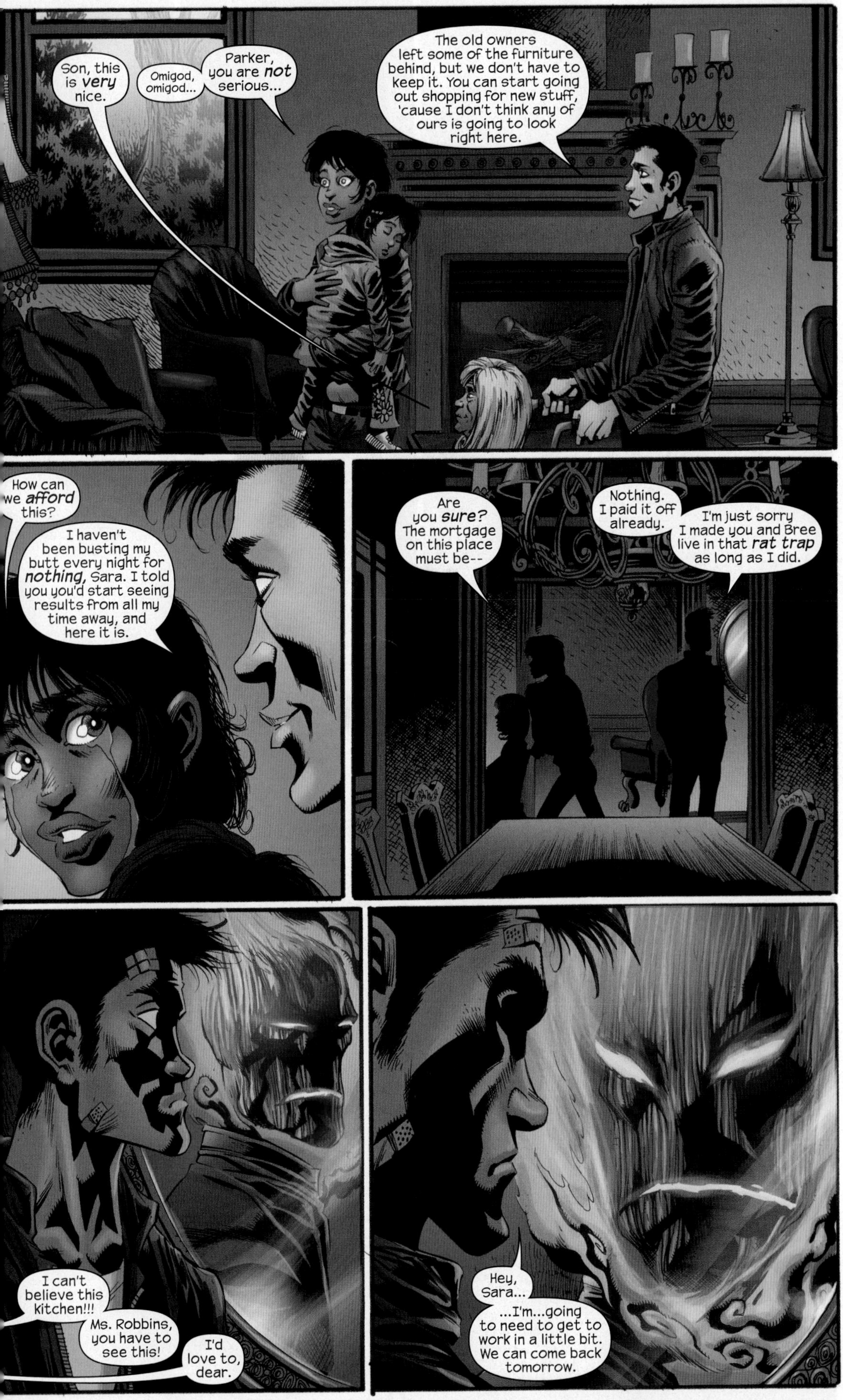

Son, this is very nice.
Omigod, omigod...
Parker, you are not serious...
The old owners left some of the furniture behind, but we don't have to keep it. You can start going out shopping for new stuff, 'cause I don't think any of ours is going to look right here.
How can we afford this?
I haven't been busting my butt every night for nothing, Sara. I told you you'd start seeing results from all my time away, and here it is.
Are you sure? The mortgage on this place must be--
Nothing. I paid it off already.
I'm just sorry I made you and Bree live in that rat trap as long as I did.
I can't believe this kitchen!!!
Ms. Robbins, you have to see this!
I'd love to, dear.
Hey, Sara...
...I'm...going to need to get to work in a little bit. We can come back tomorrow.

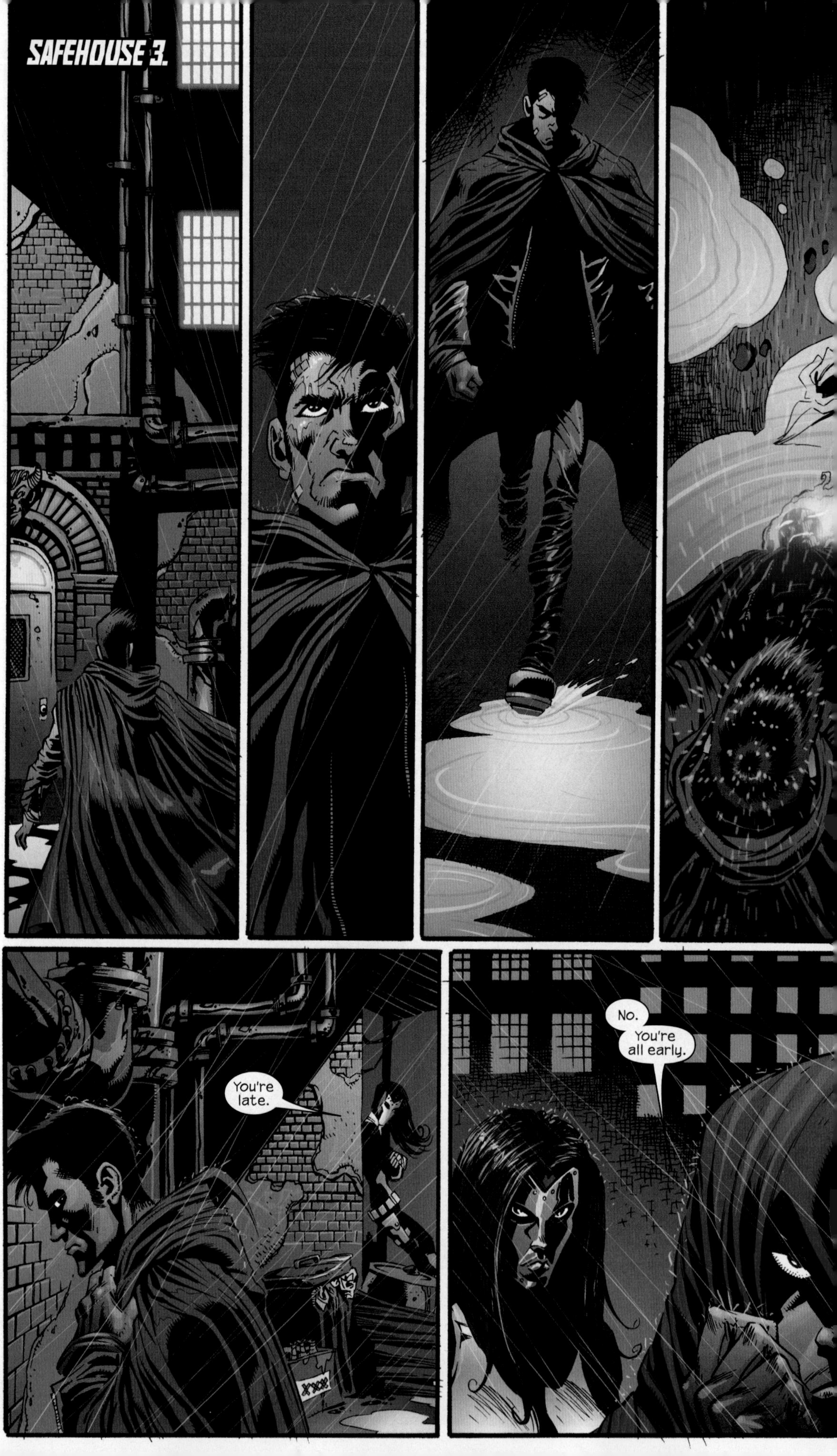
SAFEHOUSE 3.
You're late.
No.
You're all early.

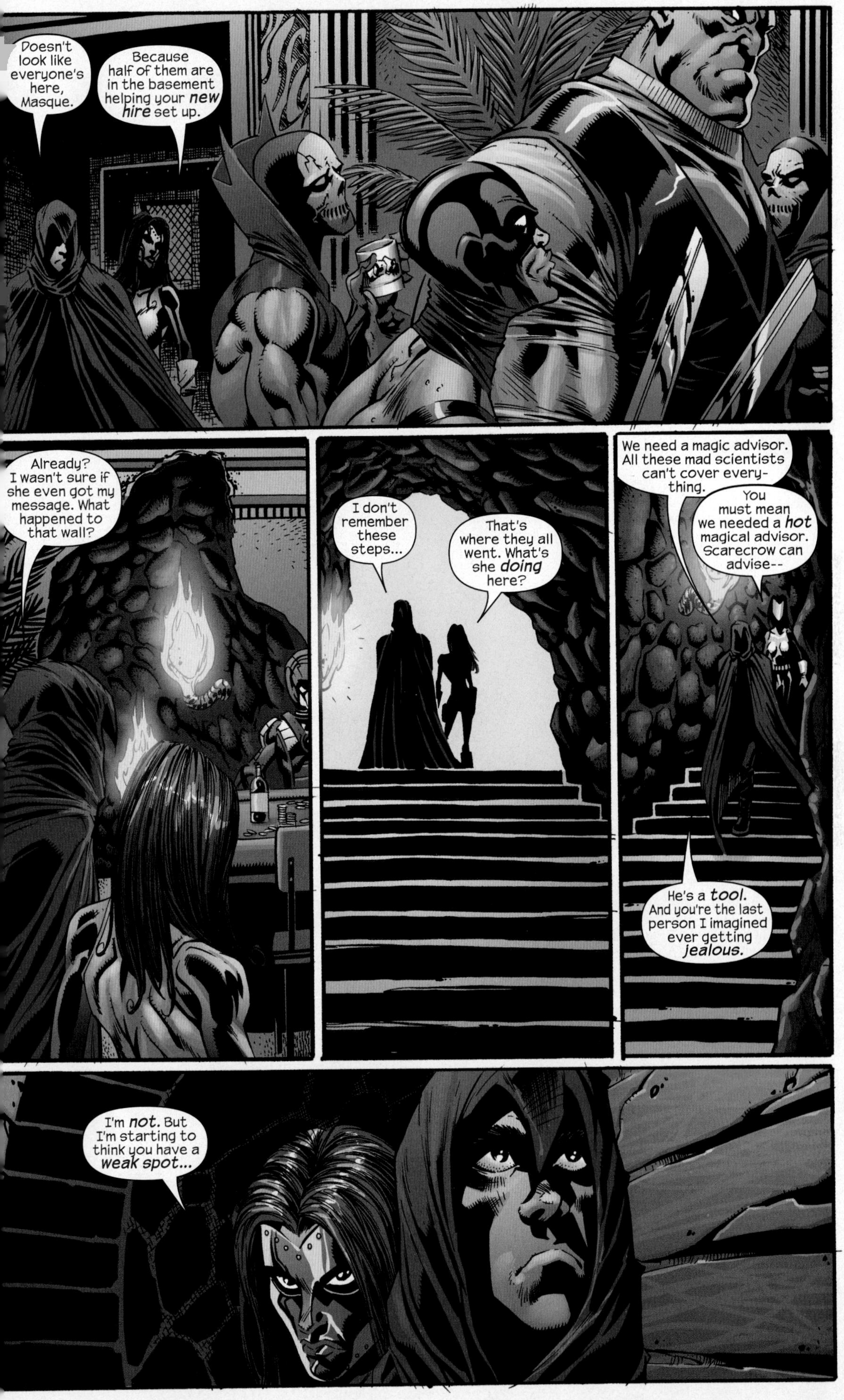
Doesn't look like everyone's here, Masque.
Because half of them are in the basement helping your *new hire* set up.
Already? I wasn't sure if she even got my message. What happened to that wall?
I don't remember these steps...
That's where they all went. What's she *doing* here?
We need a magic advisor. All these mad scientists can't cover every-thing.
You must mean we needed a *hot* magical advisor. Scarecrow can advise--
He's a *tool.* And you're the last person I imagined ever getting *jealous.*
I'm *not.* But I'm starting to think you have a *weak spot...*

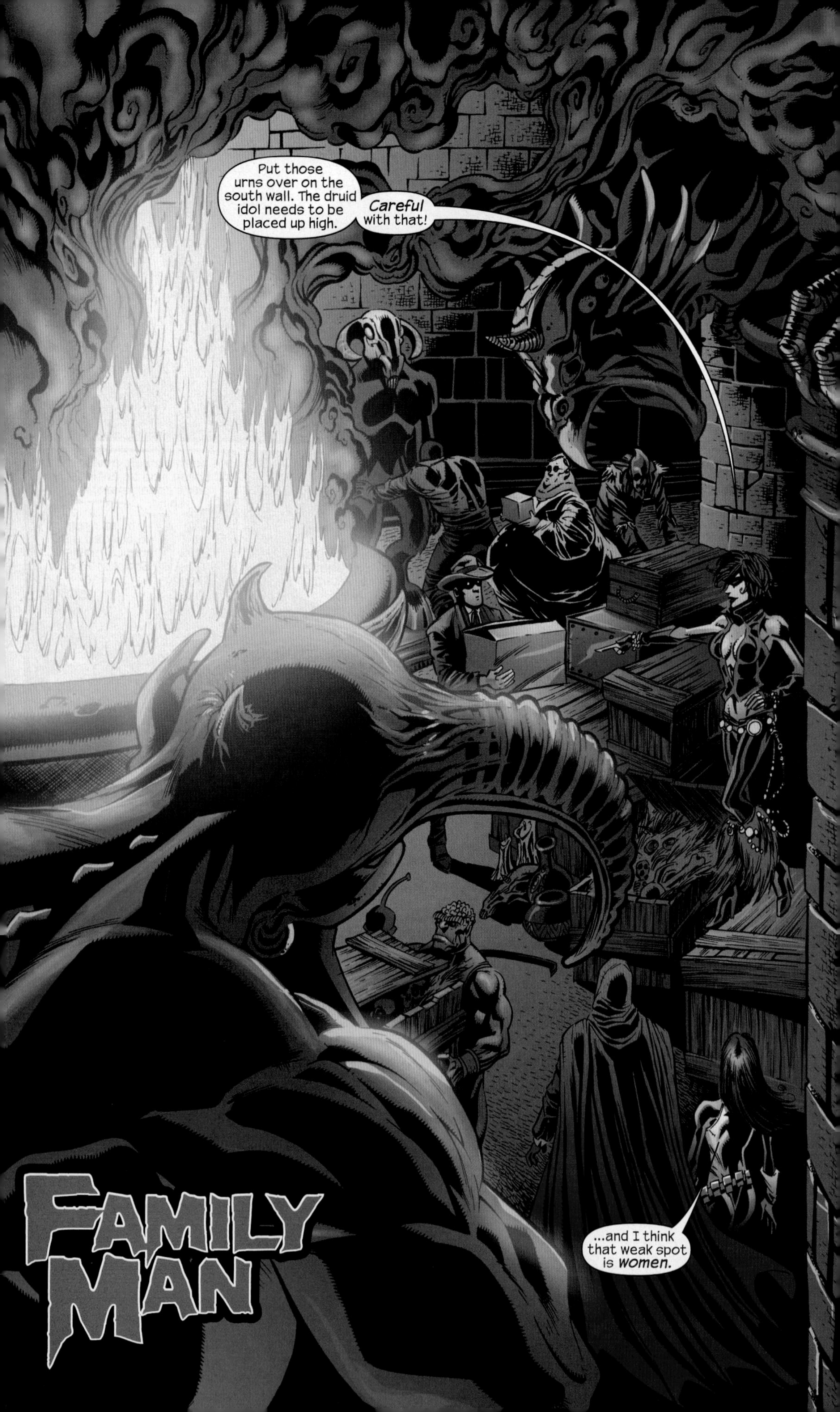
Put those urns over on the south wall. The druid idol needs to be placed up high.
Careful with that!
...and I think that weak spot is *women.*
FAMILY MAN

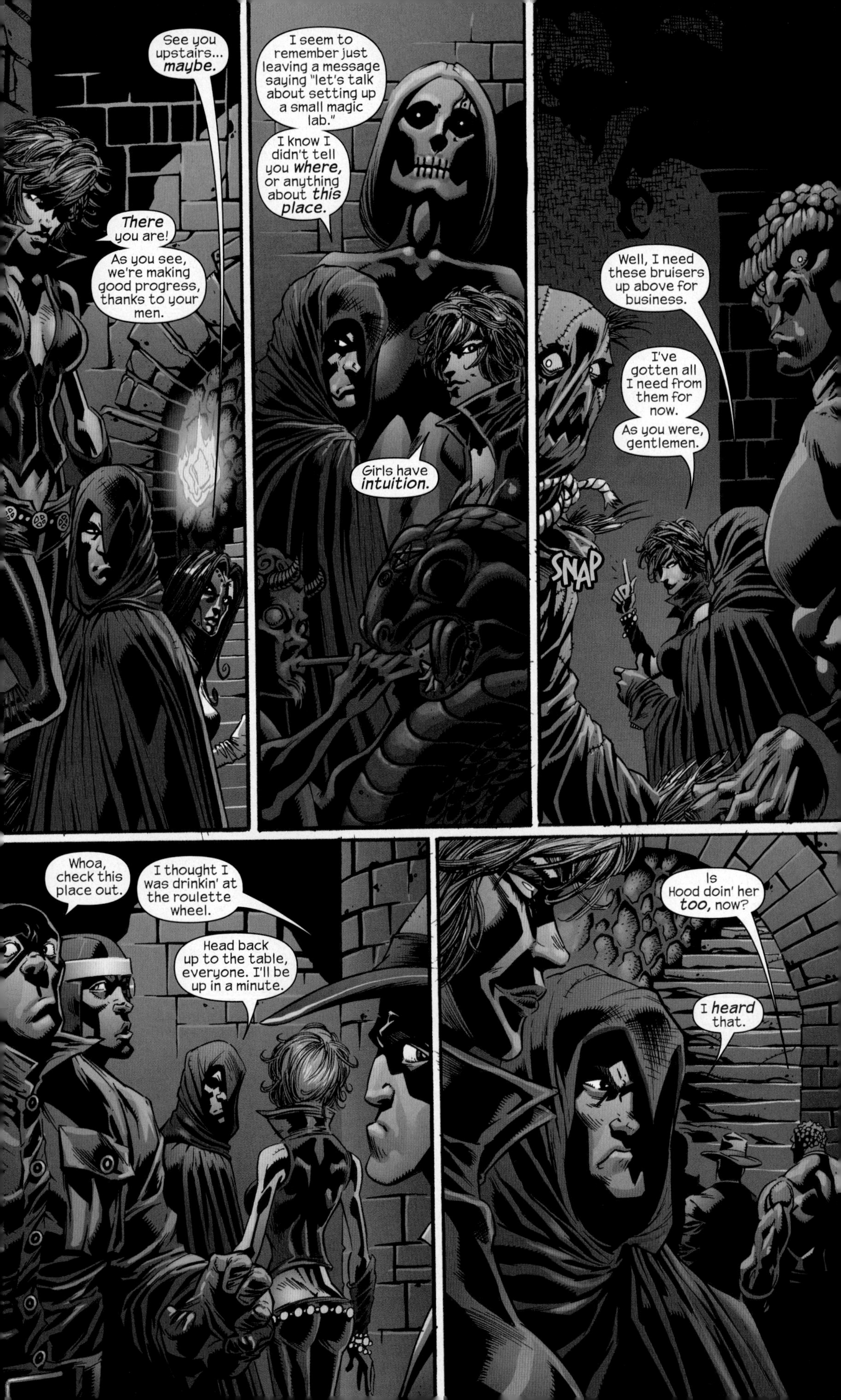
See you upstairs... maybe.
There you are!
As you see, we're making good progress, thanks to your men.
I seem to remember just leaving a message saying "let's talk about setting up a small magic lab."
I know I didn't tell you where, or anything about this place.
Girls have intuition.
Well, I need these bruisers up above for business.
I've gotten all I need from them for now.
As you were, gentlemen.
SNAP
Whoa, check this place out.
I thought I was drinkin' at the roulette wheel.
Head back up to the table, everyone. I'll be up in a minute.
Is Hood doin' her too, now?
I heard that.

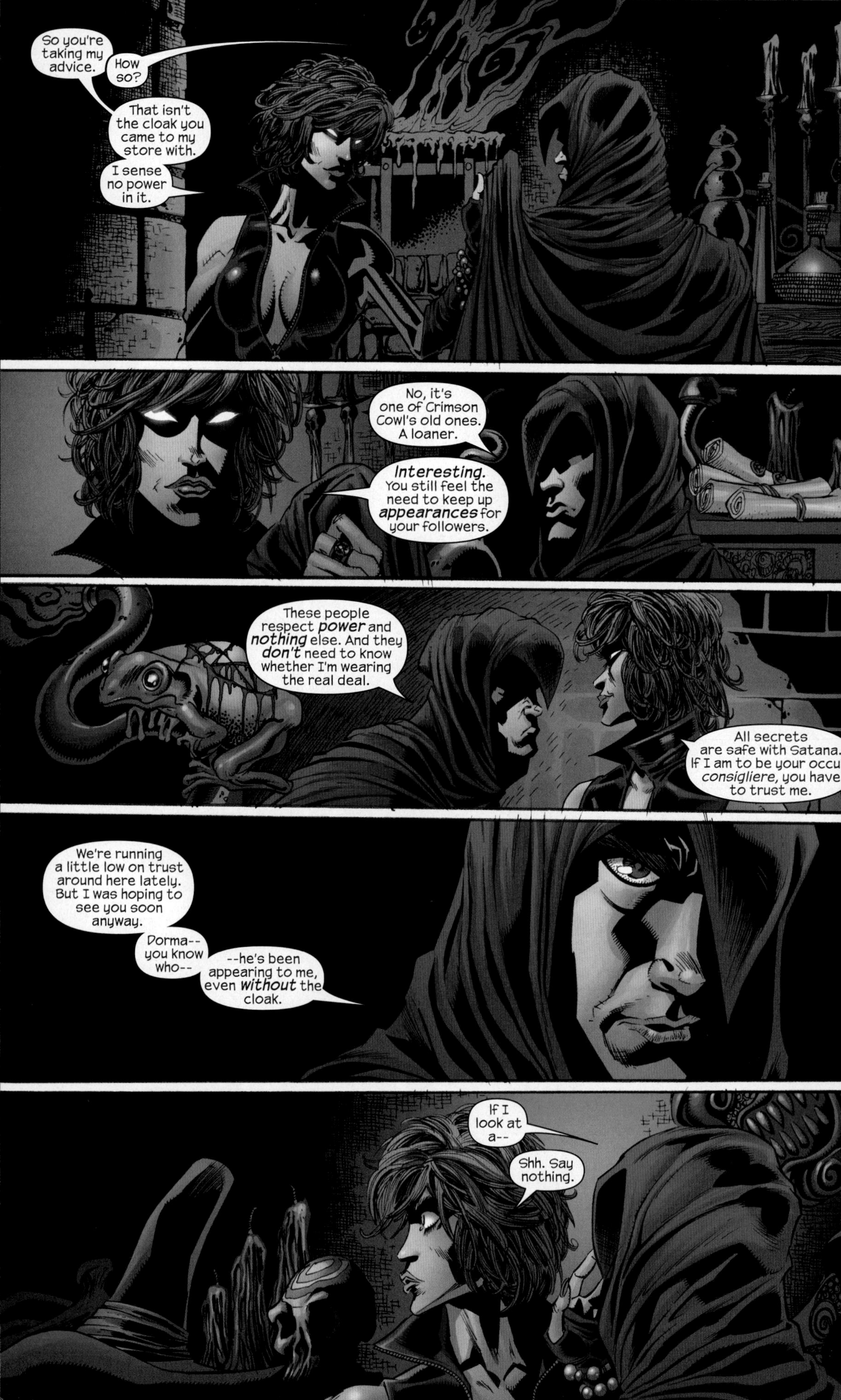

So you're taking my advice.
How so?
That isn't the cloak you came to my store with.
I sense no power in it.
No, it's one of Crimson Cowl's old ones. A loaner.
Interesting. You still feel the need to keep up *appearances* for your followers.
These people respect *power* and *nothing* else. And they *don't* need to know whether I'm wearing the real deal.
All secrets are safe with Satana. If I am to be your occu *consigliere,* you have to trust me.
We're running a little low on trust around here lately. But I was hoping to see you soon anyway.
Dorma-- you know who--
--he's been appearing to me, even *without* the cloak.
If I look at a--
Shh. Say nothing.

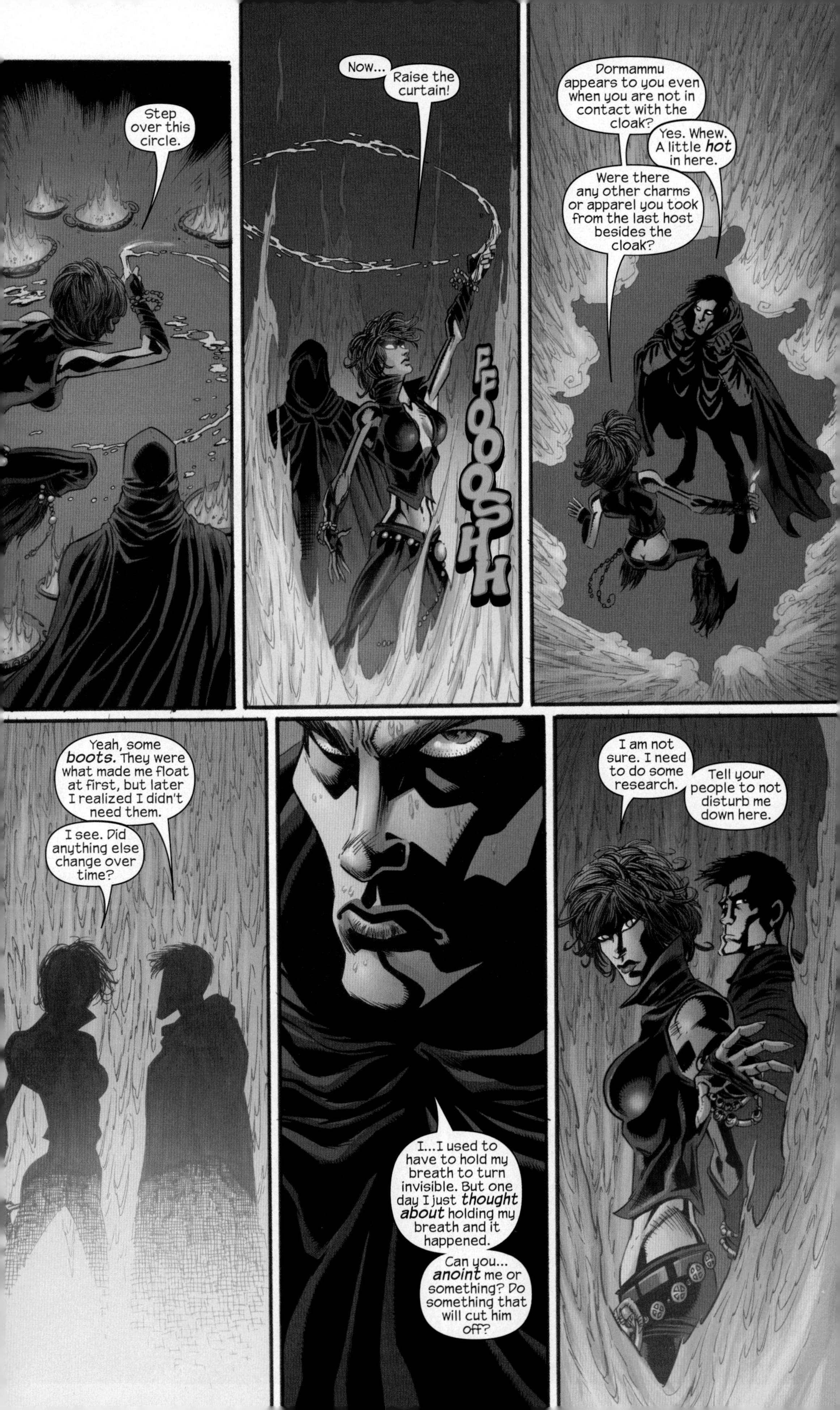

Step over this circle.
Now...
Raise the curtain!
FFOOOOSHH
Dormammu appears to you even when you are not in contact with the cloak?
Yes. Whew. A little *hot* in here.
Were there any other charms or apparel you took from the last host besides the cloak?
Yeah, some *boots.* They were what made me float at first, but later I realized I didn't need them.
I see. Did anything else change over time?
I...I used to have to hold my breath to turn invisible. But one day I just *thought about* holding my breath and it happened.
Can you... *anoint* me or something? Do something that will cut him off?
I am not sure. I need to do some research.
Tell your people to not disturb me down here.

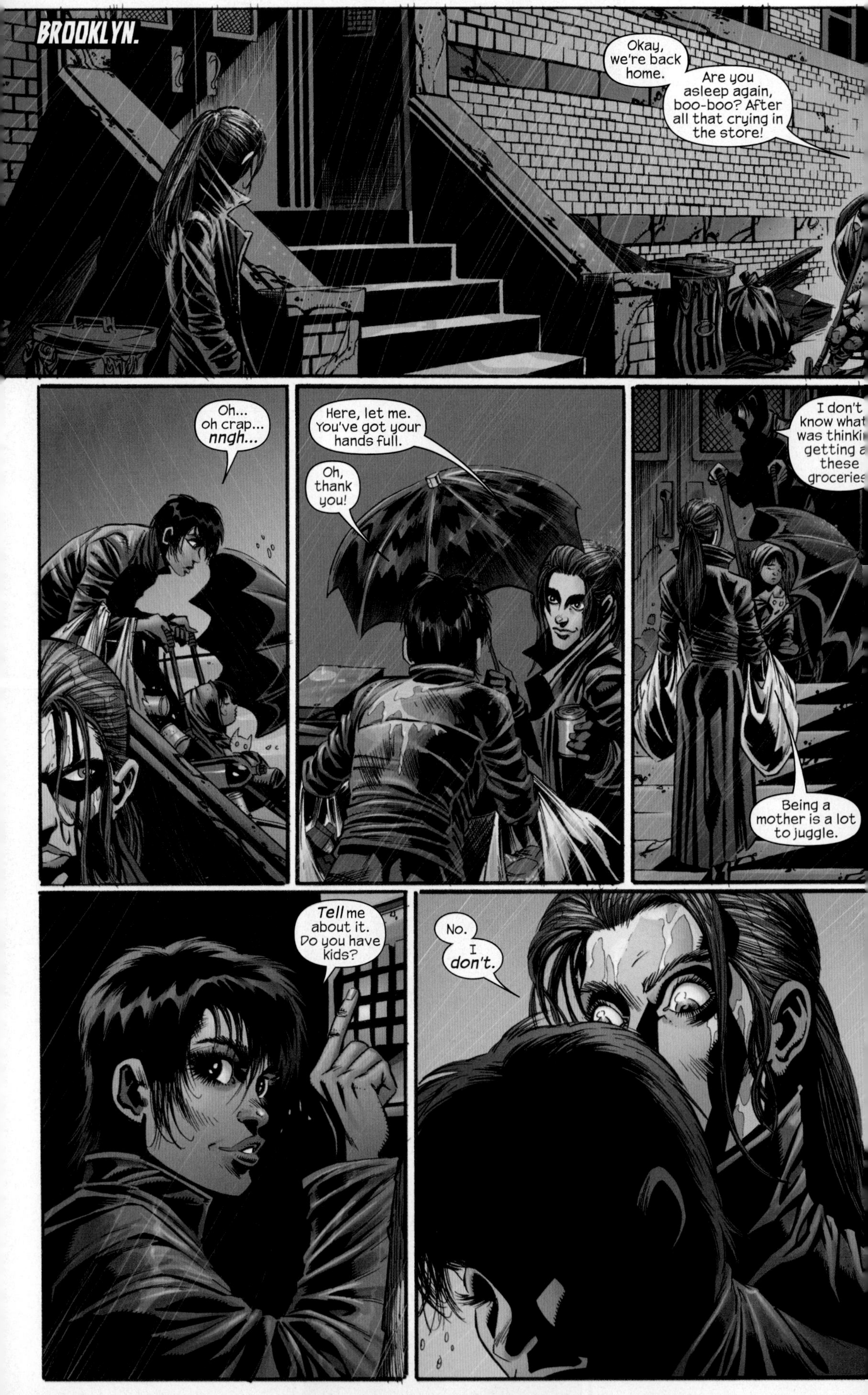
BROOKLYN.
Okay, we're back home.
Are you asleep again, boo-boo? After all that crying in the store!
Oh... oh crap... *nngh...*
Here, let me. You've got your hands full.
Oh, thank you!
I don't know what was thinki getting a these groceries
Being a mother is a lot to juggle.
Tell me about it. Do you have kids?
No. I *don't.*

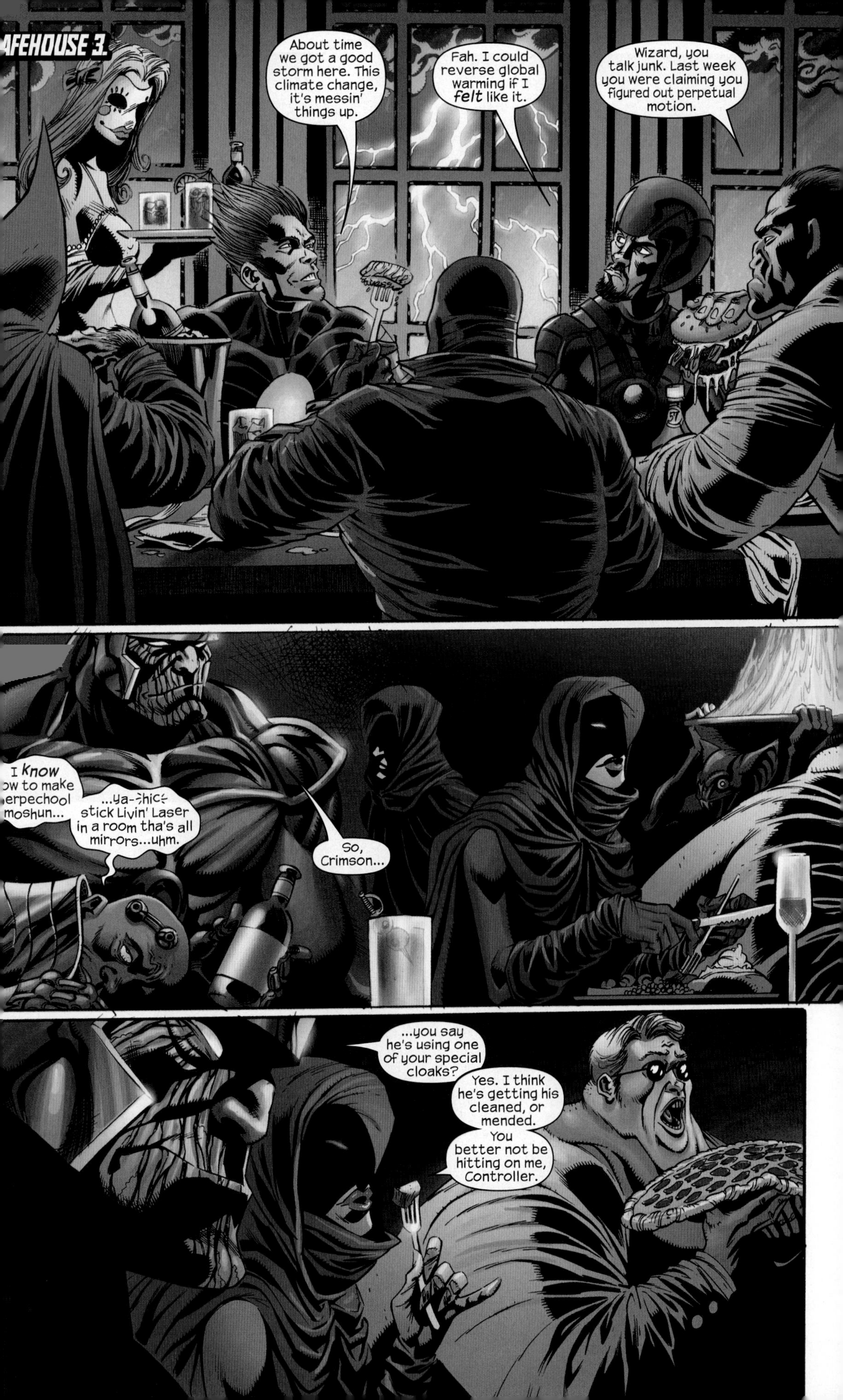
AFEHOUSE 3.
About time we got a good storm here. This climate change, it's messin' things up.
Fah. I could reverse global warming if I *felt* like it.
Wizard, you talk junk. Last week you were claiming you figured out perpetual motion.
I *know* ow to make erpechool moshun...
...ya-hic- stick Livin' Laser in a room tha's all mirrors...uhm.
So, Crimson...
...you say he's using one of your special cloaks?
Yes. I think he's getting his cleaned, or mended.
You better not be hitting on me, Controller.

I *thought* he looked different. I didn't see the little spooky doohickeys on the cape.

...spoohickeys.

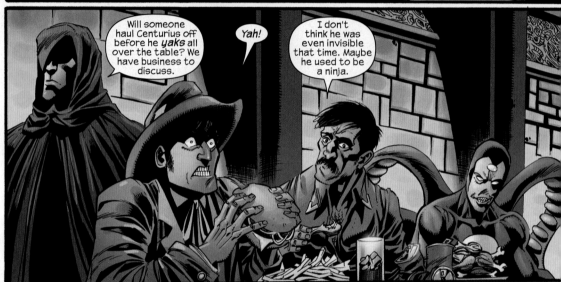

Will someone haul Centurius off before he *yaks* all over the table? We have business to discuss.

Yah!

I don't think he was even invisible that time. Maybe he used to be a ninja.

Controller. I have news for you.

Oh. Now what could *that* be?

An inside man at Stark Industri finally got us t crystal coils y need for your *slave discs.*

The rest are in the new lab. It not much, but should get yo started.

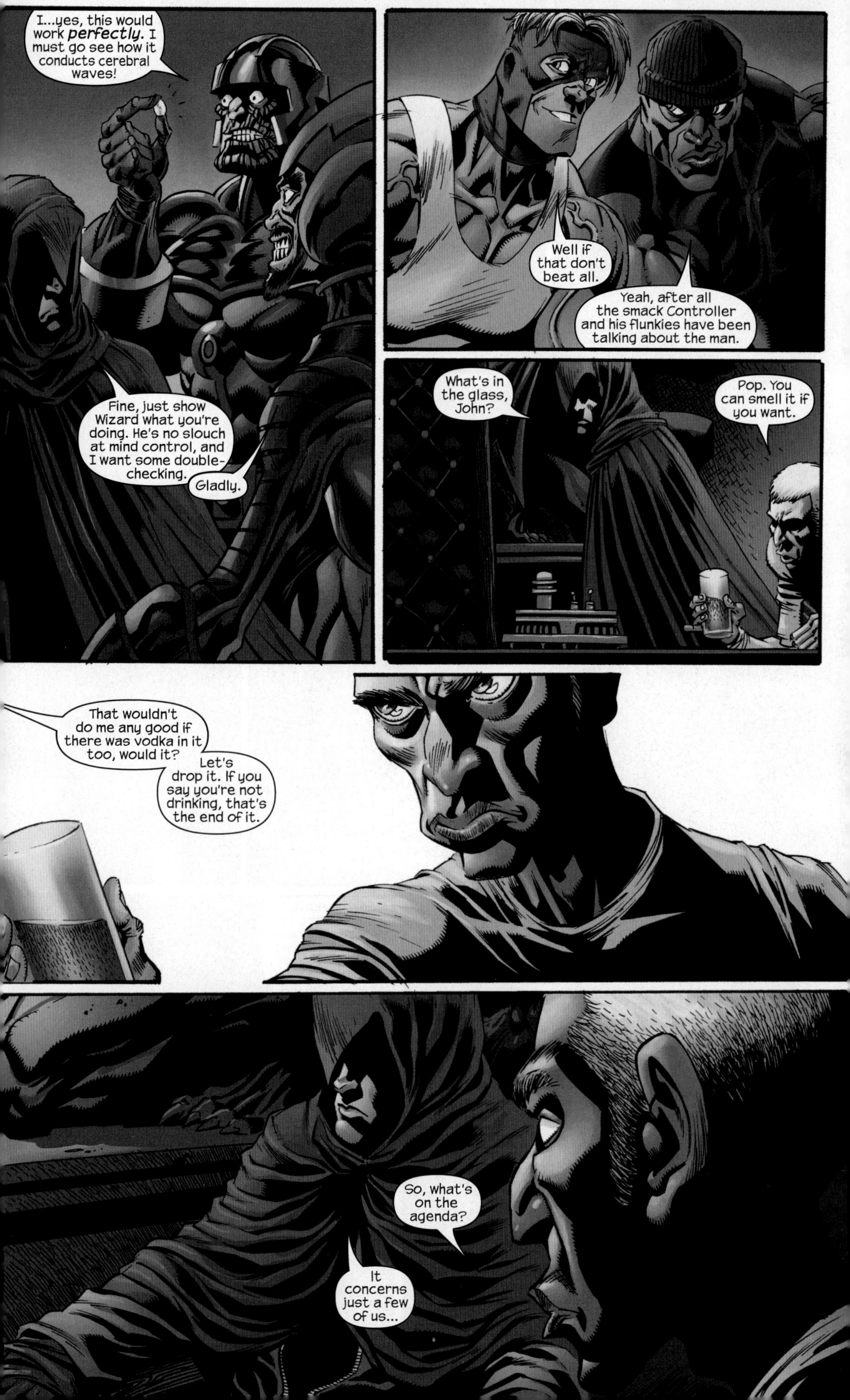

I...yes, this would work *perfectly.* I must go see how it conducts cerebral waves!
Fine, just show Wizard what you're doing. He's no slouch at mind control, and I want some double-checking.
Gladly.
Well if that don't beat all.
Yeah, after all the smack Controller and his flunkies have been talking about the man.
What's in the glass, John?
Pop. You can smell it if you want.
That wouldn't do me any good if there was vodka in it too, would it?
Let's drop it. If you say you're not drinking, that's the end of it.
So, what's on the agenda?
It concerns just a few of us...

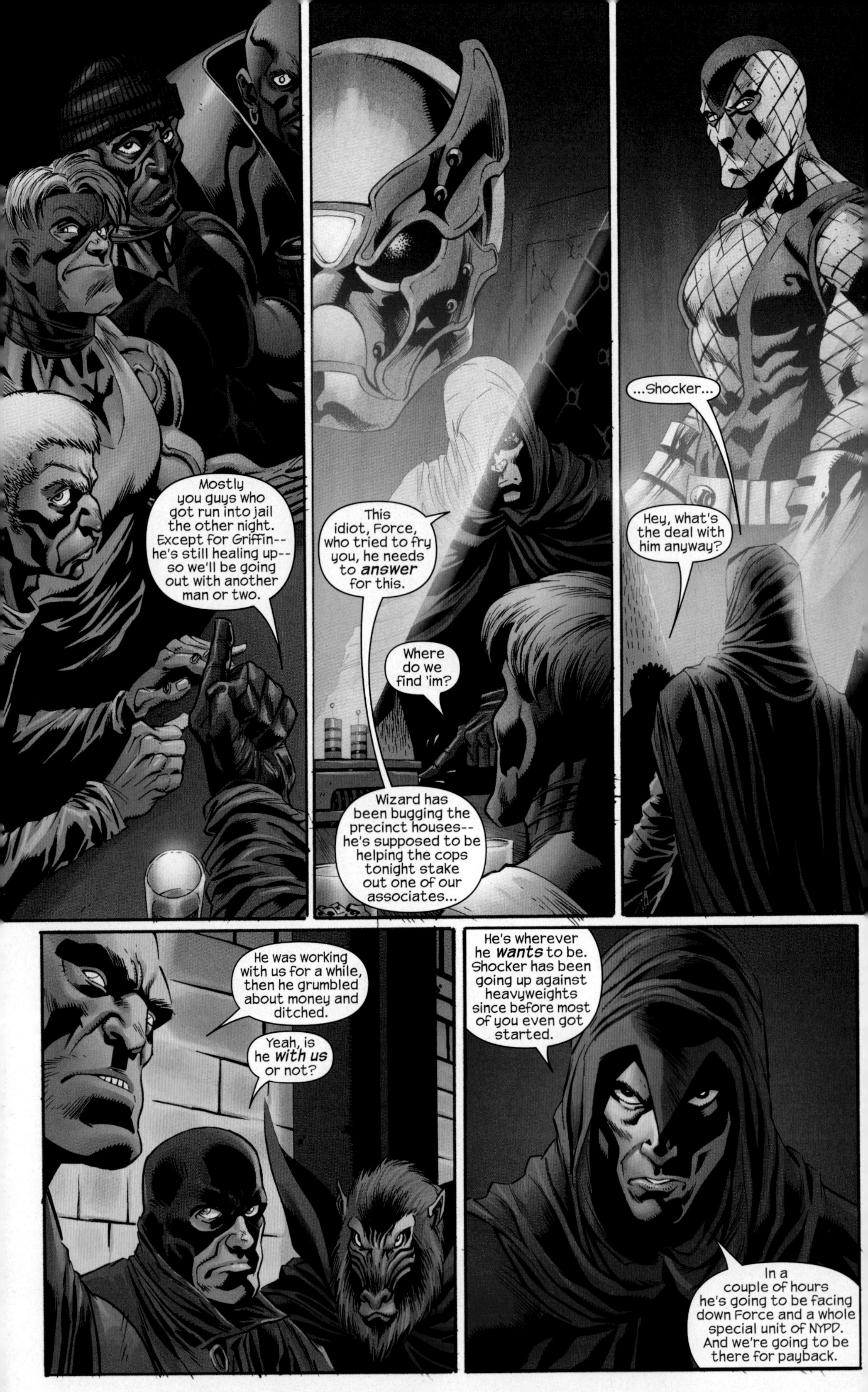
Mostly you guys who got run into jail the other night. Except for Griffin-- he's still healing up-- so we'll be going out with another man or two.
This idiot, Force, who tried to fry you, he needs to answer for this.
Where do we find 'im?
Wizard has been bugging the precinct houses-- he's supposed to be helping the cops tonight stake out one of our associates...
...Shocker...
Hey, what's the deal with him anyway?
He was working with us for a while, then he grumbled about money and ditched.
Yeah, is he with us or not?
He's wherever he wants to be. Shocker has been going up against heavyweights since before most of you even got started.
In a couple of hours he's going to be facing down Force and a whole special unit of NYPD. And we're going to be there for payback.

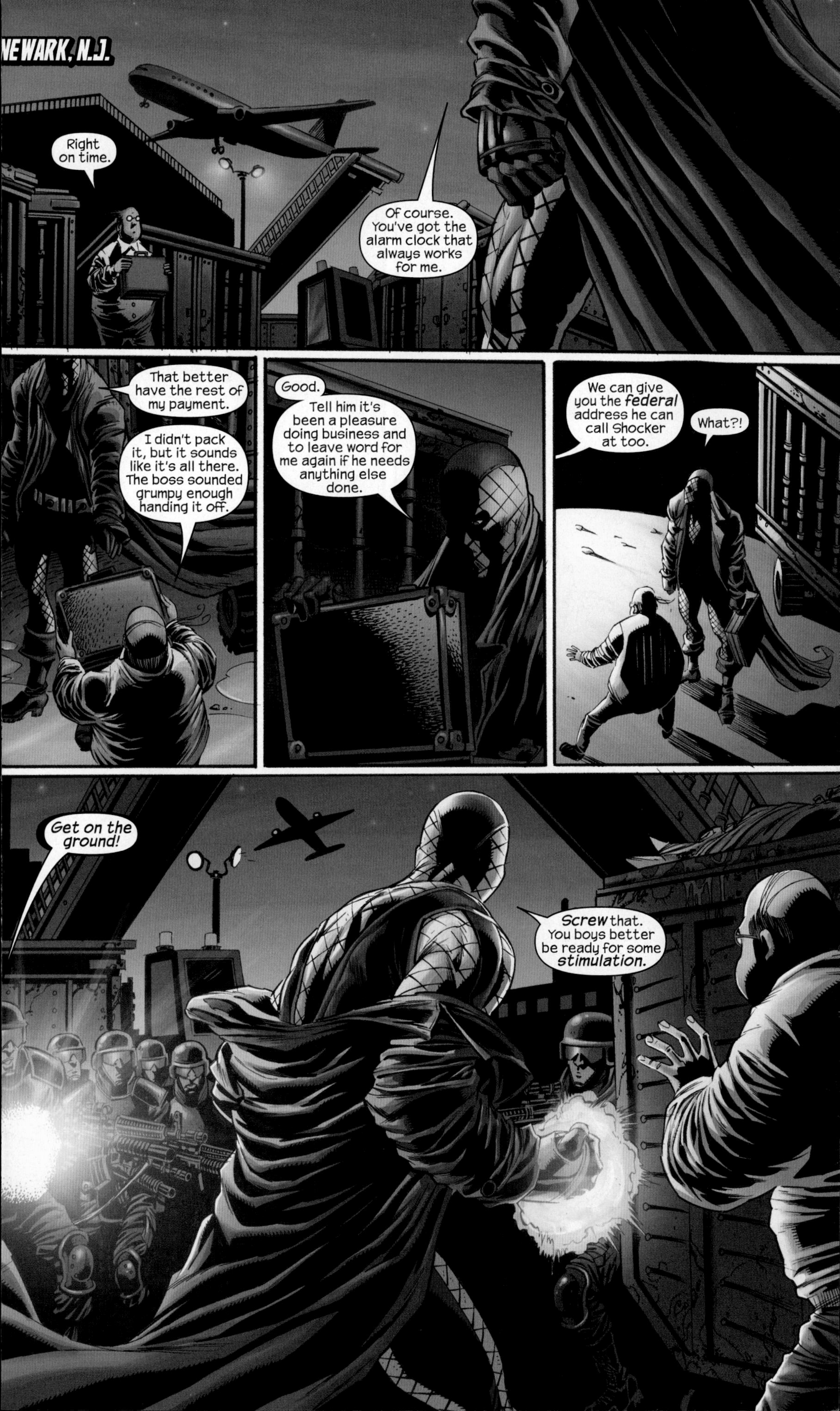
NEWARK, N.J.
Right on time.
Of course. You've got the alarm clock that always works for me.
That better have the rest of my payment.
I didn't pack it, but it sounds like it's all there. The boss sounded grumpy enough handing it off.
Good.
Tell him it's been a pleasure doing business and to leave word for me again if he needs anything else done.
We can give you the federal address he can call Shocker at too.
What?!
Get on the ground!
Screw that. You boys better be ready for some stimulation.

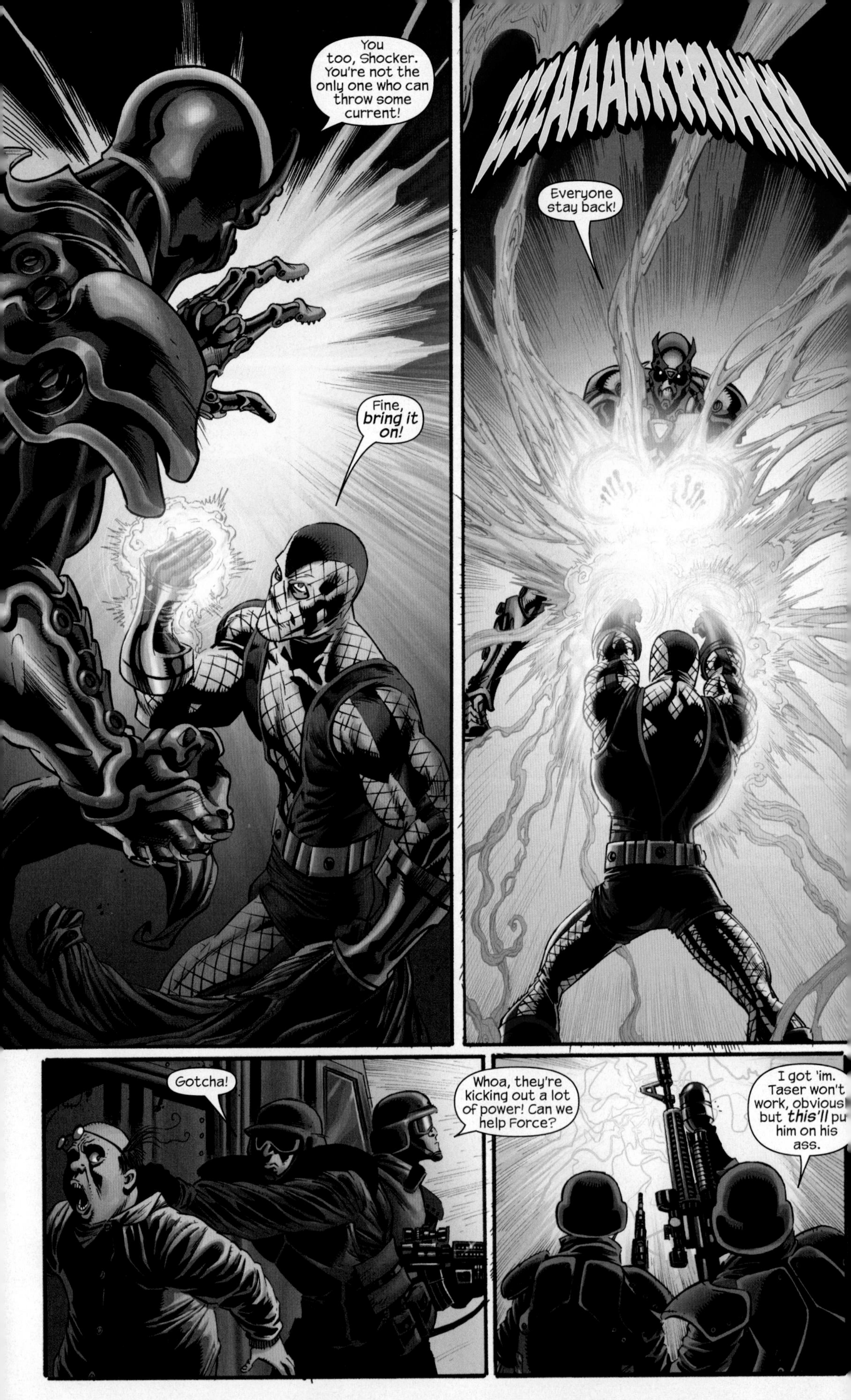
You too, Shocker. You're not the only one who can throw some current!
Fine, *bring it on!*
ZZZAAAKKRRAKK
Everyone stay back!
Gotcha!
Whoa, they're kicking out a lot of power! Can we help Force?
I got 'im. Taser won't work, obvious but *this'll* pu him on his ass.

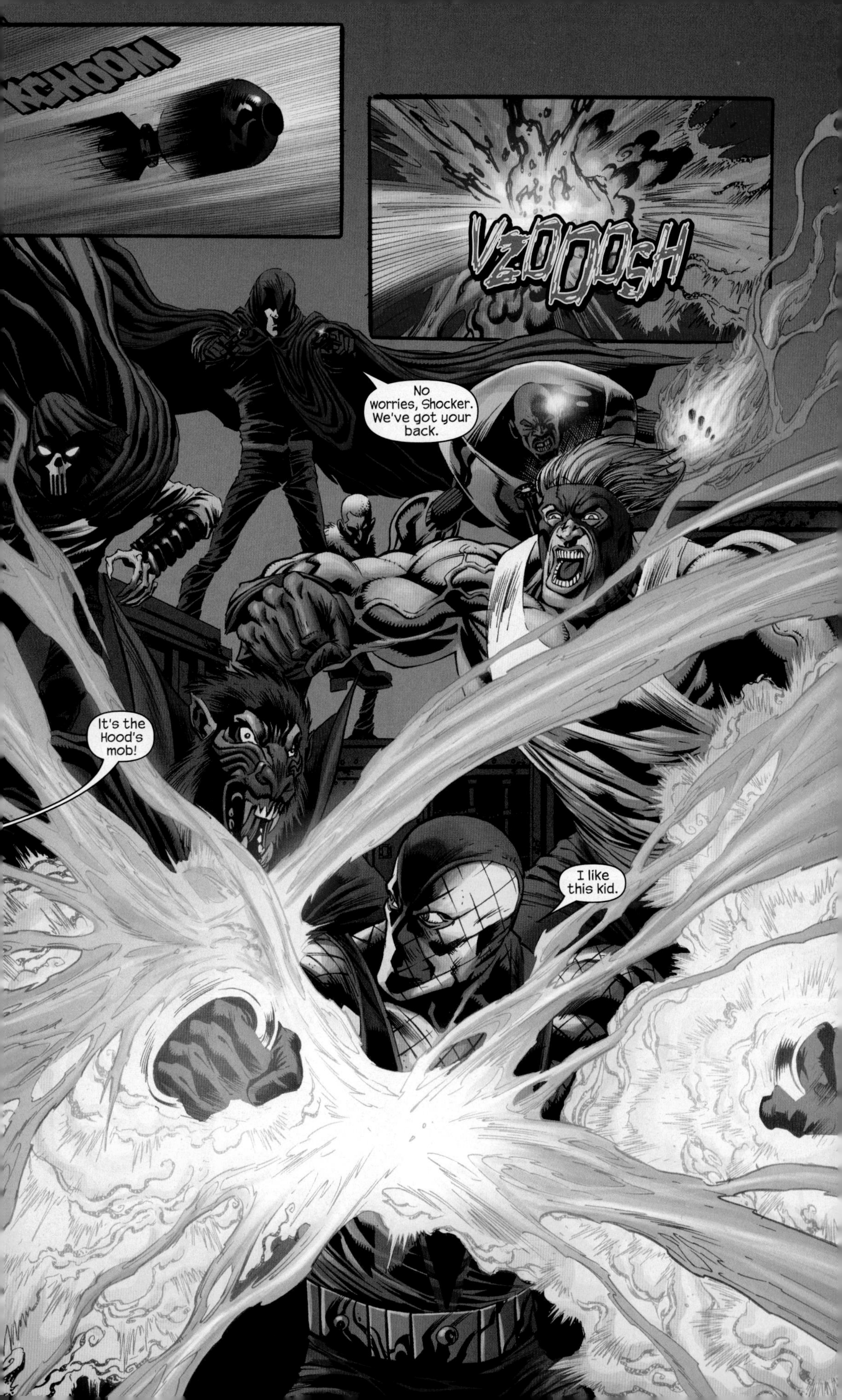

KCHOOM
VZOOOSH
No worries, Shocker. We've got your back.
It's the Hood's mob!
I like this kid.

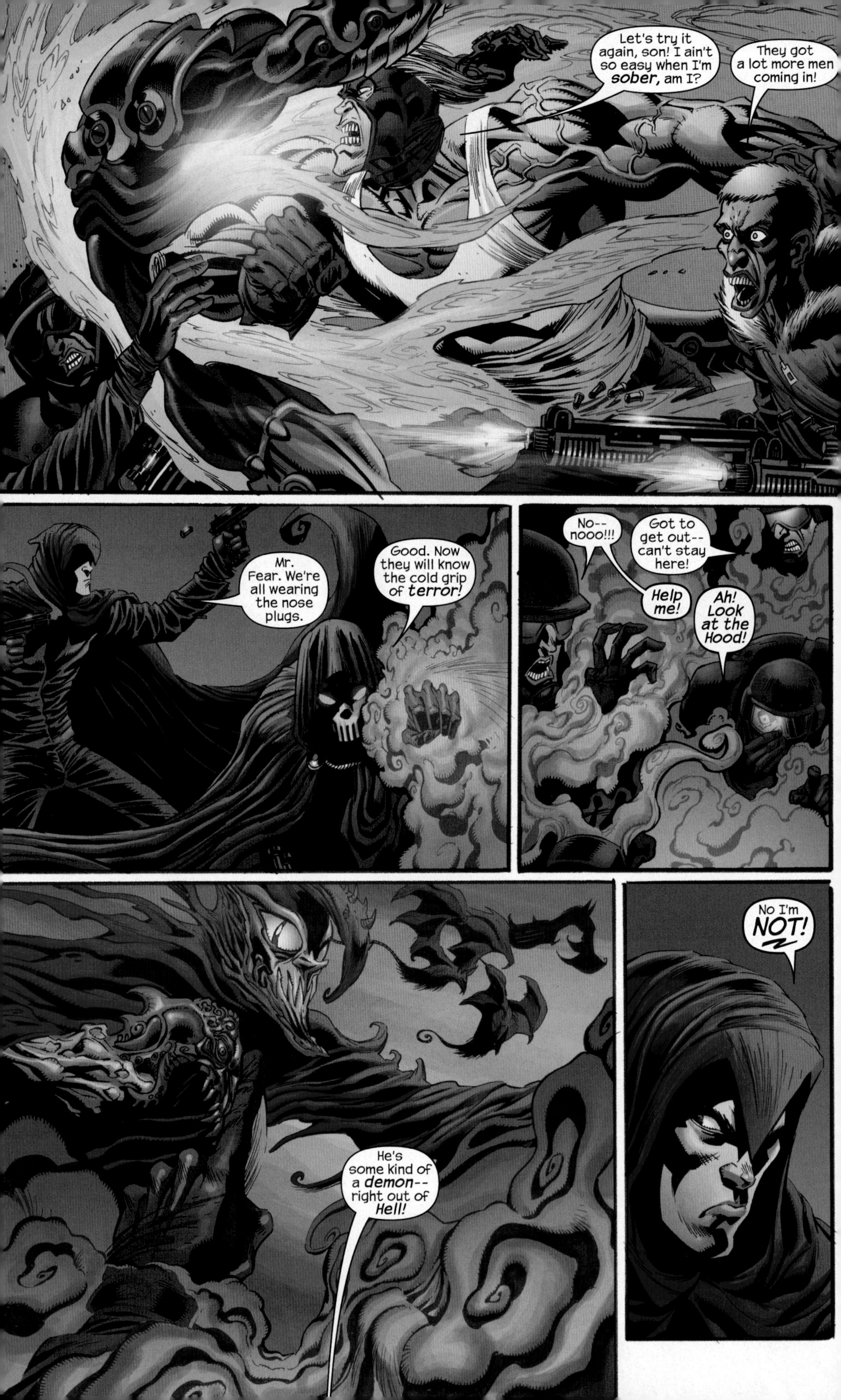
Let's try it again, son! I ain't so easy when I'm sober, am I?
They got a lot more men coming in!
Mr. Fear. We're all wearing the nose plugs.
Good. Now they will know the cold grip of terror!
No--nooo!!!
Got to get out--can't stay here!
Help me!
Ah! Look at the Hood!
He's some kind of a demon--right out of Hell!
No I'm NOT!

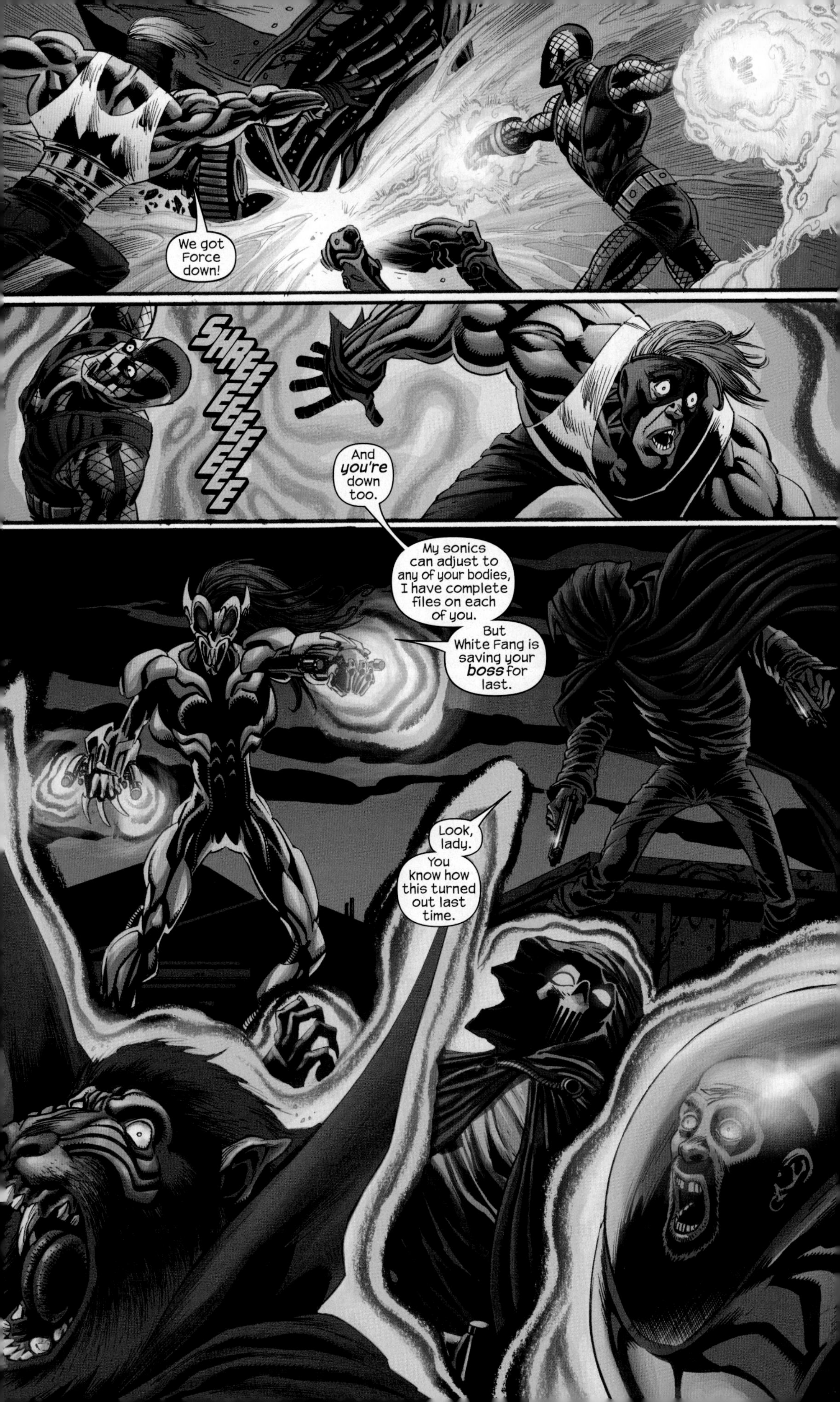
We got Force down!
SHREEEEEEEEE
And *you're* down too.
My sonics can adjust to any of your bodies, I have complete files on each of you.
But White Fang is saving your *boss* for last.
Look, lady.
You know how this turned out last time.

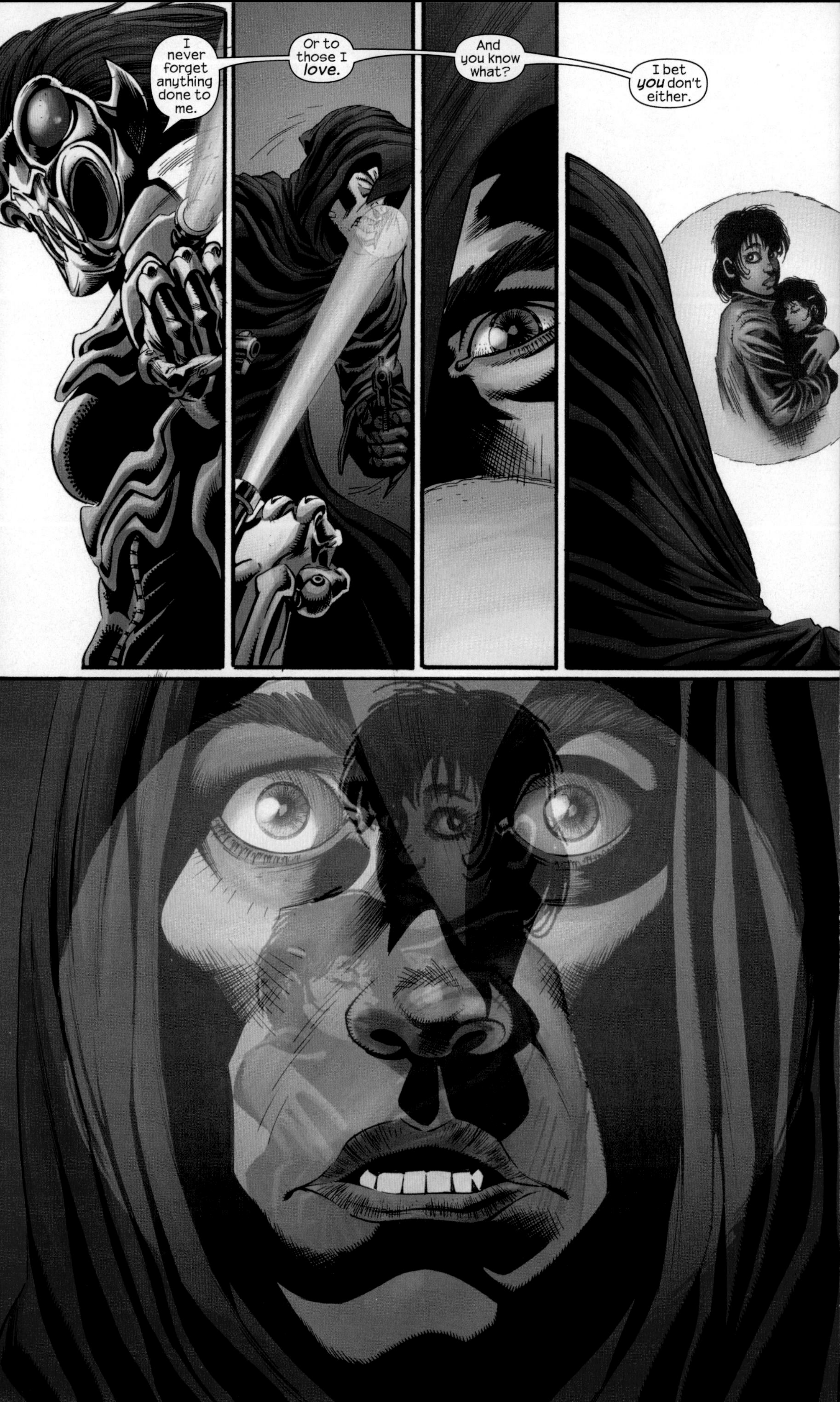
I never forget anything done to me.
Or to those I love.
And you know what?
I bet you don't either.

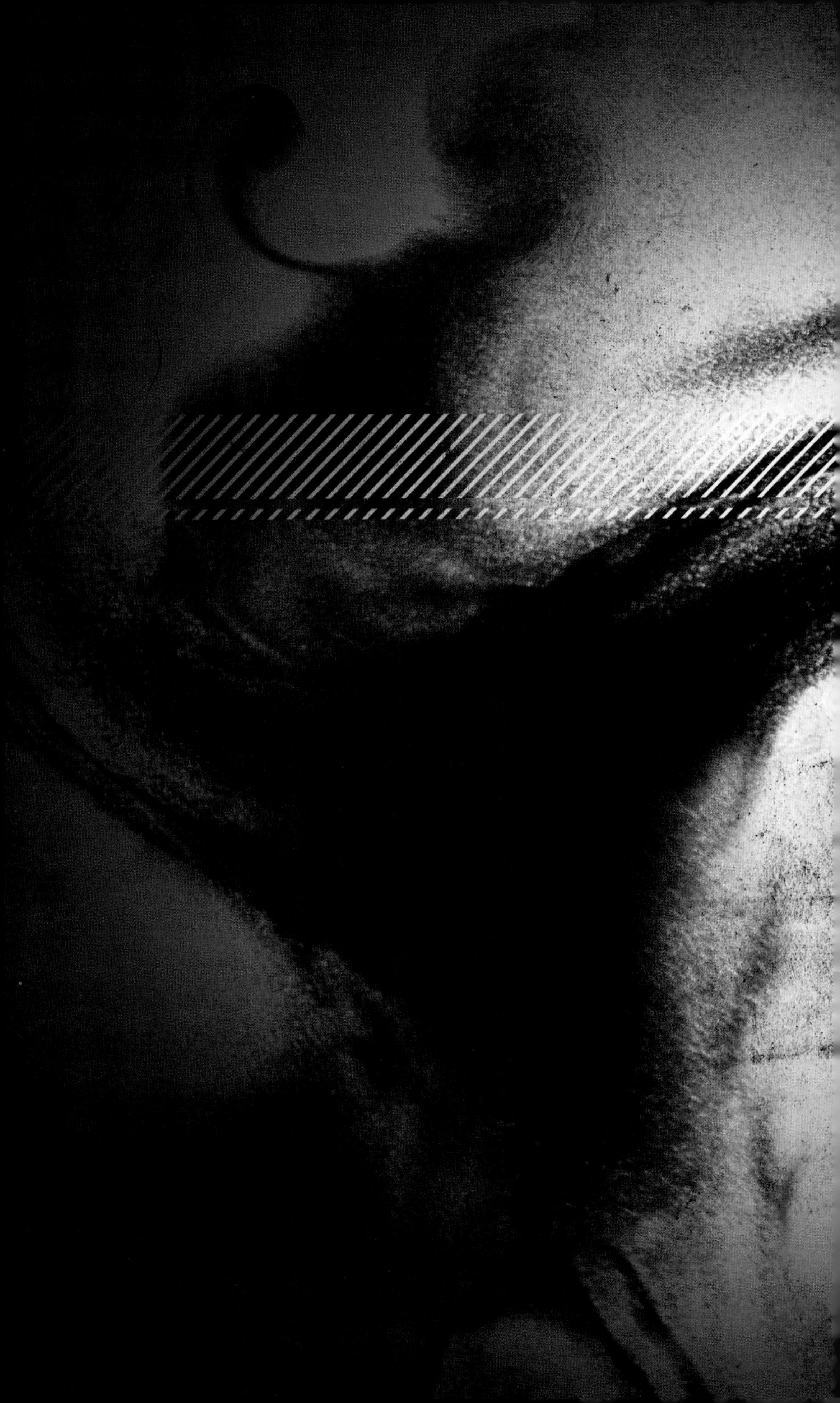

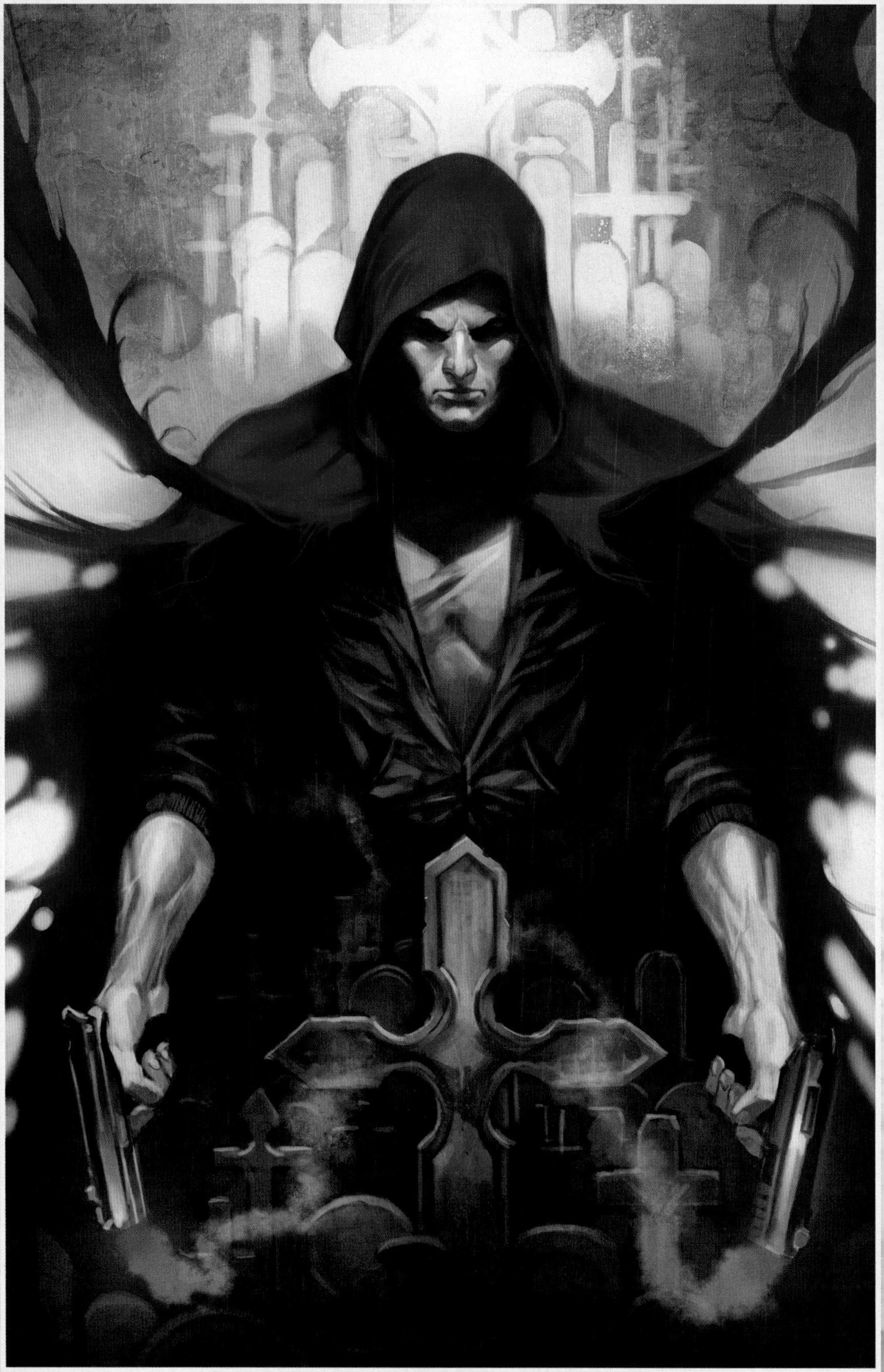

DARK REIGN: THE HOOD #5

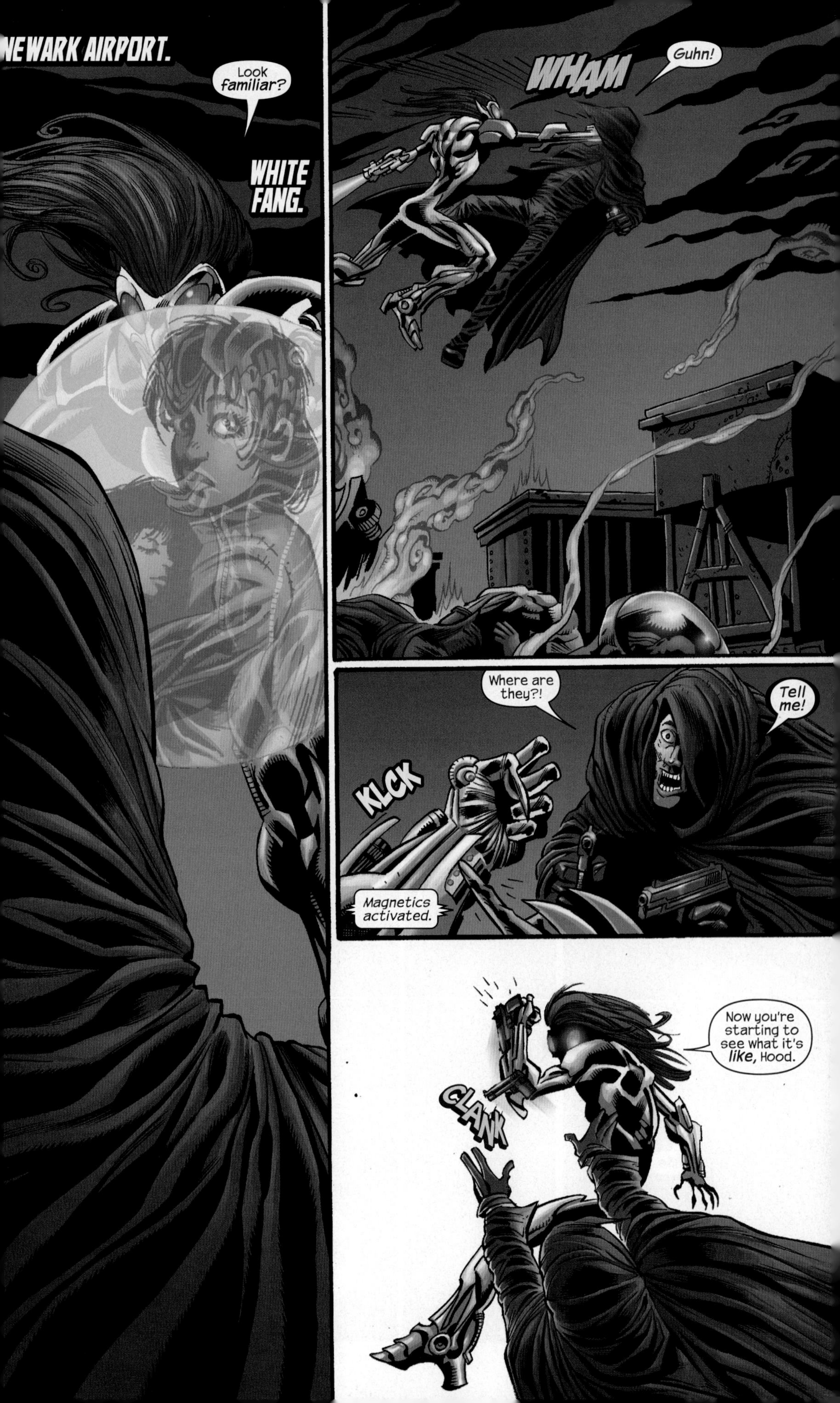
NEWARK AIRPORT.
Look familiar?
WHITE FANG.
WHAM
Guhn!
Where are they?!
Tell me!
KLCK
Magnetics activated.
Now you're starting to see what it's like, Hood.
CLANK

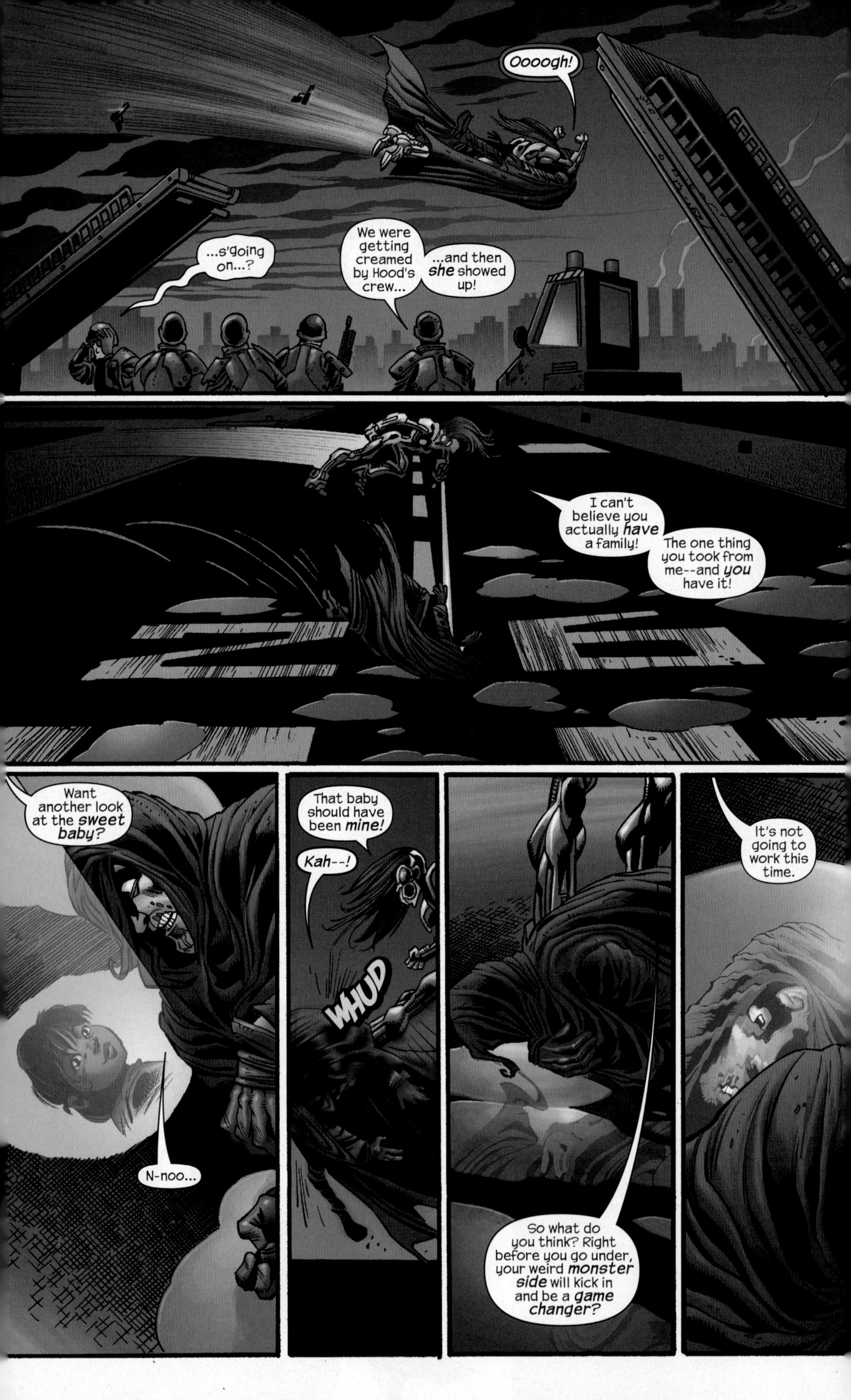

Oooogh!
...s'going on...?
We were getting creamed by Hood's crew...
...and then she showed up!
I can't believe you actually have a family!
The one thing you took from me--and you have it!
Want another look at the sweet baby?
N-noo...
That baby should have been mine!
Kah--!
WHUD
So what do you think? Right before you go under, your weird monster side will kick in and be a game changer?
It's not going to work this time.

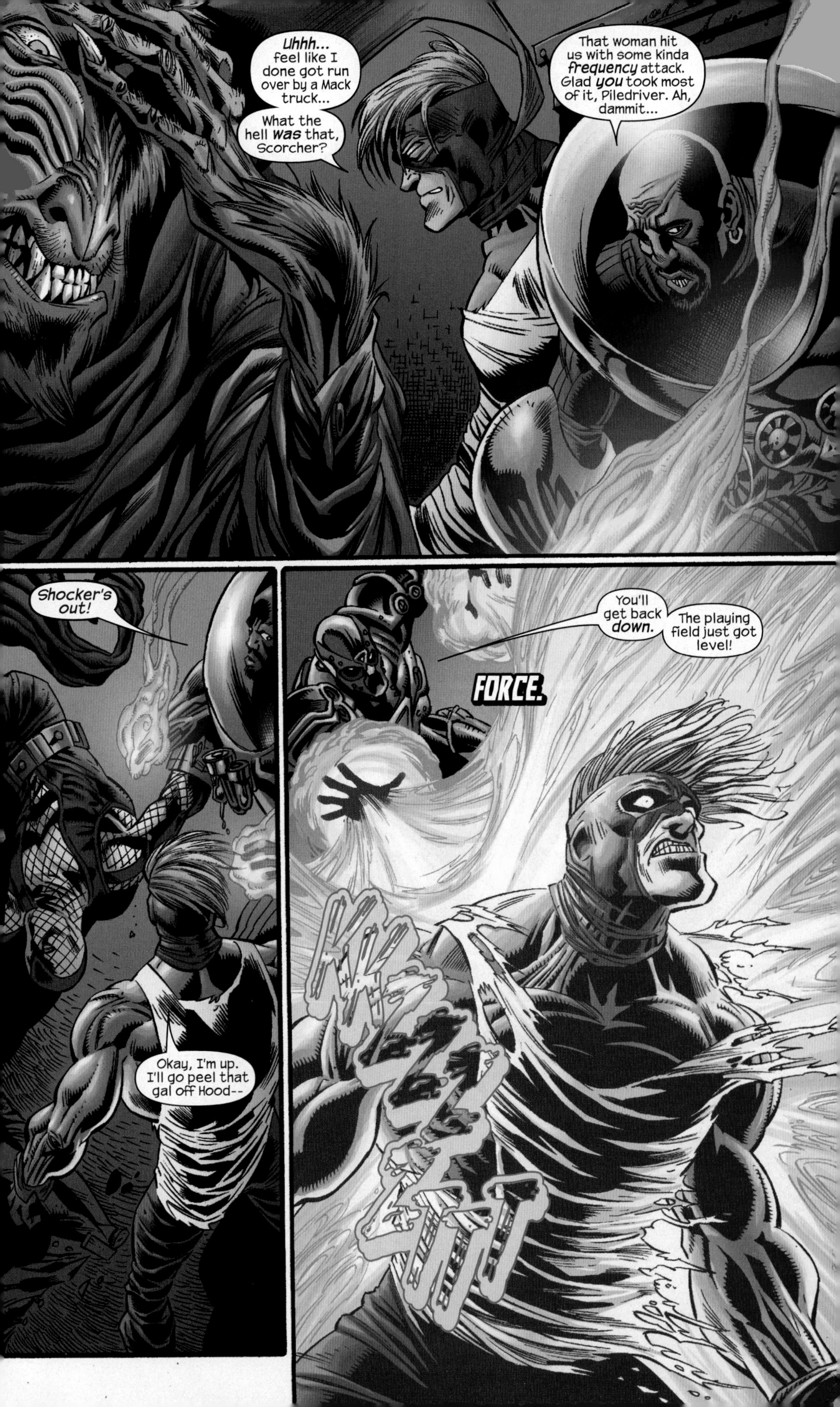
Uhhh... feel like I done got run over by a Mack truck...
What the hell was that, Scorcher?
That woman hit us with some kinda frequency attack. Glad you took most of it, Piledriver. Ah, dammit...
Shocker's out!
Okay, I'm up. I'll go peel that gal off Hood--
You'll get back down.
The playing field just got level!
FORCE.

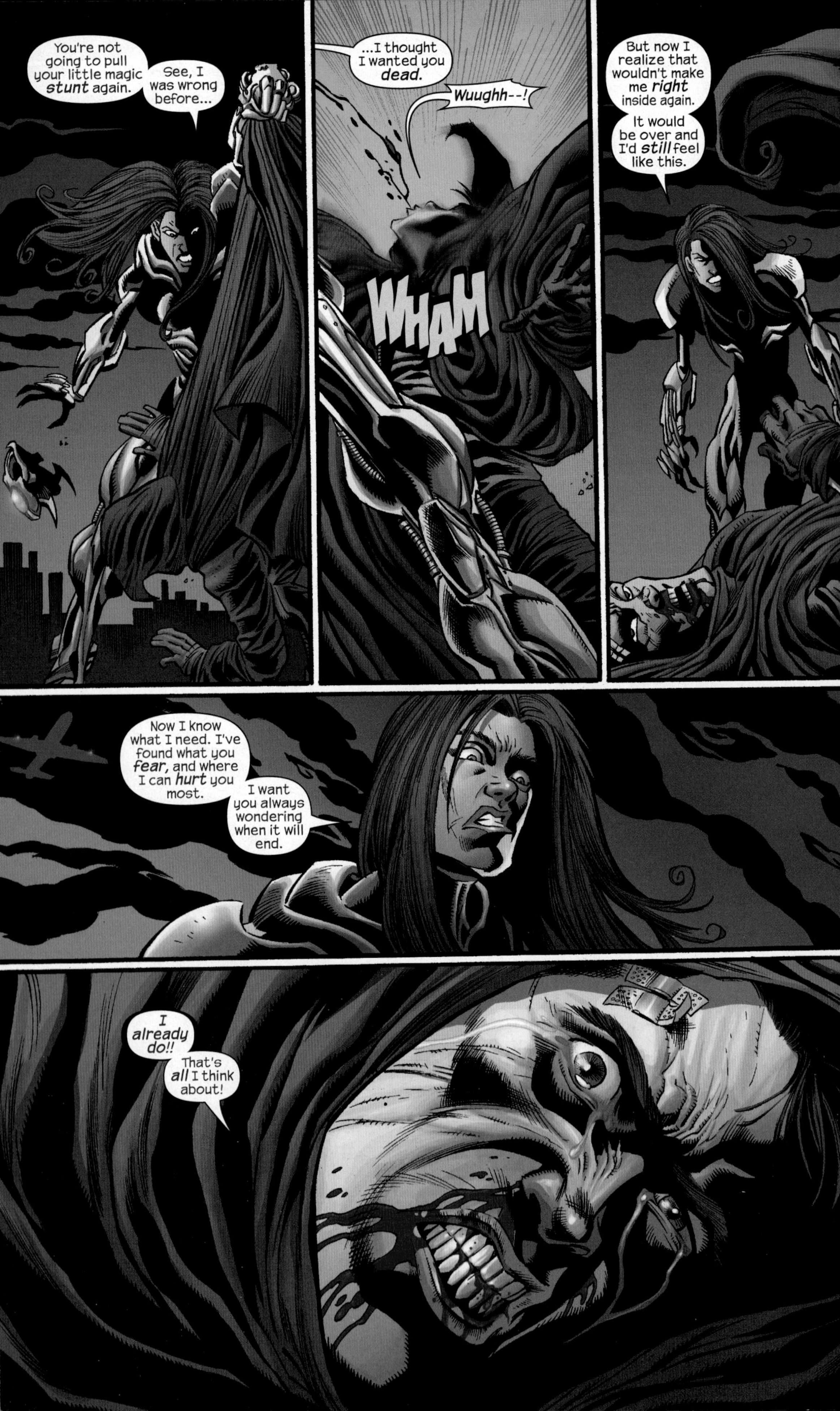
You're not going to pull your little magic *stunt* again.
See, I was wrong before...
...I thought I wanted you *dead*.
Wuughh--!
WHAM
But now I realize that wouldn't make me *right* inside again.
It would be over and I'd *still* feel like this.
Now I know what I need. I've found what you *fear*, and where I can *hurt* you most.
I want you always wondering when it will end.
I already do!!
That's *all* I think about!

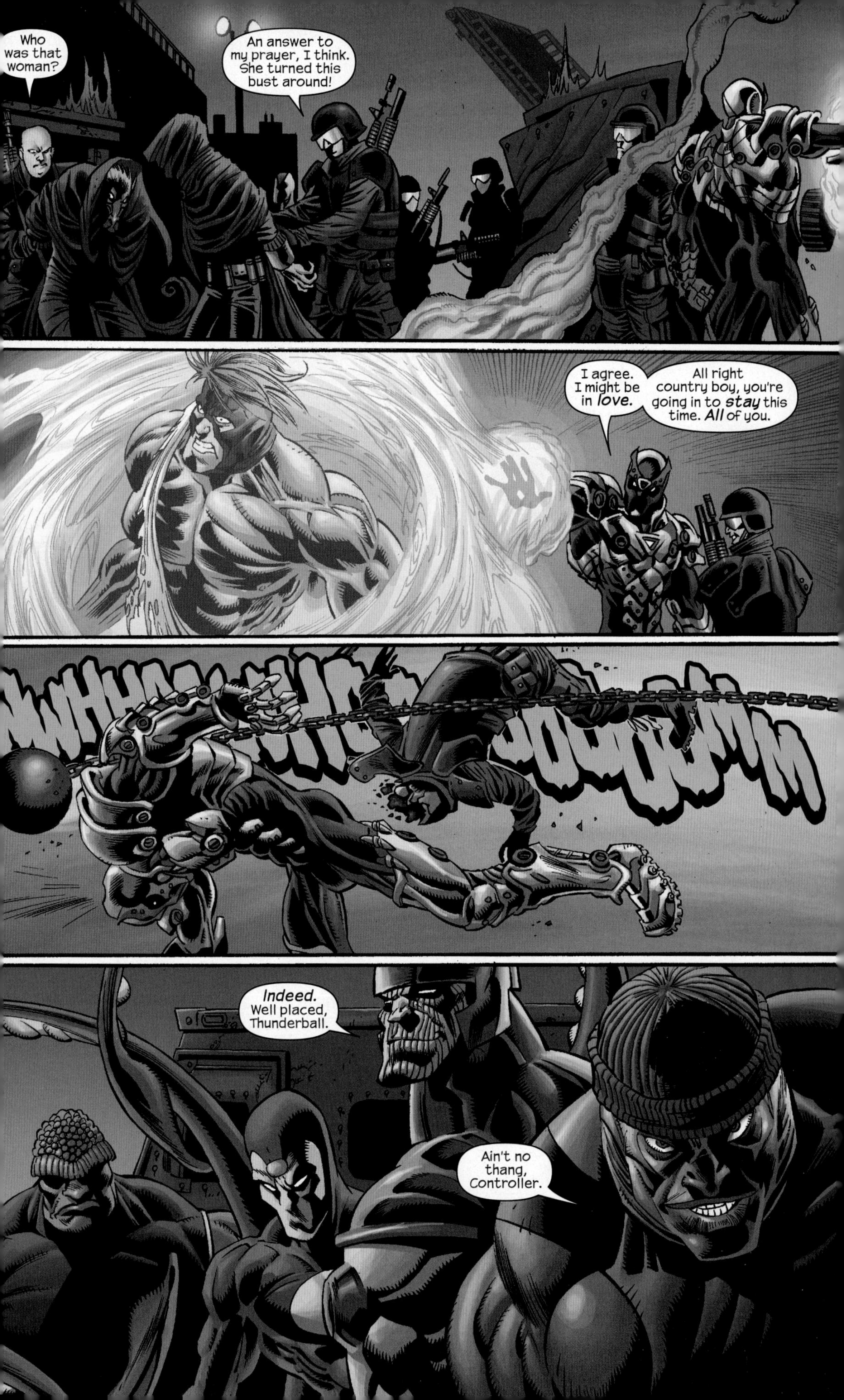
Who was that woman?
An answer to my prayer, I think. She turned this bust around!
I agree. I might be in *love.*
All right country boy, you're going in to *stay* this time. *All* of you.
Indeed. Well placed, Thunderball.
Ain't no thang, Controller.

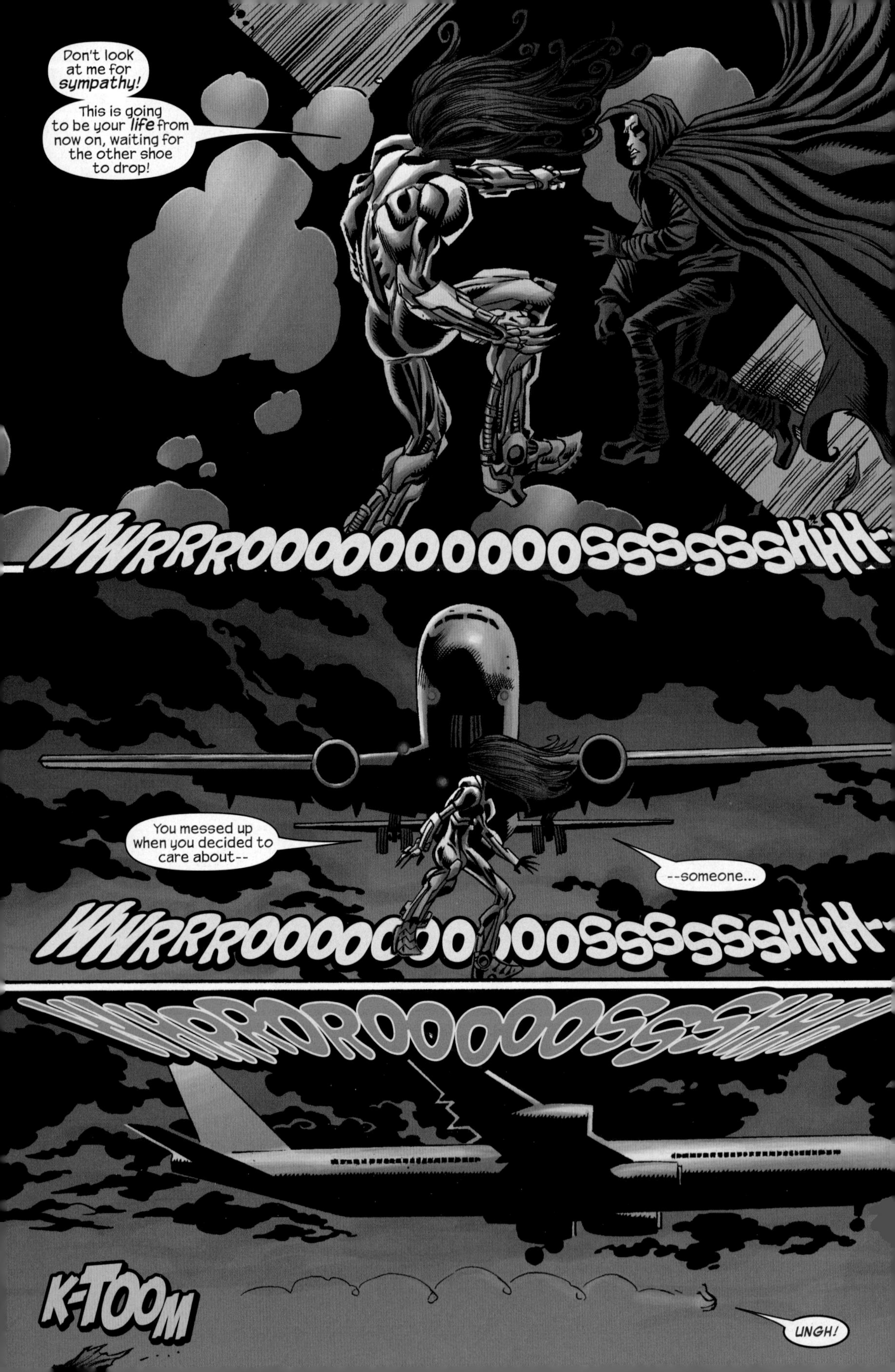
Don't look at me for *sympathy!*
This is going to be your *life* from now on, waiting for the other shoe to drop!
WWRRROOOOOOOOOOOSSSSSSHHH--
You messed up when you decided to care about--
--someone...
WWRRROOOOOOOOOOOSSSSSSHHH--
K-TOOM
UNGH!

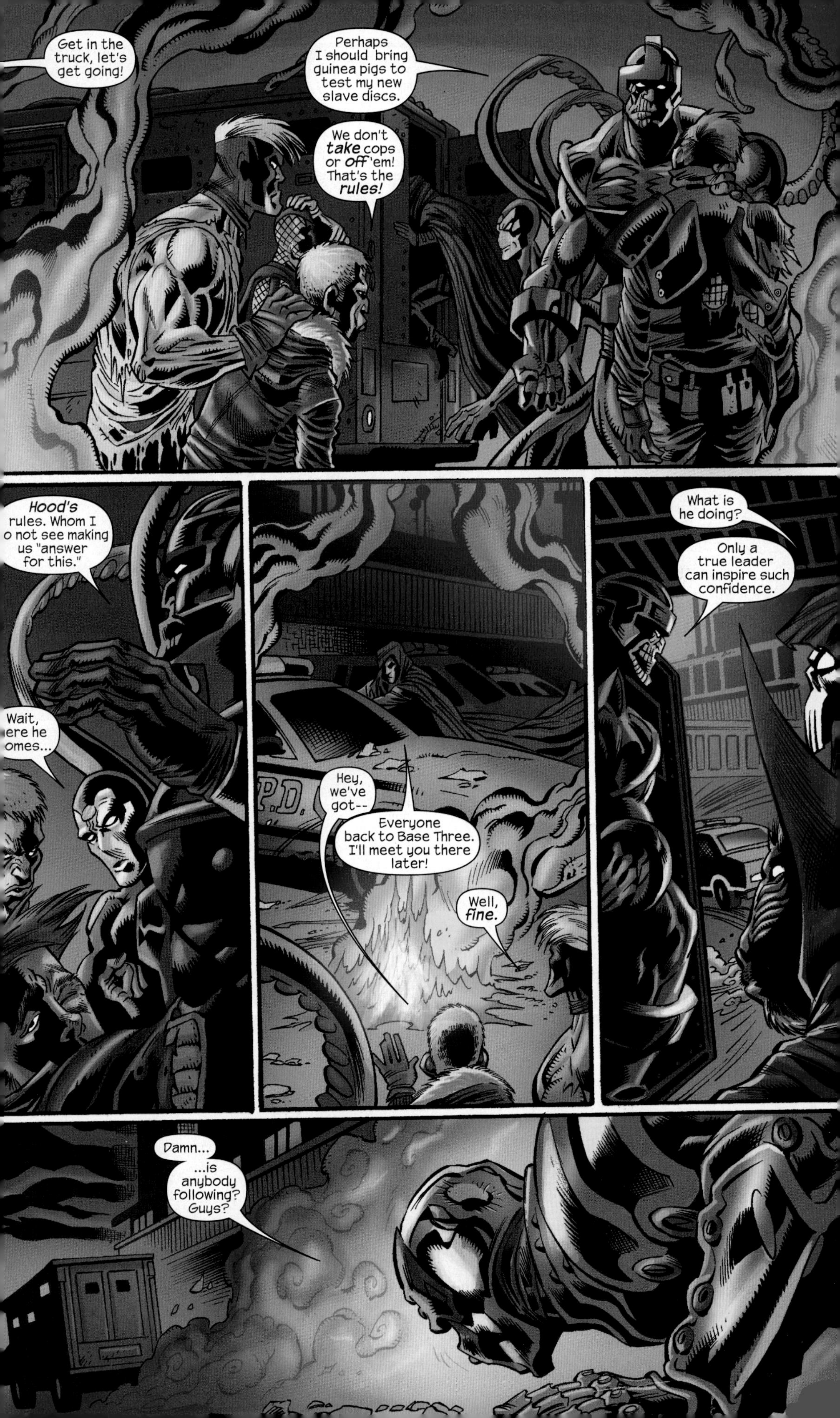
Get in the truck, let's get going!
Perhaps I should bring guinea pigs to test my new slave discs.
We don't *take* cops or *off* 'em! That's the *rules!*
Hood's rules. Whom I o not see making us "answer for this."
Wait, ere he omes...
Hey, we've got--
Everyone back to Base Three. I'll meet you there later!
Well, *fine.*
What is he doing?
Only a true leader can inspire such confidence.
Damn...
...is anybody following? Guys?

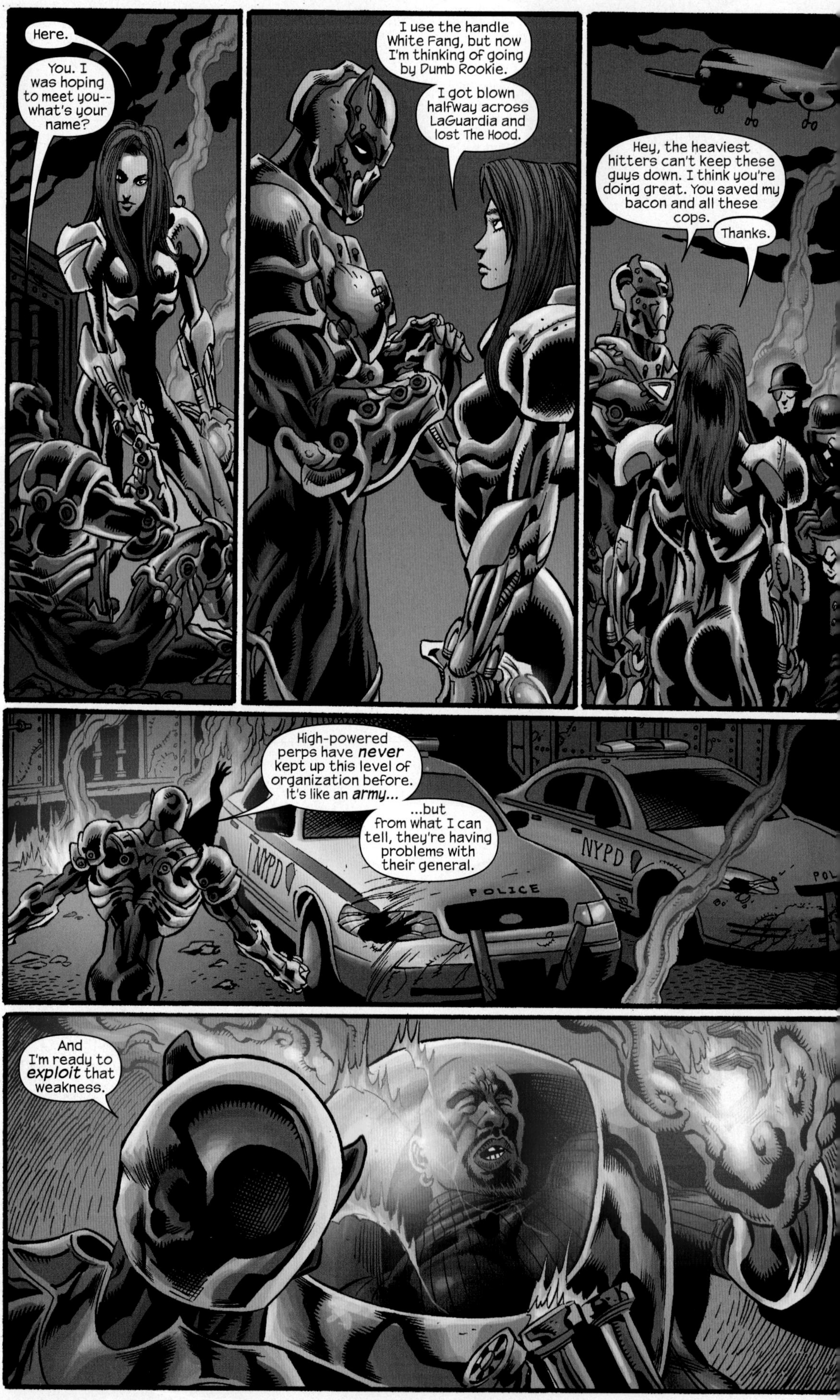
Here.
You. I was hoping to meet you--what's your name?
I use the handle White Fang, but now I'm thinking of going by Dumb Rookie.
I got blown halfway across LaGuardia and lost The Hood.
Hey, the heaviest hitters can't keep these guys down. I think you're doing great. You saved my bacon and all these cops.
Thanks.
High-powered perps have ***never*** kept up this level of organization before. It's like an ***army...***
...but from what I can tell, they're having problems with their general.
NYPD
POLICE
NYPD
POL
And I'm ready to ***exploit*** that weakness.

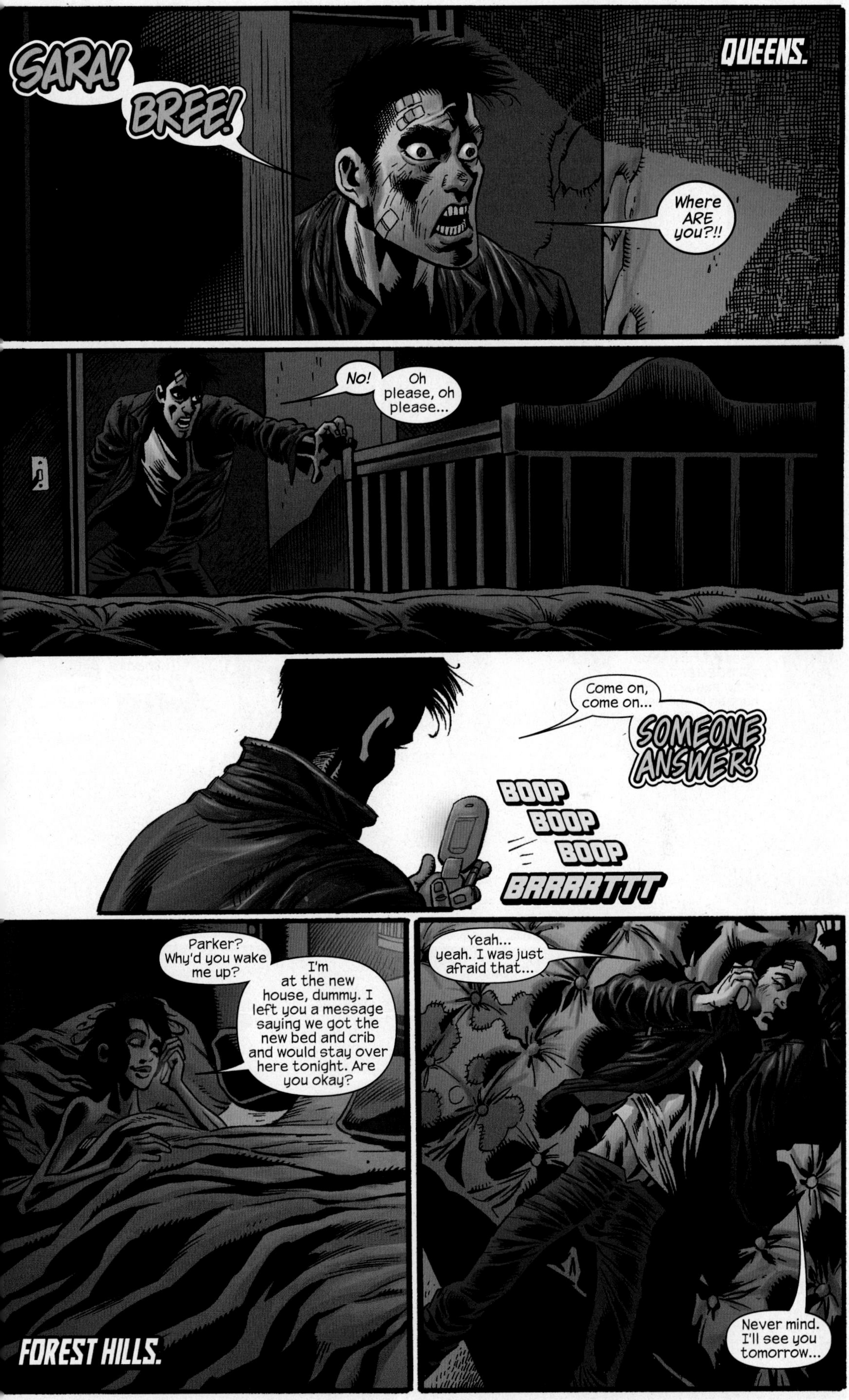

SARA!
BREE!
QUEENS.
Where ARE you?!!
No!
Oh please, oh please...
Come on, come on...
SOMEONE ANSWER!
BOOP
BOOP
BOOP
BRRRRTTT
Parker? Why'd you wake me up?
I'm at the new house, dummy. I left you a message saying we got the new bed and crib and would stay over here tonight. Are you okay?
FOREST HILLS.
Yeah... yeah. I was just afraid that...
Never mind. I'll see you tomorrow...

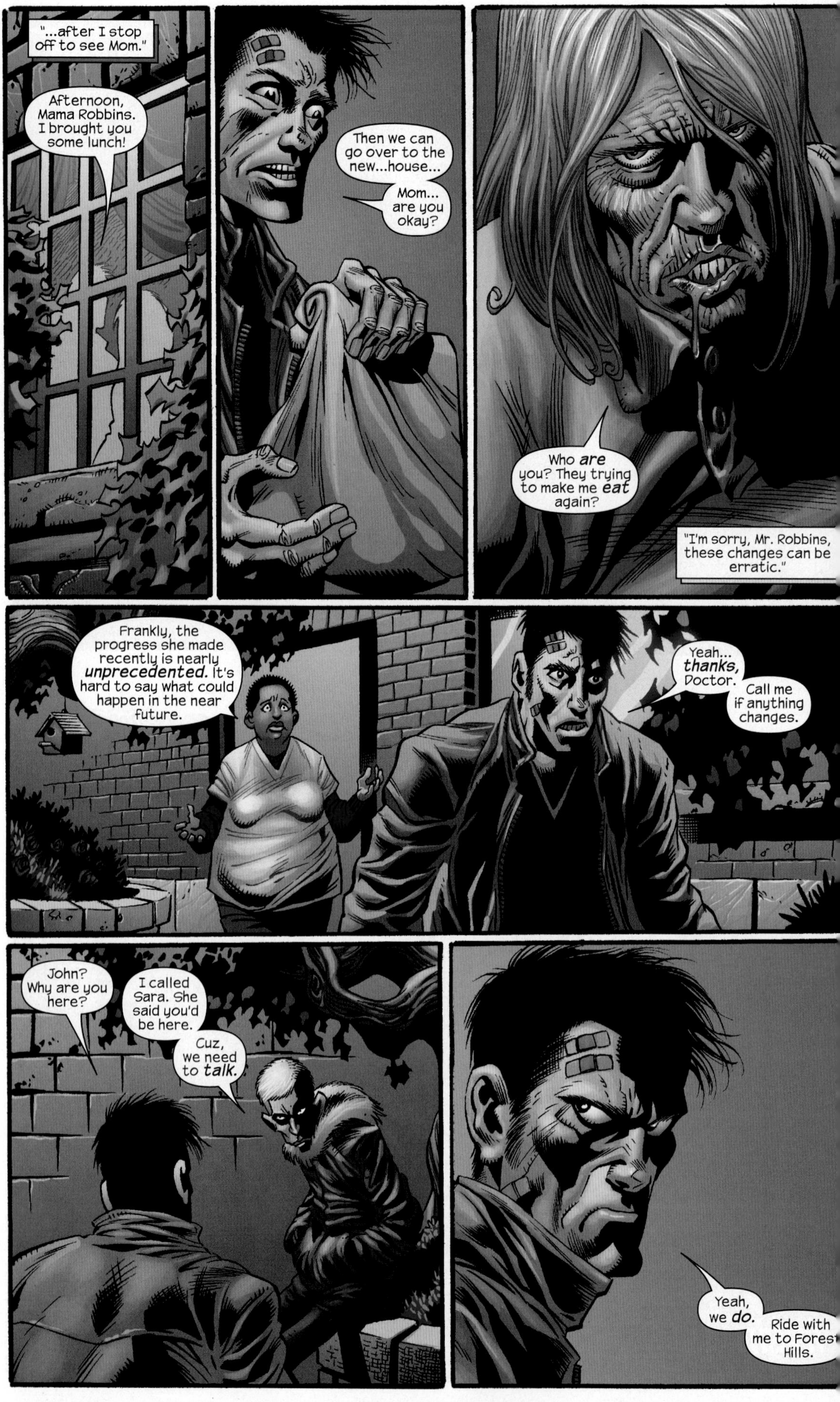
"...after I stop off to see Mom."
Afternoon, Mama Robbins. I brought you some lunch!
Then we can go over to the new...house...
Mom... are you okay?
Who *are* you? They trying to make me *eat* again?
"I'm sorry, Mr. Robbins, these changes can be erratic."
Frankly, the progress she made recently is nearly *unprecedented.* It's hard to say what could happen in the near future.
Yeah... *thanks,* Doctor.
Call me if anything changes.
John? Why are you here?
I called Sara. She said you'd be here.
Cuz, we need to *talk.*
Yeah, we *do.*
Ride with me to Forest Hills.

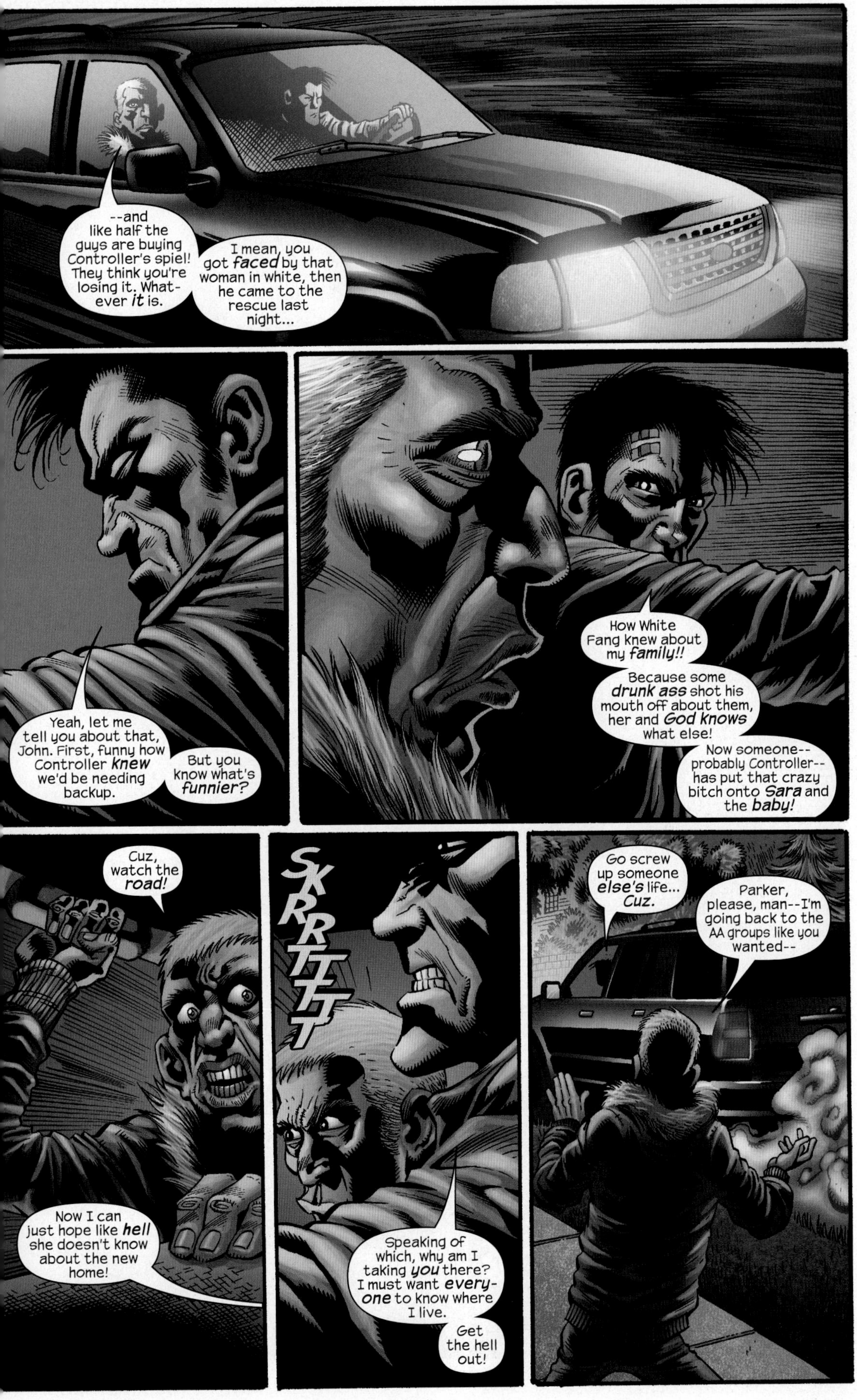
--and like half the guys are buying Controller's spiel! They think you're losing it. What-ever it is.
I mean, you got faced by that woman in white, then he came to the rescue last night...
Yeah, let me tell you about that, John. First, funny how Controller knew we'd be needing backup.
But you know what's funnier?
How White Fang knew about my family!!
Because some drunk ass shot his mouth off about them, her and God knows what else!
Now someone--probably Controller--has put that crazy bitch onto Sara and the baby!
Cuz, watch the road!
Now I can just hope like hell she doesn't know about the new home!
SKRRTTTT
Speaking of which, why am I taking you there? I must want every-one to know where I live.
Get the hell out!
Go screw up someone else's life... Cuz.
Parker, please, man--I'm going back to the AA groups like you wanted--

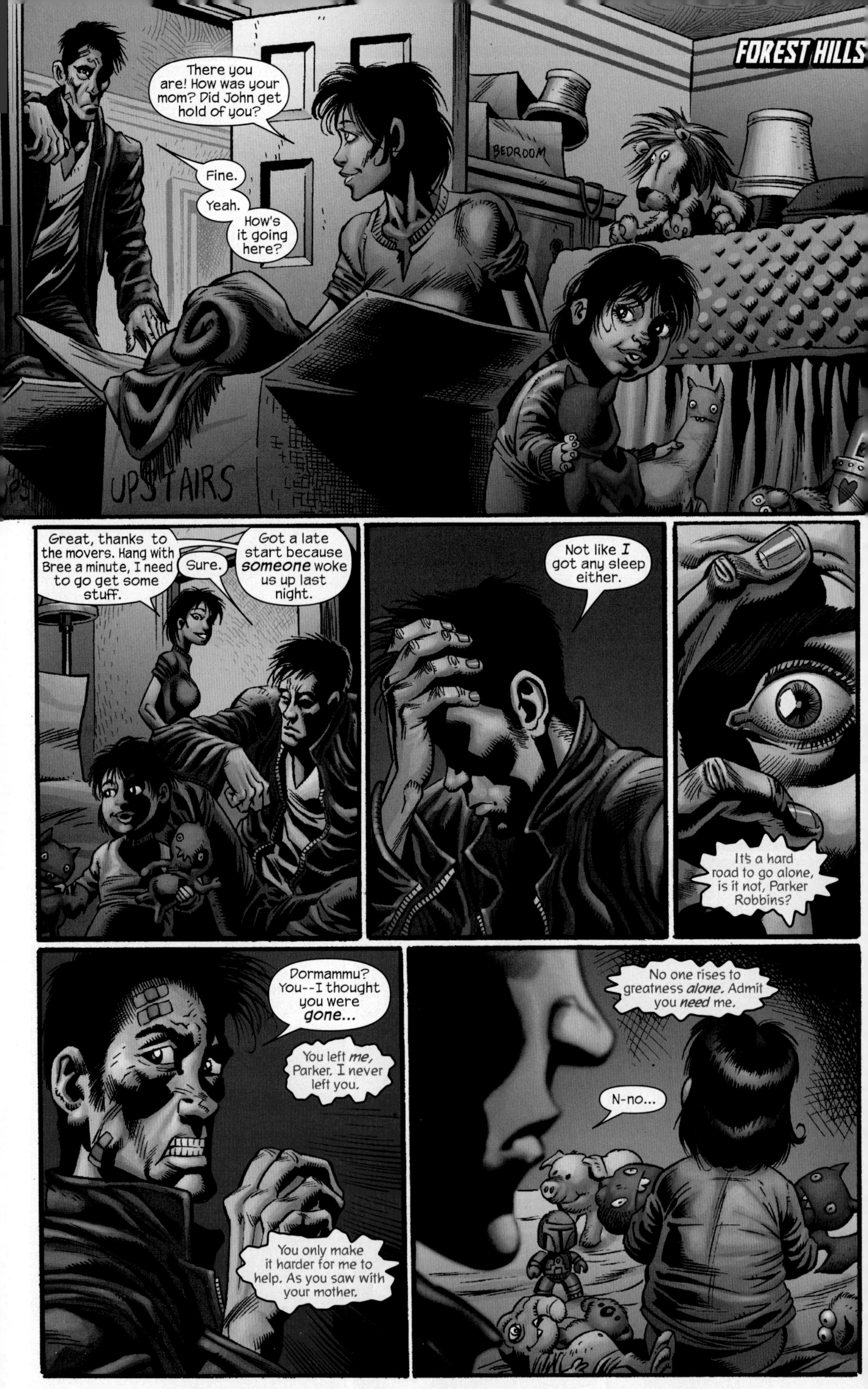
FOREST HILLS
There you are! How was your mom? Did John get hold of you?
Fine.
Yeah.
How's it going here?
BEDROOM
UPSTAIRS
Great, thanks to the movers. Hang with Bree a minute, I need to go get some stuff.
Sure.
Got a late start because *someone* woke us up last night.
Not like *I* got any sleep either.
It's a hard road to go alone, is it not, Parker Robbins?
Dormammu? You--I thought you were *gone...*
You left *me,* Parker. I never left you.
You only make it harder for me to help. As you saw with your mother.
No one rises to greatness *alone.* Admit you *need* me.
N-no...

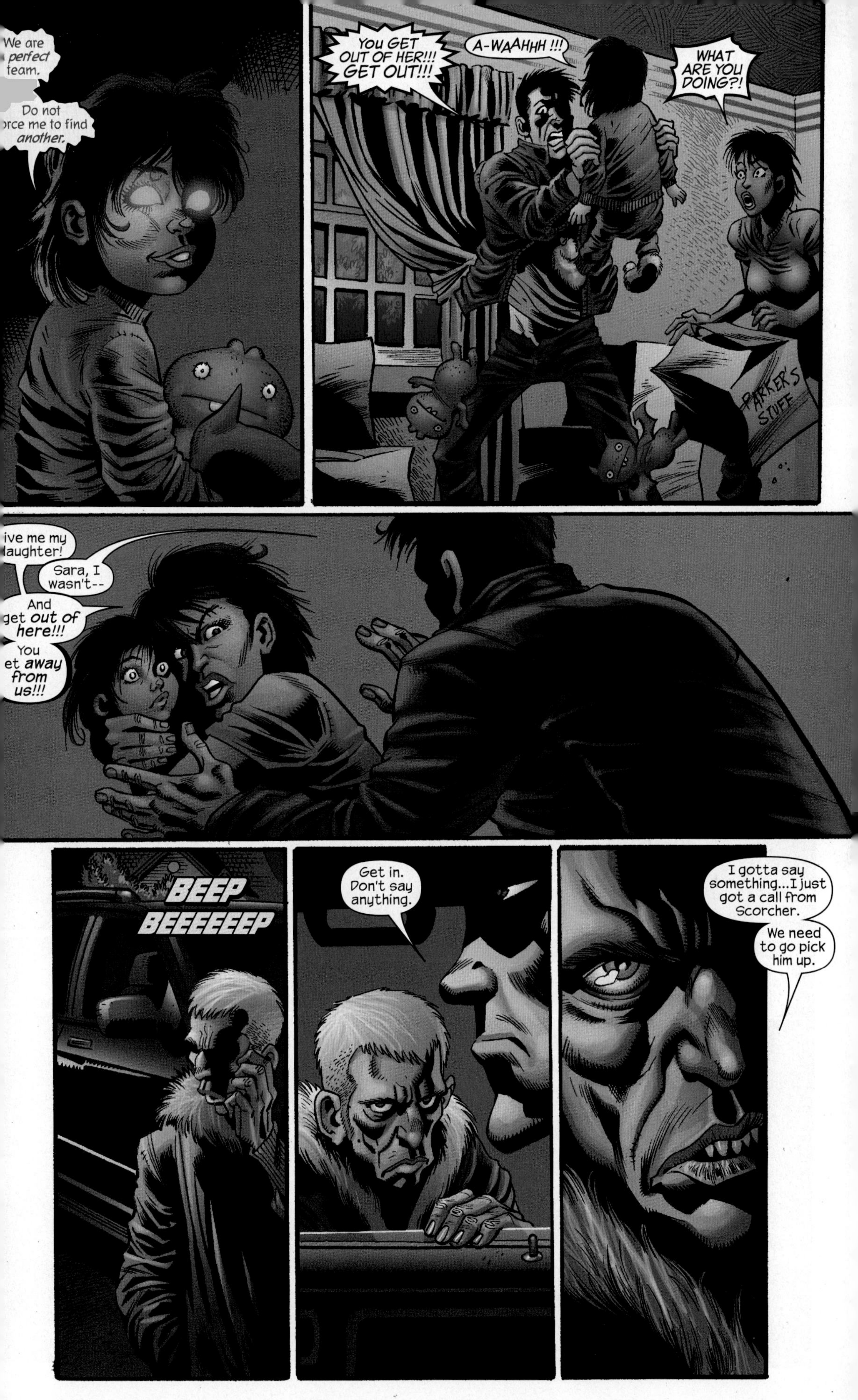

We are perfect team.
Do not force me to find another.
YOU GET OUT OF HER!!! GET OUT!!!
A-WAAHHH !!!
WHAT ARE YOU DOING?!
PARKER'S STUFF
ive me my daughter!
Sara, I wasn't--
And get out of here!!!
You et away from us!!!
BEEP BEEEEEEP
Get in. Don't say anything.
I gotta say something...I just got a call from Scorcher.
We need to go pick him up.

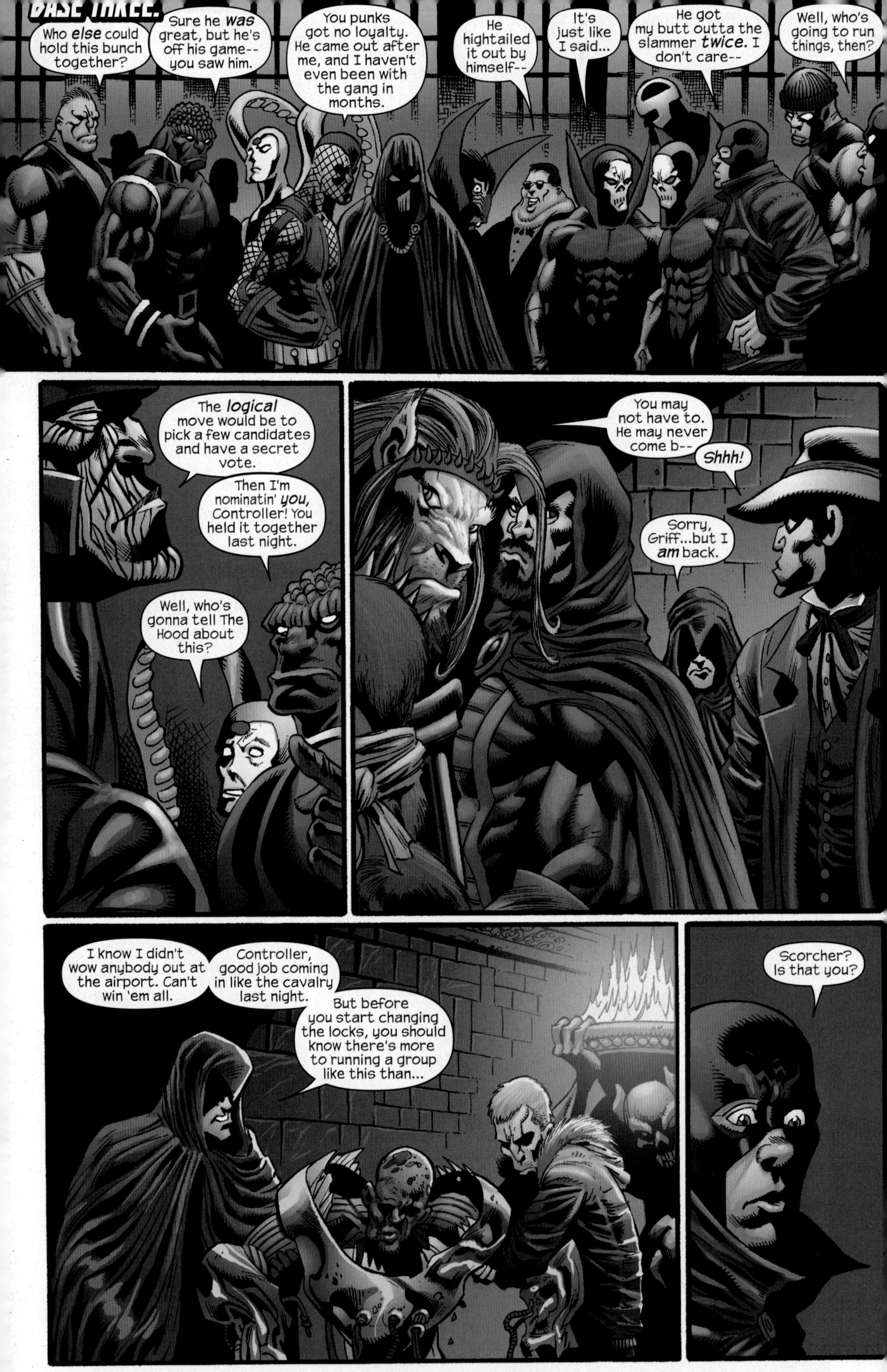
Who else could hold this bunch together?
Sure he was great, but he's off his game-- you saw him.
You punks got no loyalty. He came out after me, and I haven't even been with the gang in months.
He hightailed it out by himself--
It's just like I said...
He got my butt outta the slammer twice. I don't care--
Well, who's going to run things, then?
The logical move would be to pick a few candidates and have a secret vote.
Then I'm nominatin' you, Controller! You held it together last night.
Well, who's gonna tell The Hood about this?
You may not have to. He may never come b--
Shhh!
Sorry, Griff...but I am back.
I know I didn't wow anybody out at the airport. Can't win 'em all.
Controller, good job coming in like the cavalry last night.
But before you start changing the locks, you should know there's more to running a group like this than...
Scorcher? Is that you?

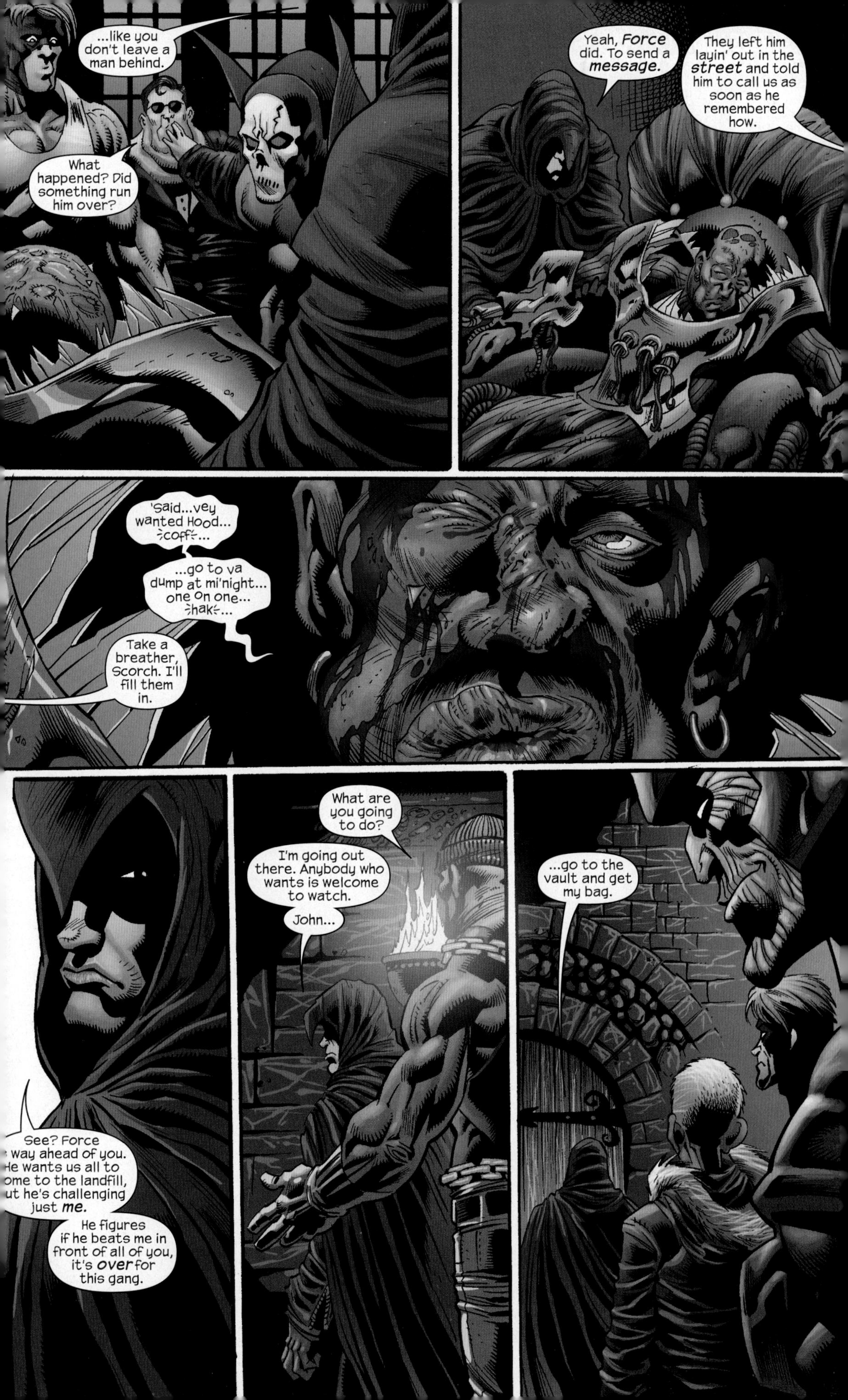

...like you don't leave a man behind.
What happened? Did something run him over?
Yeah, Force did. To send a message.
They left him layin' out in the street and told him to call us as soon as he remembered how.
'Said...vey wanted Hood... coff...
...go to va dump at mi'night... one on one... hak...
Take a breather, Scorch. I'll fill them in.
See? Force way ahead of you. He wants us all to come to the landfill, but he's challenging just me.
He figures if he beats me in front of all of you, it's over for this gang.
What are you going to do?
I'm going out there. Anybody who wants is welcome to watch.
John...
...go to the vault and get my bag.

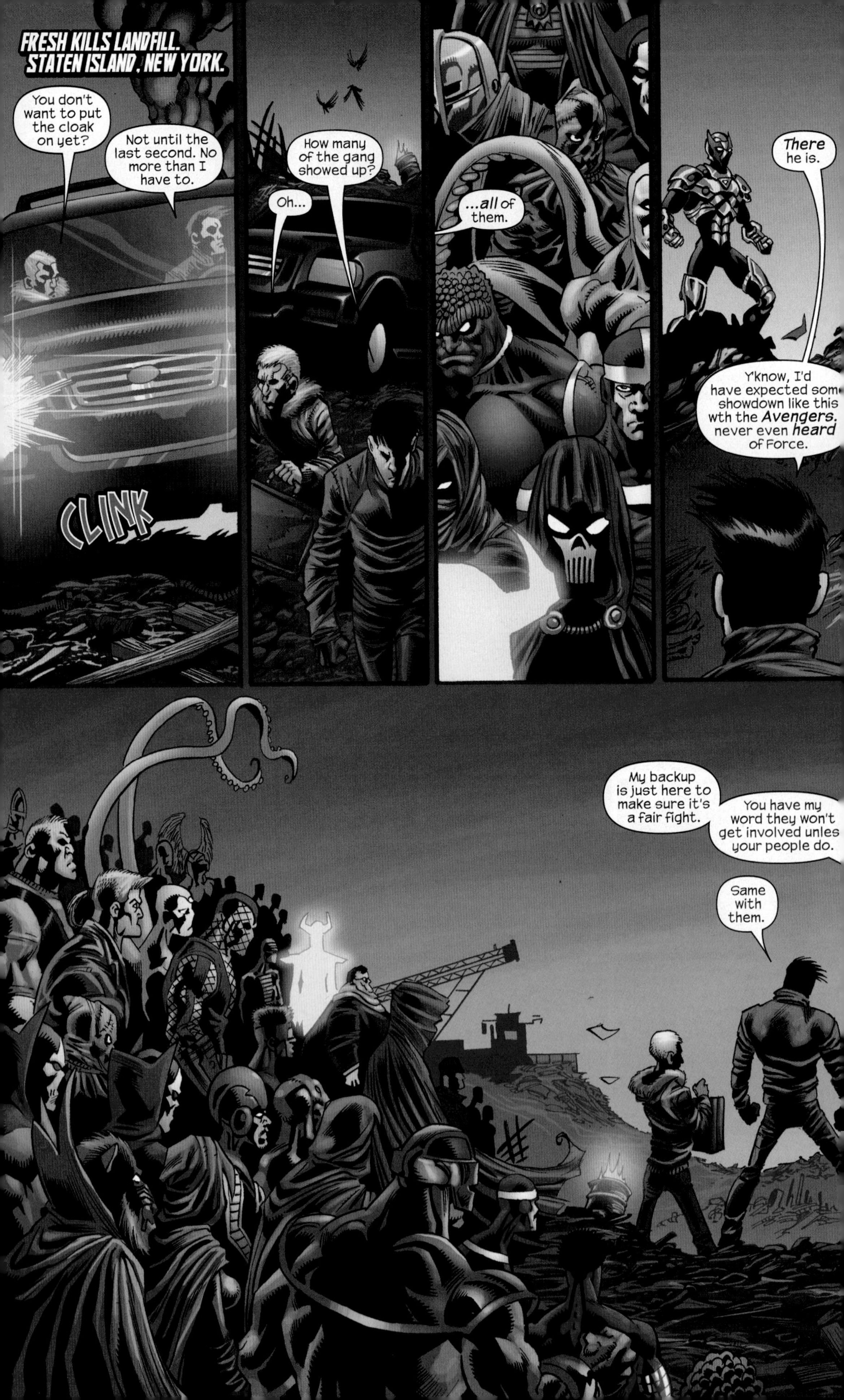
FRESH KILLS LANDFILL. STATEN ISLAND, NEW YORK.
You don't want to put the cloak on yet?
Not until the last second. No more than I have to.
CLINK
How many of the gang showed up?
Oh...
...all of them.
There he is.
Y'know, I'd have expected som showdown like this wth the Avengers. never even heard of Force.
My backup is just here to make sure it's a fair fight.
You have my word they won't get involved unles your people do.
Same with them.

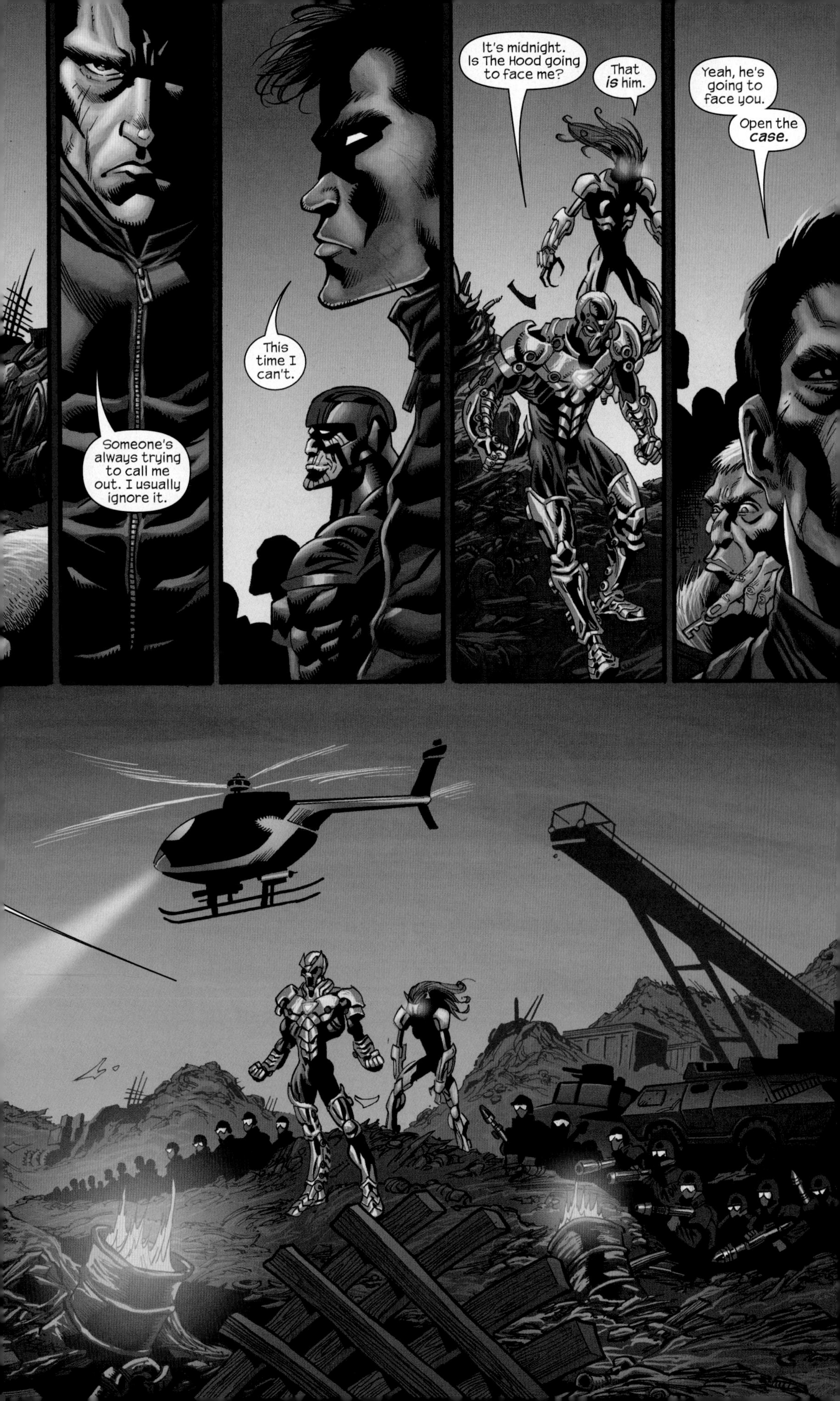

Someone's always trying to call me out. I usually ignore it.
This time I can't.
It's midnight. Is The Hood going to face me?
That *is* him.
Yeah, he's going to face you.
Open the *case.*

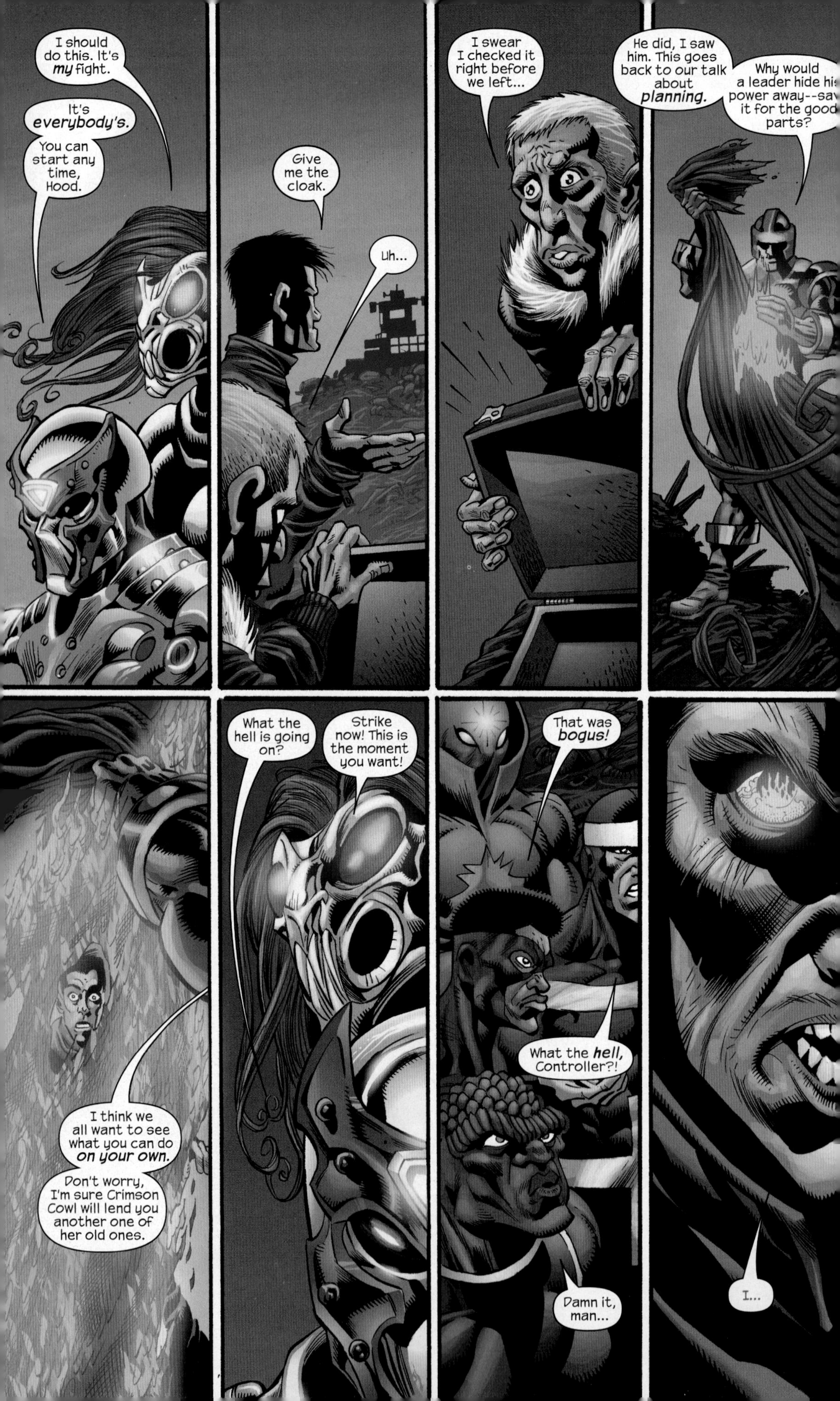
I should do this. It's *my* fight.
It's *everybody's.*
You can start any time, Hood.
Give me the cloak.
Uh...
I swear I checked it right before we left...
He did, I saw him. This goes back to our talk about *planning.*
Why would a leader hide his power away--save it for the good parts?
I think we all want to see what you can do *on your own.*
Don't worry, I'm sure Crimson Cowl will lend you another one of her old ones.
What the hell is going on?
Strike now! This is the moment you want!
That was *bogus!*
What the *hell,* Controller?!
Damn it, man...
I...

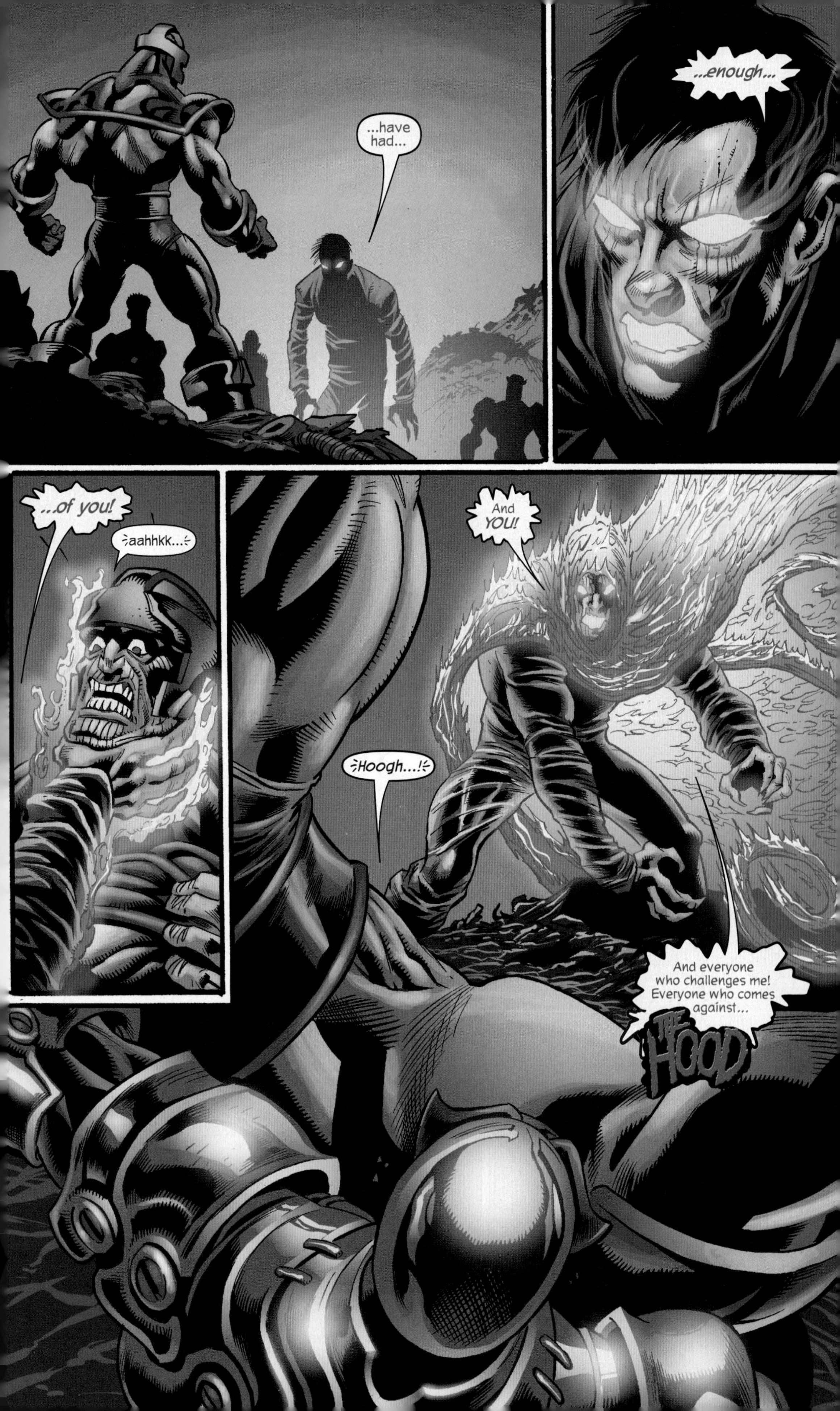
...have had...
...enough...
...of you!
aahhkk...
Hoogh...!
And YOU!
And everyone who challenges me! Everyone who comes against...
THE HOOD

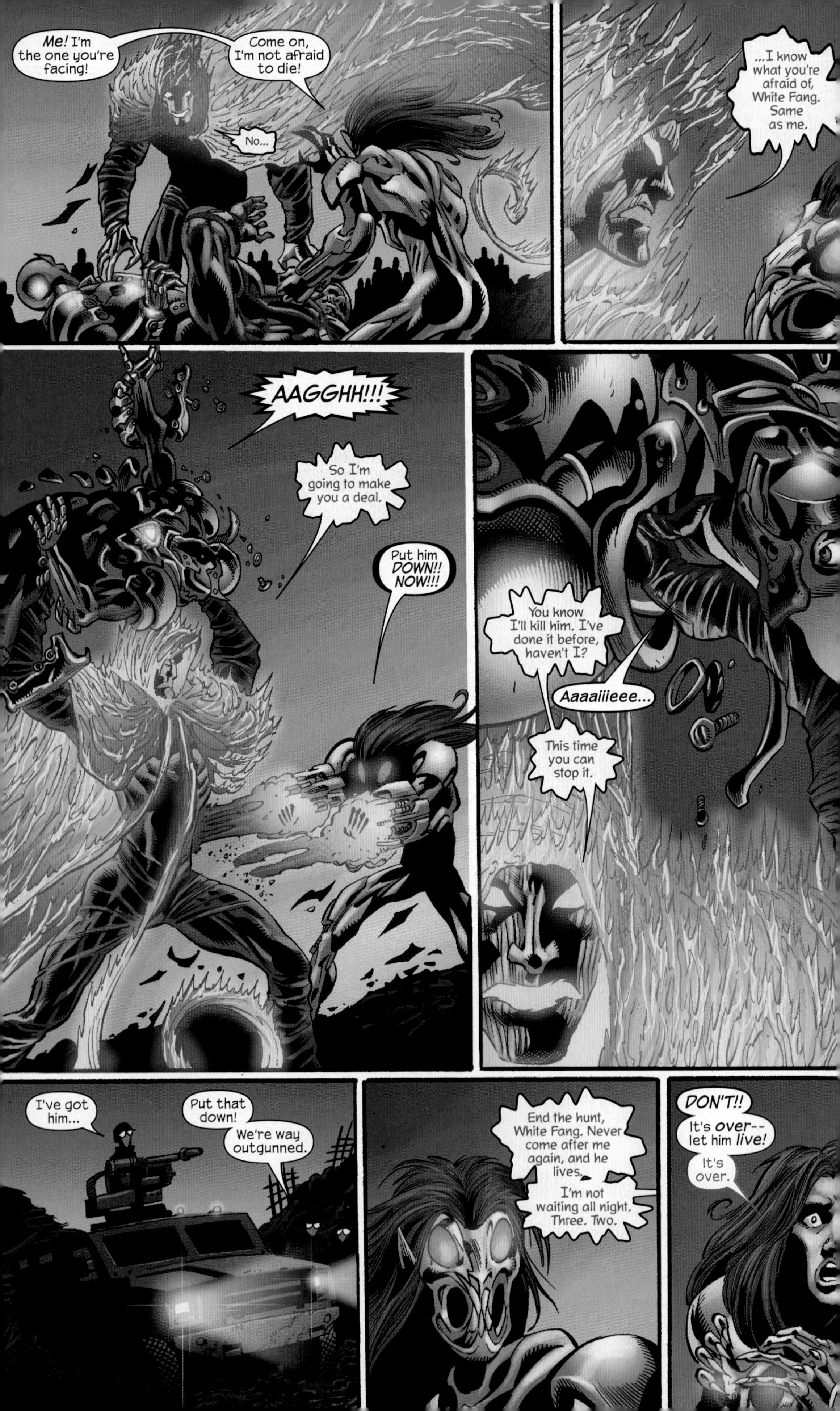
Me! I'm the one you're facing!
Come on, I'm not afraid to die!
No...
...I know what you're afraid of, White Fang. Same as me.
AAGGHH!!!
So I'm going to make you a deal.
Put him DOWN!! NOW!!!
You know I'll kill him. I've done it before, haven't I?
Aaaaiiieee...
This time you can stop it.
I've got him...
Put that down!
We're way outgunned.
End the hunt, White Fang. Never come after me again, and he lives.
I'm not waiting all night. Three. Two.
DON'T!!
It's over-- let him live!
It's over.

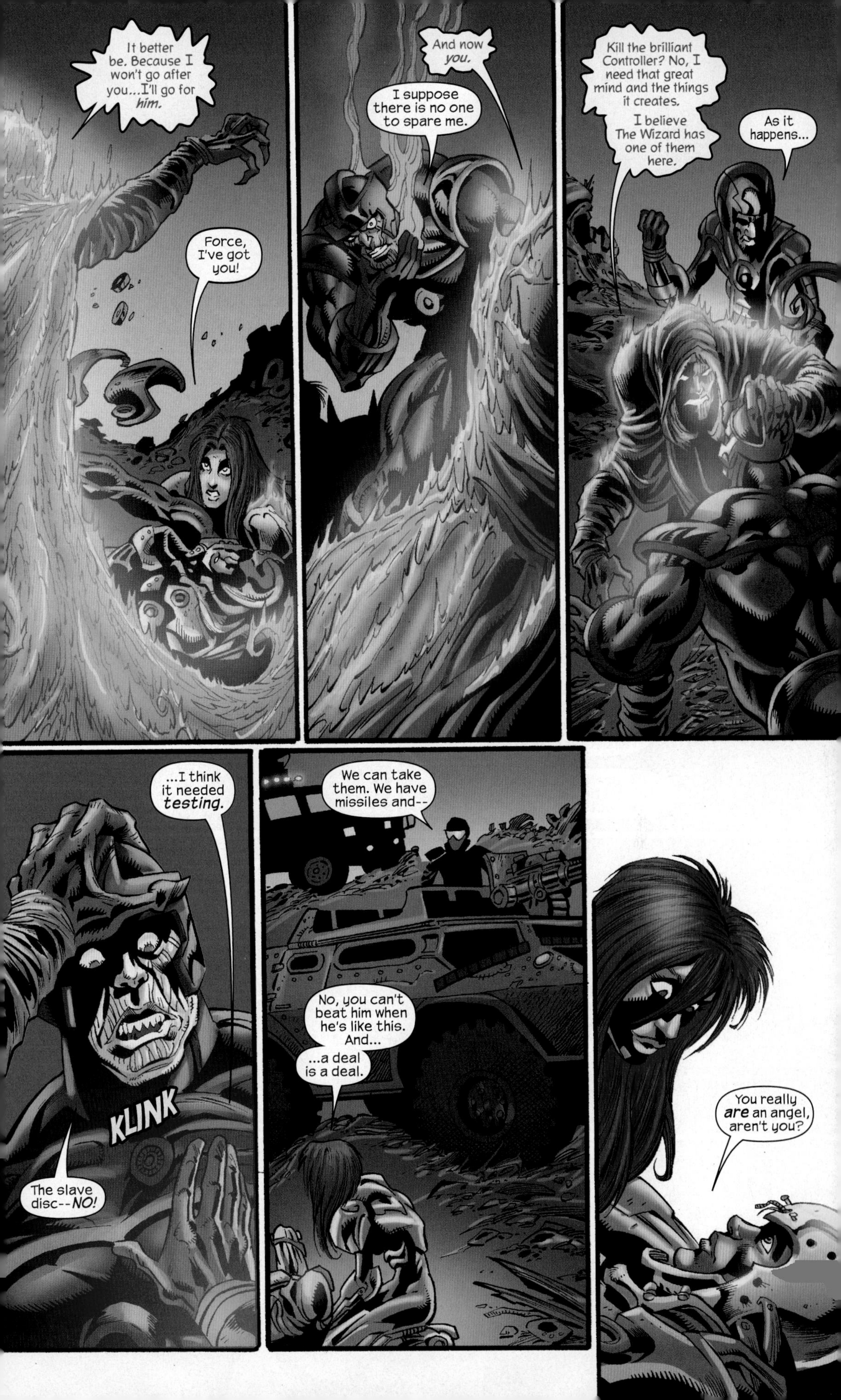
It better be. Because I won't go after you...I'll go for *him.*
Force, I've got you!
And now *you.*
I suppose there is no one to spare me.
Kill the brilliant Controller? No, I need that great mind and the things it creates.
I believe The Wizard has one of them here.
As it happens...
...I think it needed *testing.*
KLINK
The slave disc--*NO!*
We can take them. We have missiles and--
No, you can't beat him when he's like this. And...
...a deal is a deal.
You really *are* an angel, aren't you?

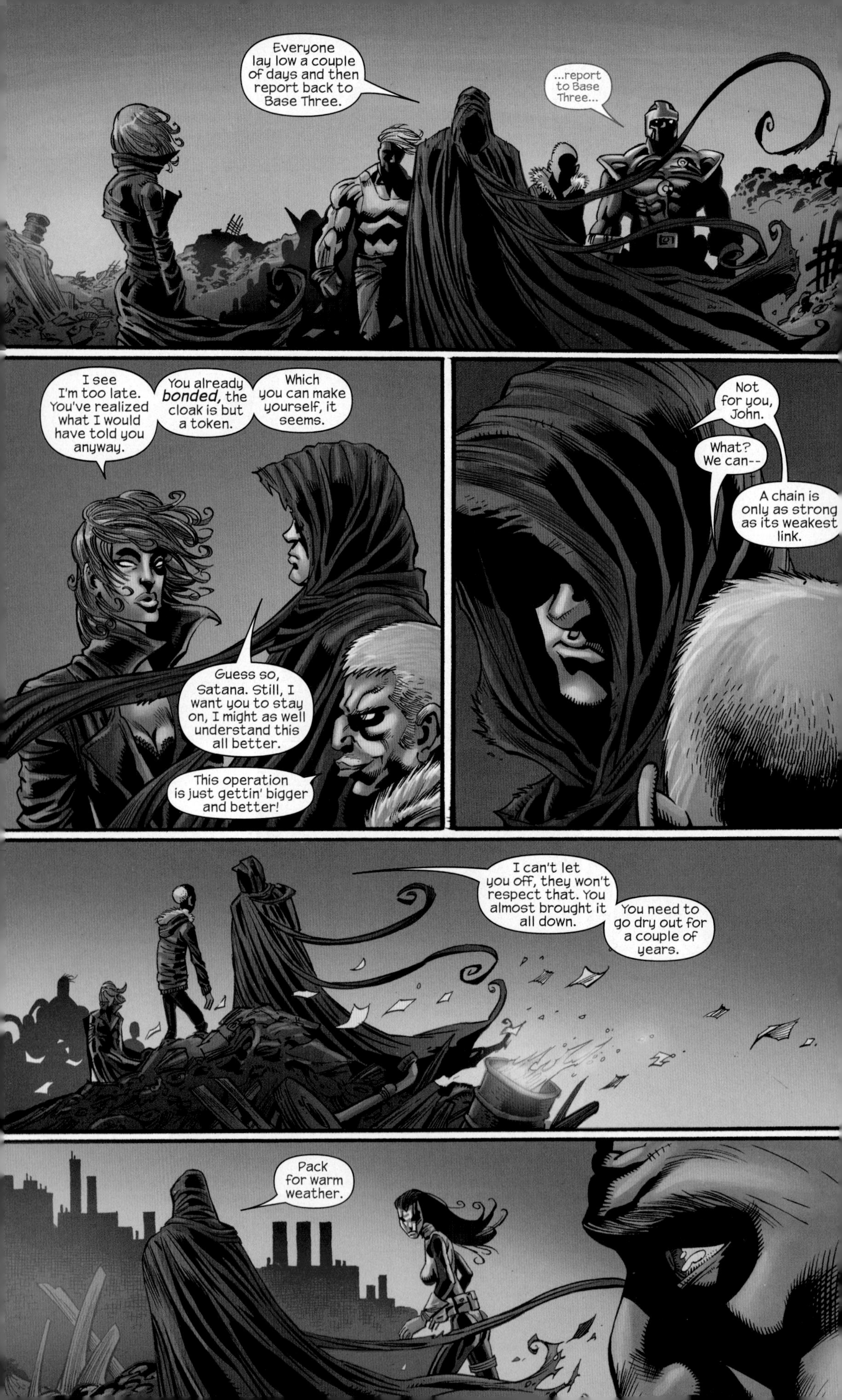

Everyone lay low a couple of days and then report back to Base Three.
...report to Base Three...
I see I'm too late. You've realized what I would have told you anyway.
You already **bonded,** the cloak is but a token.
Which you can make yourself, it seems.
Guess so, Satana. Still, I want you to stay on, I might as well understand this all better.
This operation is just gettin' bigger and better!
Not for you, John.
What? We can--
A chain is only as strong as its weakest link.
I can't let you off, they won't respect that. You almost brought it all down.
You need to go dry out for a couple of years.
Pack for warm weather.

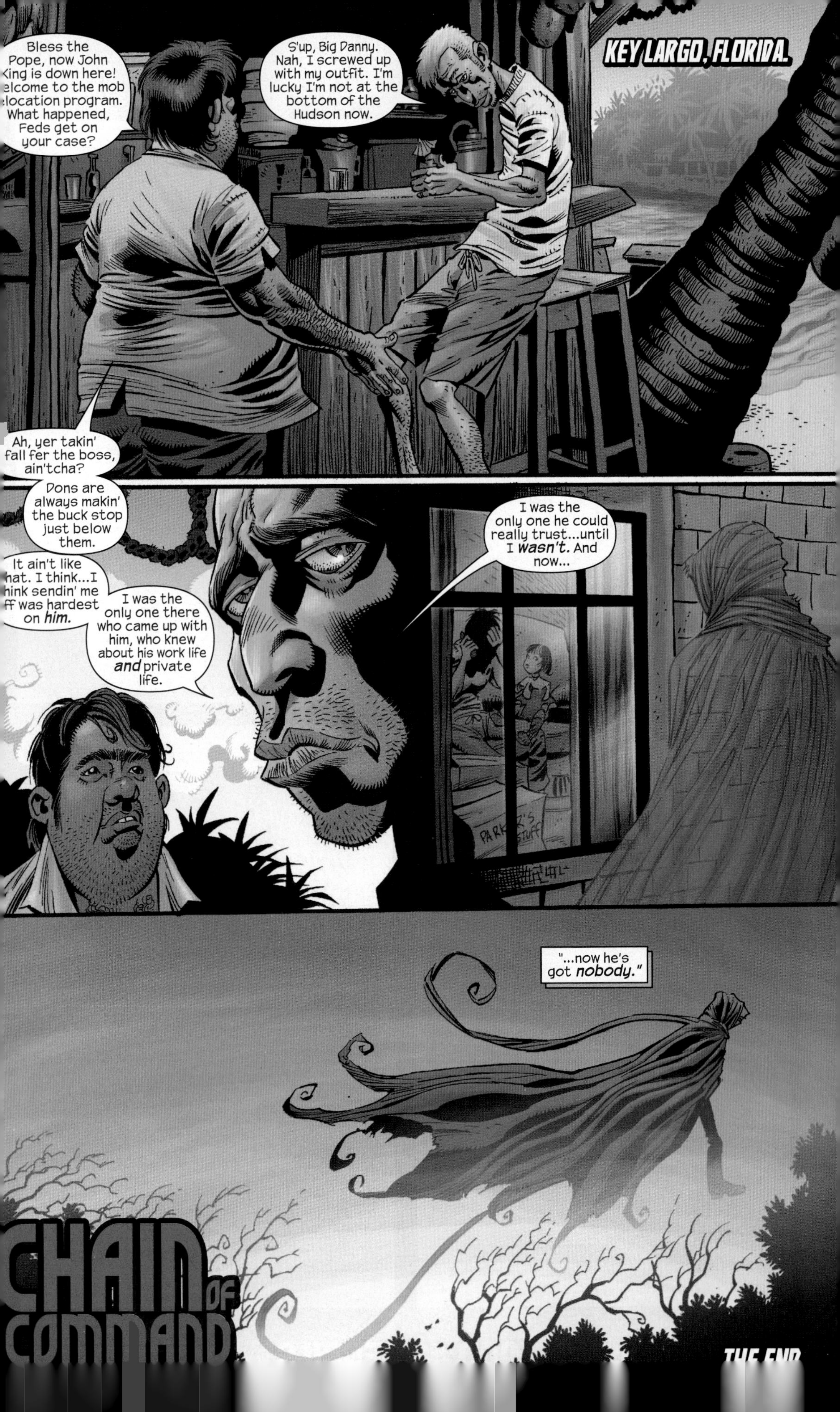
KEY LARGO, FLORIDA.
Bless the Pope, now John King is down here! elcome to the mob location program. What happened, Feds get on your case?
S'up, Big Danny. Nah, I screwed up with my outfit. I'm lucky I'm not at the bottom of the Hudson now.
Ah, yer takin' fall fer the boss, ain'tcha?
Dons are always makin' the buck stop just below them.
It ain't like that. I think...I think sendin' me off was hardest on *him*.
I was the only one there who came up with him, who knew about his work life *and* private life.
I was the only one he could really trust...until I *wasn't*. And now...
PARKER'S STUFF
"...now he's got *nobody*."
CHAIN OF COMMAND
THE END

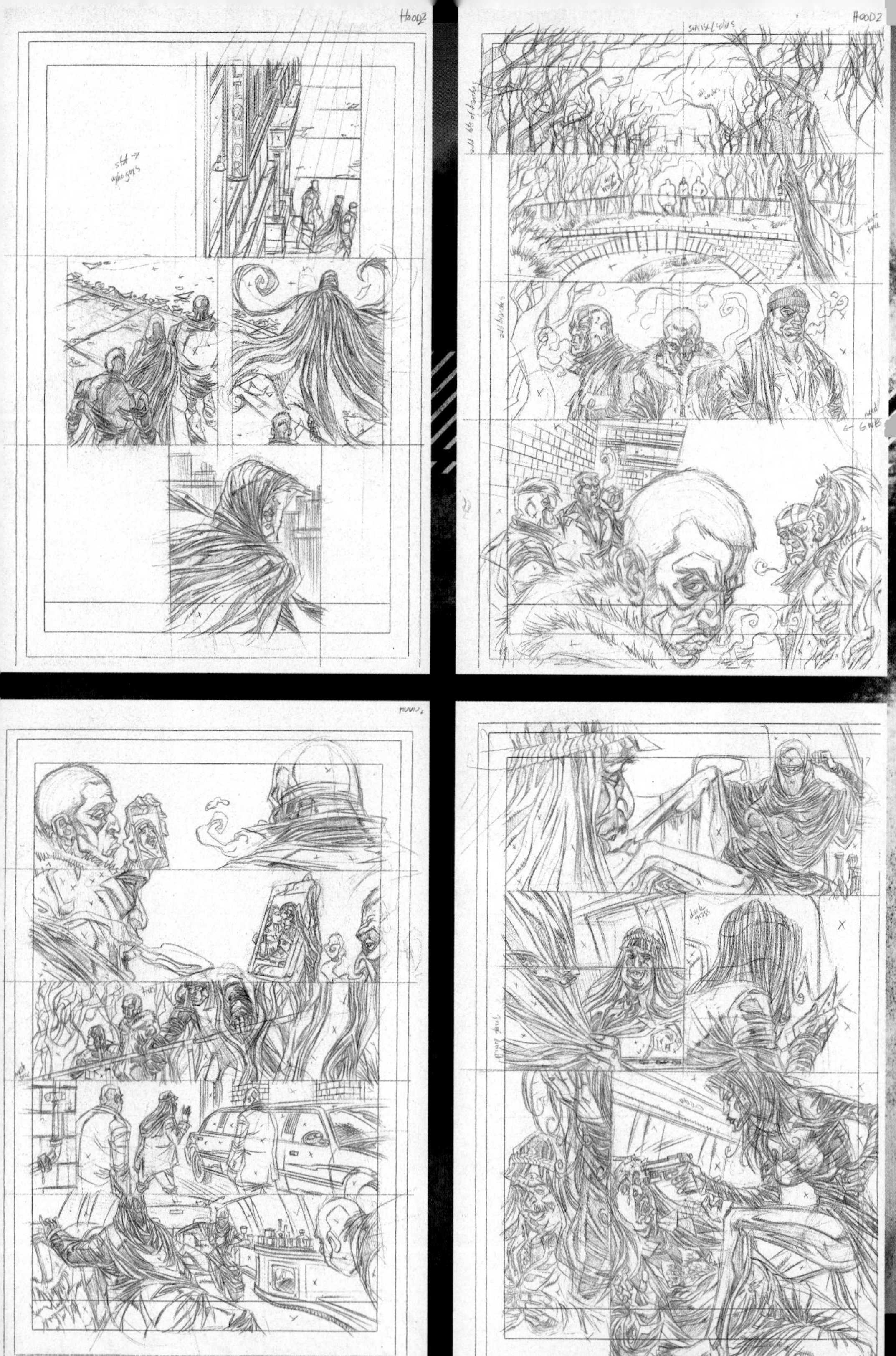

DARK REIGN: THE HOOD #1 PENCILS BY KYLE HOTZ

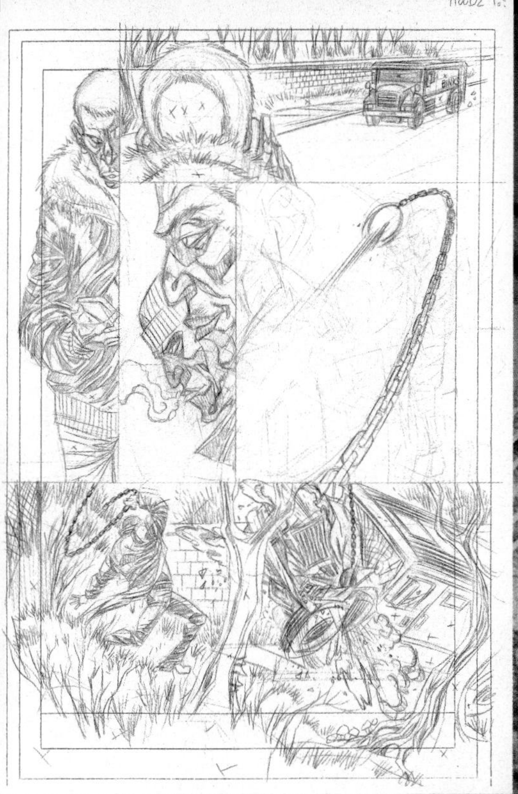
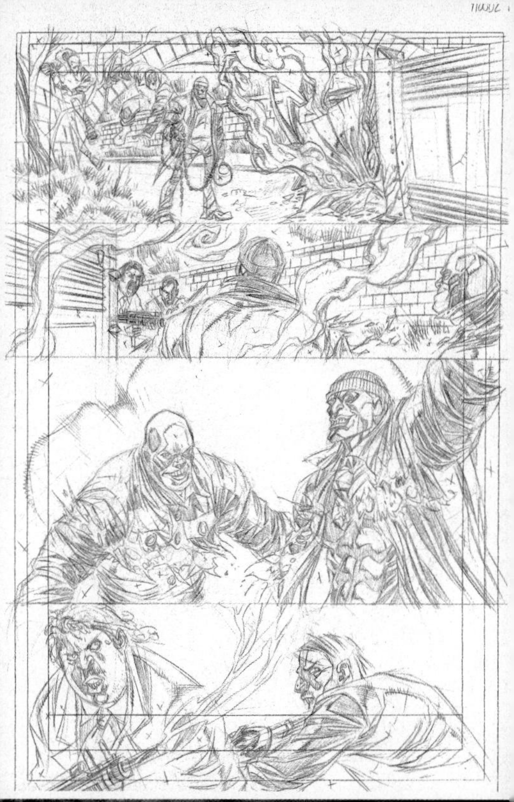
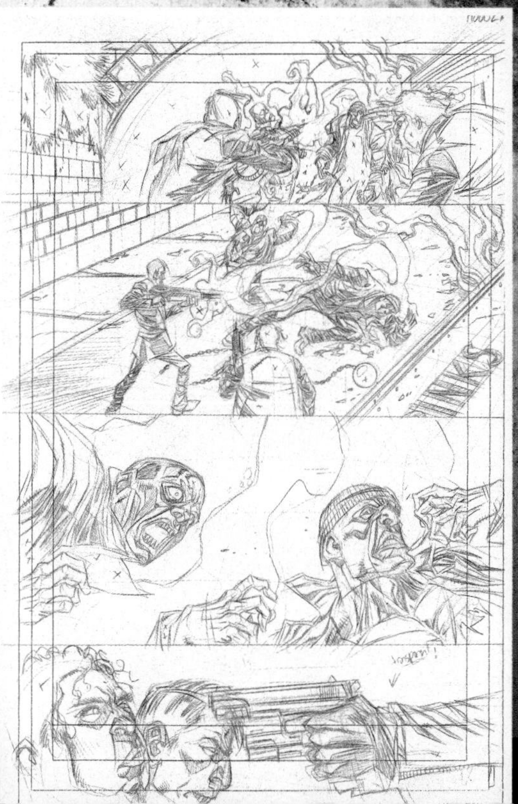
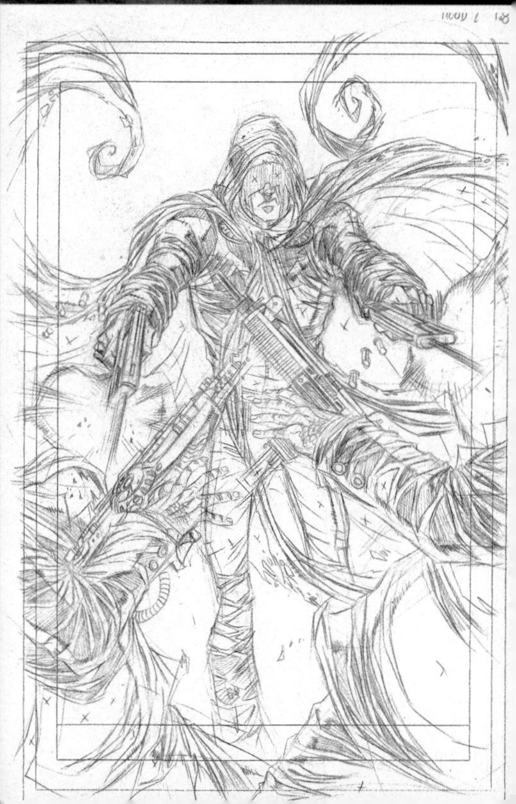

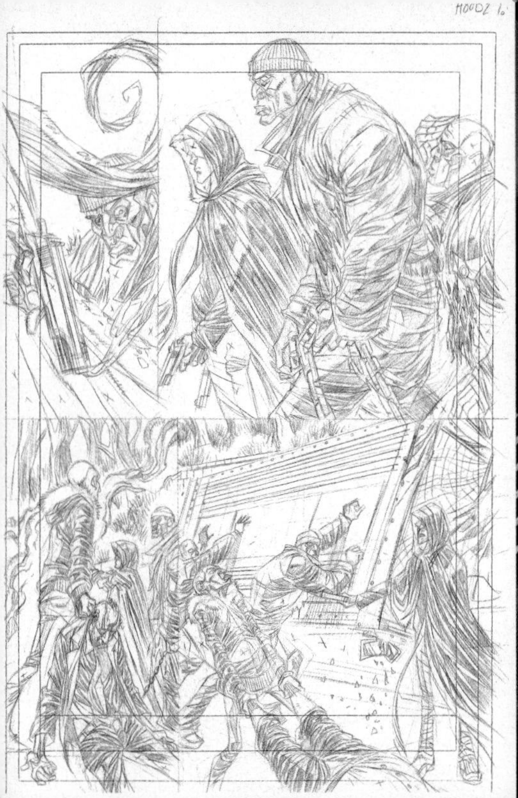

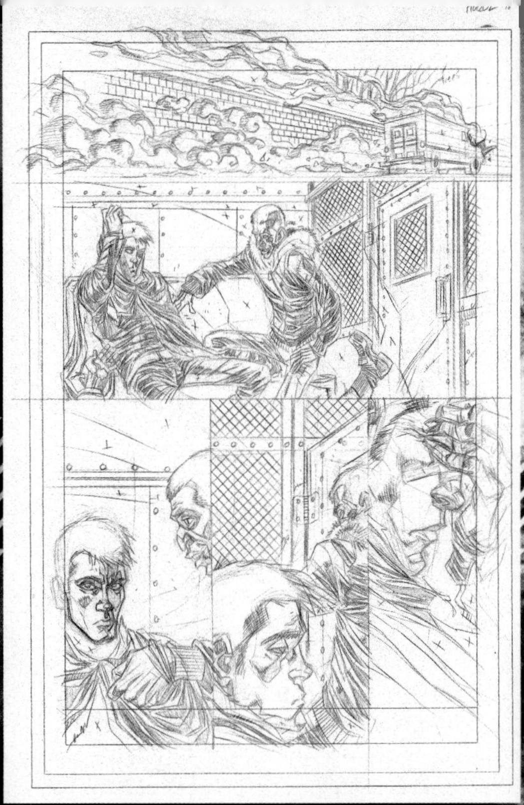

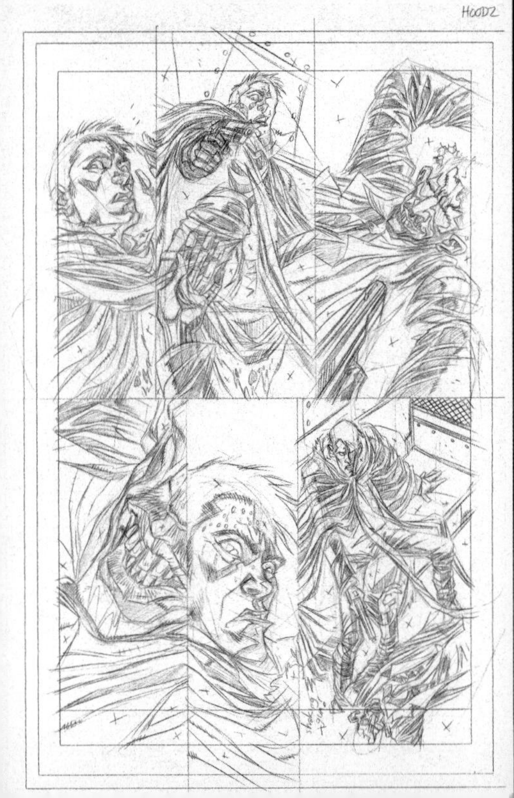

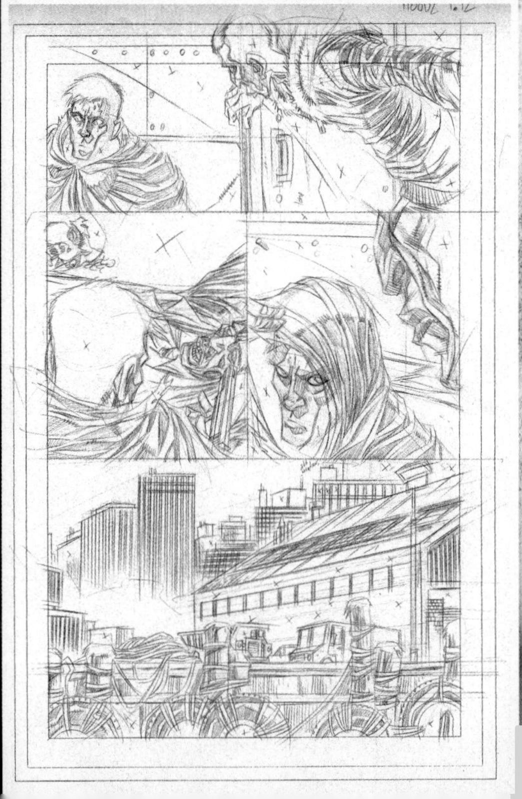

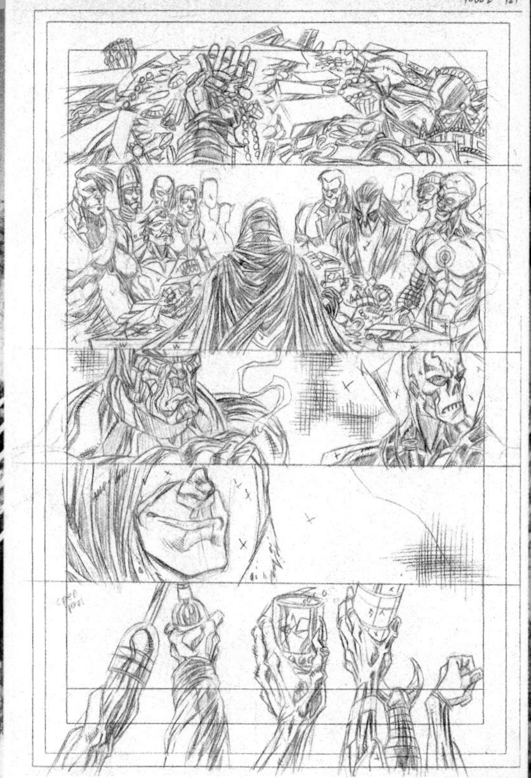

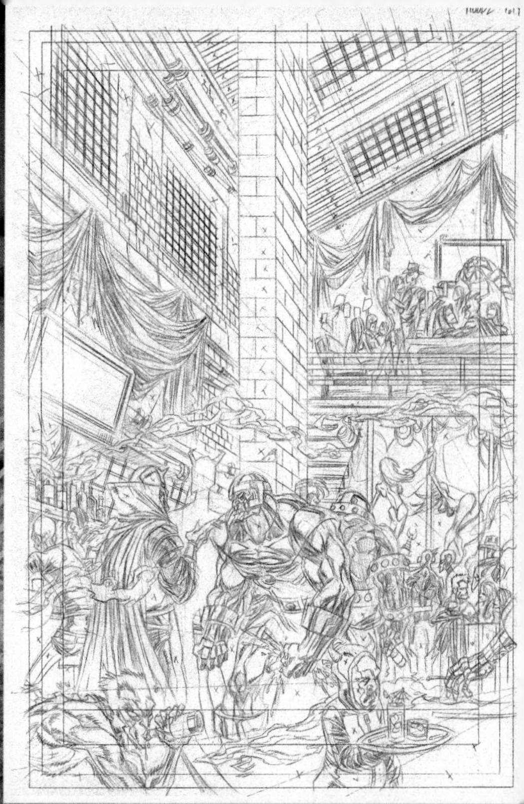

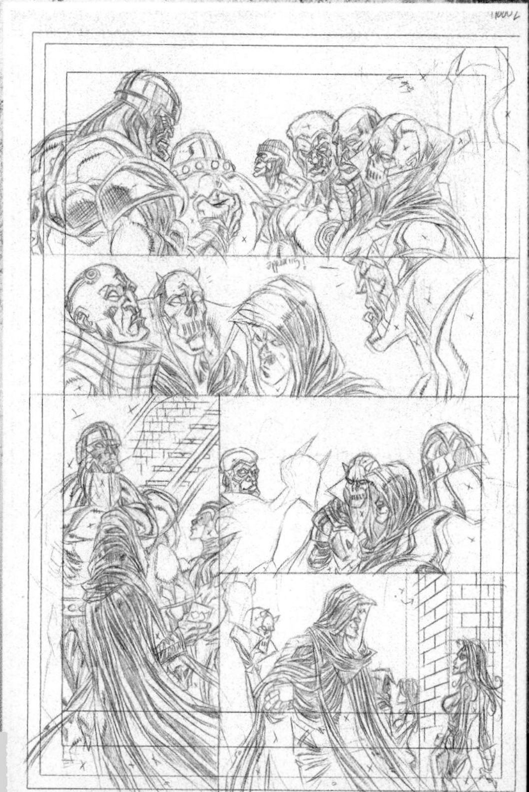

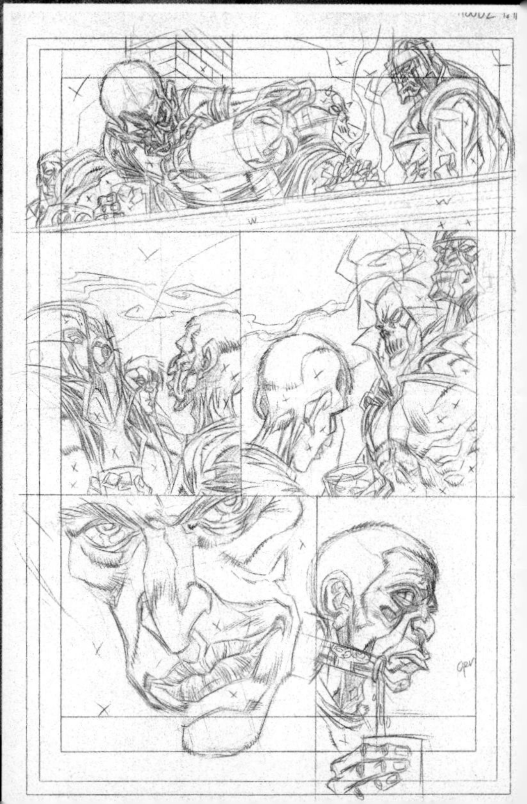

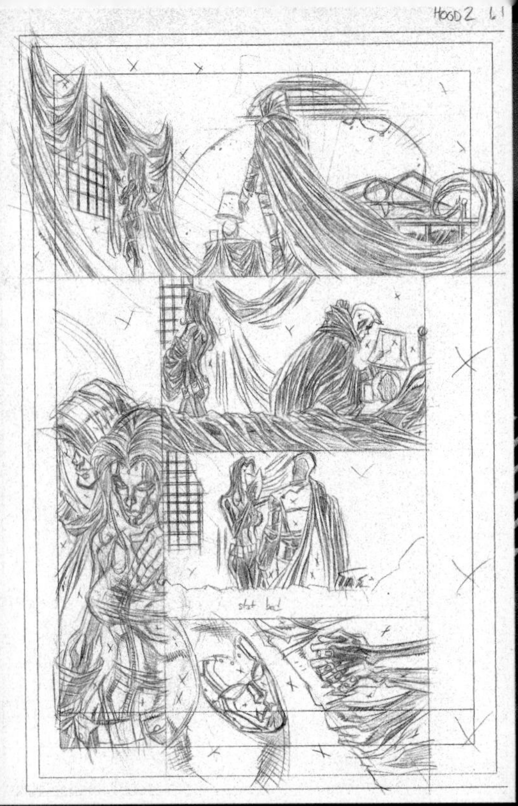
HOOD2 61
stat bed

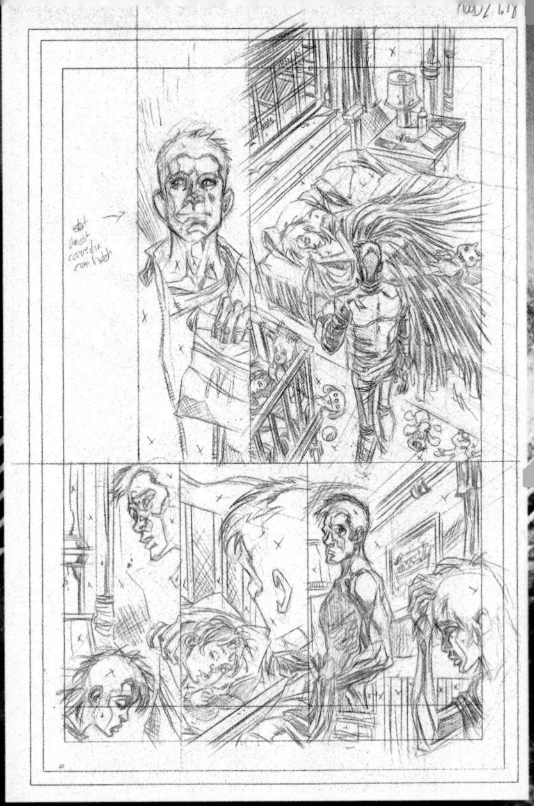

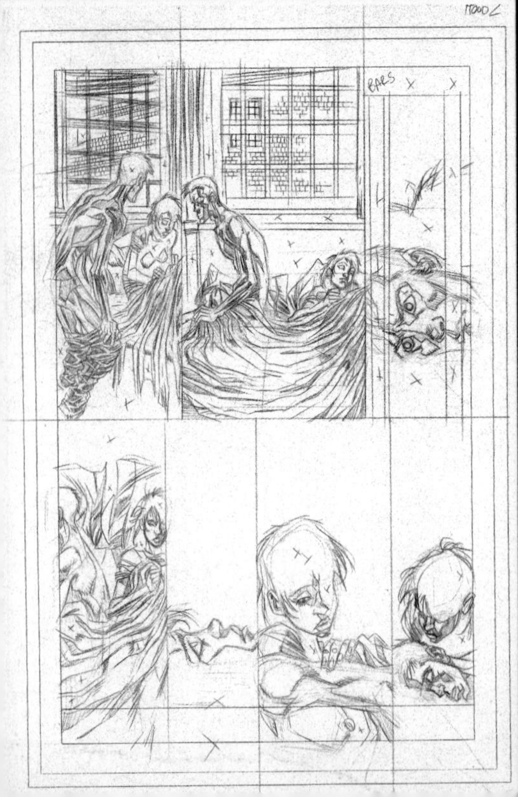
BARS

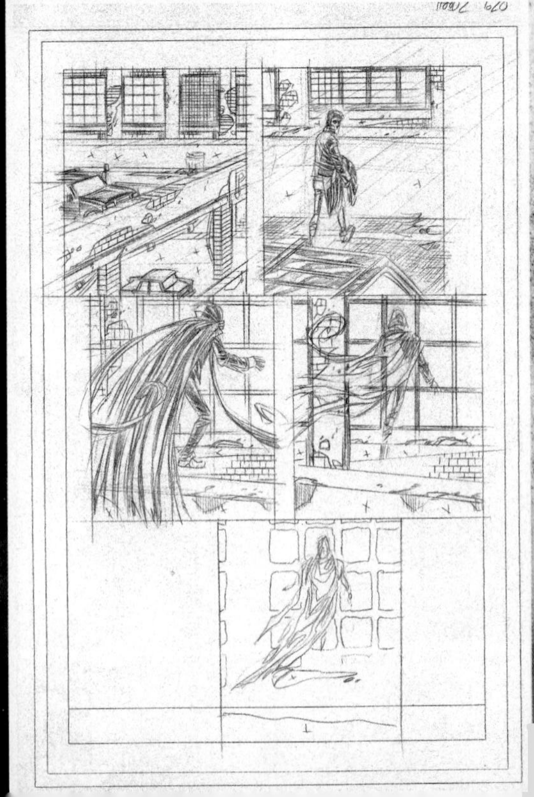

Hood2 1.21
add tons of glass

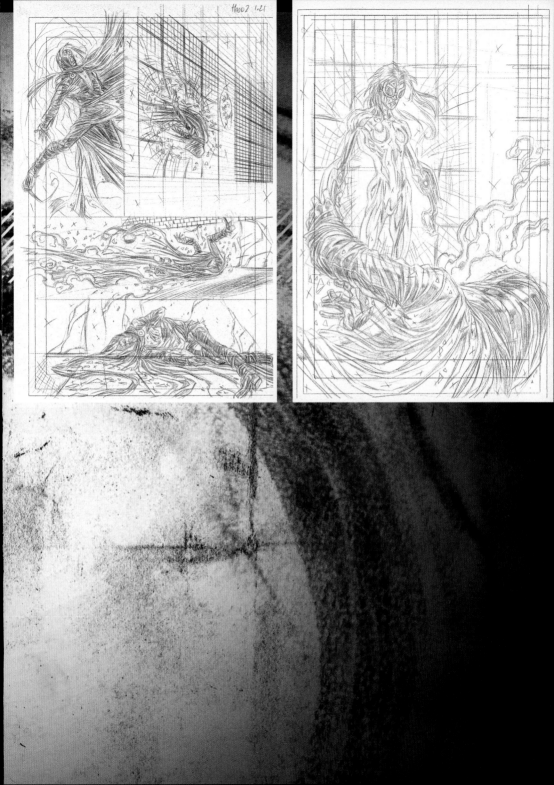

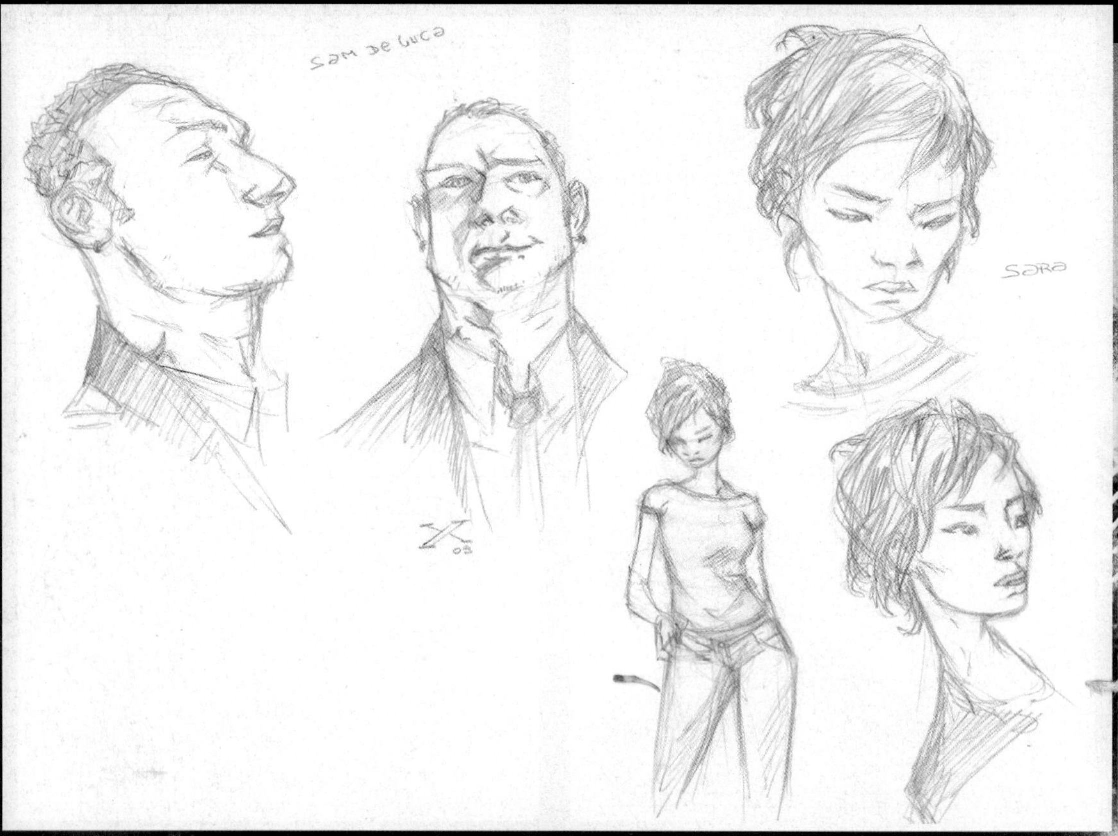
Sam De Luca
Sara

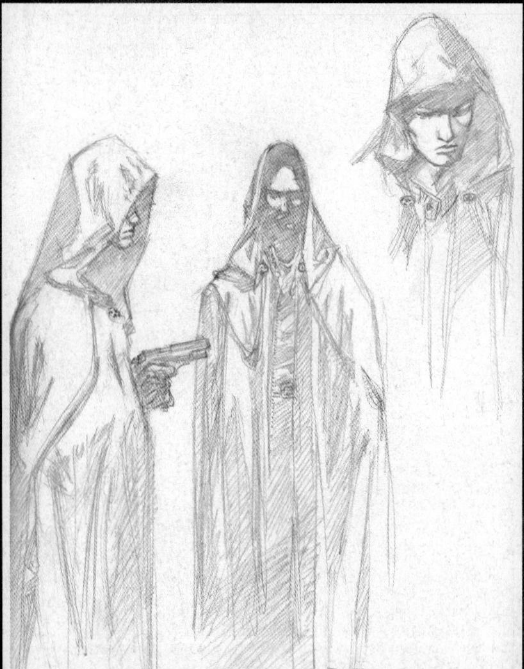

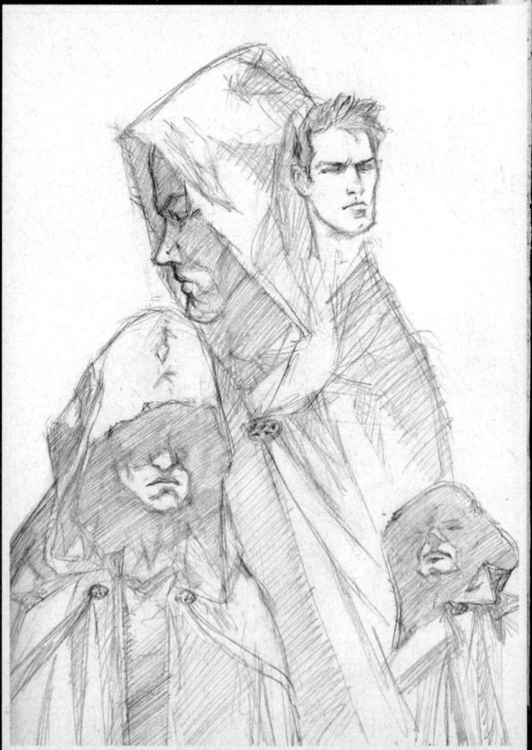

CHARACTER SKETCHES BY MAX FIUMARA